D1498354

The Britannica Guide to
Numbers and
Measurement

MATH EXPLAINED

The Britannica Guide to
Numbers and
Measurement

EDITED BY WILLIAM L. HOSCH,
ASSOCIATE EDITOR, MATHEMATICS AND COMPUTER SCIENCES

Britannica®
Educational Publishing

IN ASSOCIATION WITH

ROSEN
EDUCATIONAL SERVICES

Published in 2011 by Britannica Educational Publishing
(a trademark of Encyclopædia Britannica, Inc.)
in association with Rosen Educational Services, LLC
29 East 21st Street, New York, NY 10010.

Distributed exclusively by Rosen Educational Services.
For a listing of additional Britannica Educational Publishing titles, call toll free (800) 237-9932.

First Edition

Britannica Educational Publishing
Michael I. Levy: Executive Editor
J.E. Luebering: Senior Manager
Marilyn L. Barton: Senior Coordinator, Production Control
Steven Bosco: Director, Editorial Technologies
Lisa S. Braucher: Senior Producer and Data Editor
Yvette Charboneau: Senior Copy Editor
Kathy Nakamura: Manager, Media Acquisition
William L. Hosch: Associate Editor, Mathematics and Computer Sciences

Rosen Educational Services
Alexandra Hanson-Harding: Senior Editor
Nelson Sá: Art Director
Cindy Reiman: Photography Manager
Matthew Cauli: Designer, Cover Design
Introduction by Sean D. McCollum

Library of Congress Cataloging-in-Publication Data

The Britannica guide to numbers and measurement / edited by William L. Hosch.—1st ed.
    p. cm.—(Math explained)
"In association with Britannica Educational Publishing, Rosen Educational Services."
Includes bibliographical references and index.
ISBN 978-1-61530-108-9 (lib. bdg.)
1. Number theory—History. 2. Set theory—History. I. Hosch, William L.
QA241.B7885 2010
512.7—dc22

                                                                2009044217

Manufactured in the United States of America

Cover © www.istockphoto.com/Tommaso Colia; page 12 © www.istockphoto.com/Jiri Moucka; pages 21, 97, 150, 201, 230, 237, 271, 274, 278 © www.istockphoto.com/Norebbo

On page 20: This engraving shows the Exchequer at Westminster (England) during the reign of King Henry VII (1485–1509). The Exchequer, or treasury department, created new standards of measurements for merchants in the late 15th century. *SSPL via Getty Images*

CONTENTS

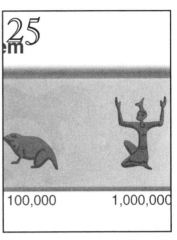

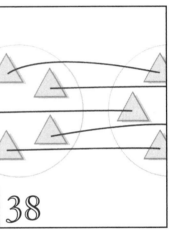

**Chapter 2: Great Arithmeticians and
Number Theorists** 97

109

122

148

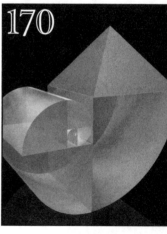

232

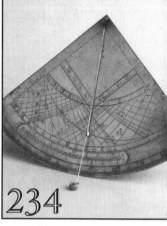

234

239

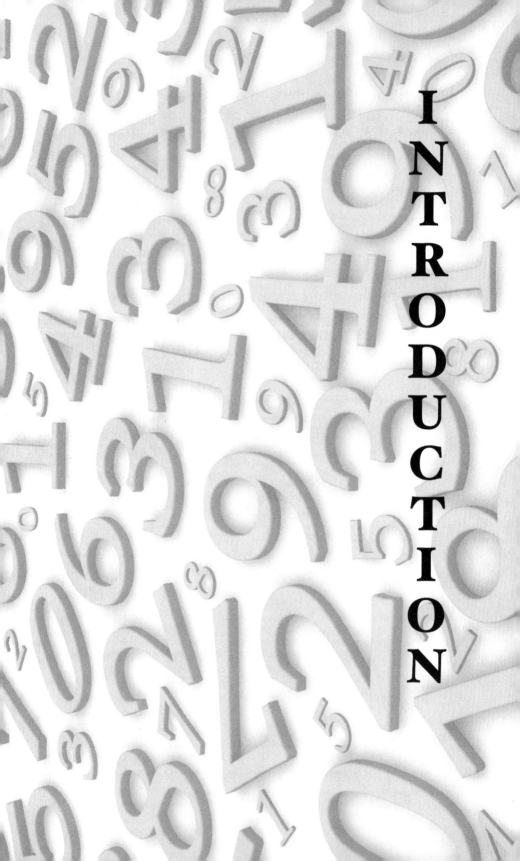

INTRODUCTION

Numbers have frequently been called a universal language for their ability to transmit information across cultures. The scoreboard at an Olympic basketball game, for example, needs no translation no matter the number of languages spoken by the fans. When asked "What time is it?" in a foreign city, all a tourist must do is hold up her watch to provide the answer. For everything from sports to shopping to computer cryptography, numbers are fundamental to everyday life today. This book offers an overview of the development of numbers, their expression in mathematics and measurement, and profiles of visionaries who saw order amidst the numbers.

Like language, numbers arose along with human civilization, and in turn helped civilization rise. Their use developed from people's desires to count up their chickens and other important possessions and, perhaps, measure their humble dwelling. Most early number systems were based on the most handy counting device available—ten fingers—the inspiration for the decimal system that still dominates today. Notable exceptions to the base-10 scheme formed in Mesopotamia where they established a base-60 system that still thrives in the measurement of time and angles and the base-20 system the Maya later developed in North America.

Increasing trade and commerce helped drive the need for numbers as people settled in towns and cities. At first, people most likely scratched tallies on stones or put simple notches on a stick to count important objects. But soon, merchants, traders, and tax collectors in every budding civilization required better ways to manage their accounts.

In a huge conceptual shift, numbers gradually evolved from concrete tools for counting and measuring to become abstract ideas in their own right. This shift in thinking began to appear in discrete notations for the numbers themselves. Symbols for specific numbers appear in Egypt beginning in about 3400 BCE, in Mesopotamia about 400 years after that, and in China around 1600 BCE. Number symbols appear in Crete beginning in about 1200 BCE. Like most useful ideas, this knowledge of numbers and mathematics flowed between cultures, regions, and continents as trade expanded, and also cross-pollinated with existing counting and number systems.

Number symbols did not appear in India until later, about 300 BCE. But over the next 1,000 years, Indian scholars laid claim to three revolutionary ideas that energized the field of mathematics: 1) a more efficient notational system, 2) the place-value system, and 3) a functioning concept of zero.

India was the primary source of the number notations 1, 2, 3, 4, 5, 6, 7, 8, 9, and eventually 0, used almost universally today. These digits are commonly known as the Hindu-Arabic system, in part because the Arab-Muslim world greatly aided its dissemination.

Some mathematicians had already employed the notion of zero, but Indian scholars fully developed its conception and function. The existence and value of zero goes unquestioned today, but it was a high conceptual hurdle for early thinkers. They struggled with a symbol that could represent nothing and act as a placeholder for an empty value in the place-value system.

Even while these fundamental concepts were being put forth, mathematicians had been making advances in understanding algebra and geometry. Pythagoras, according to tradition, had hashed out his theorem regarding right triangles in the 6th century BCE. Euclid's work around 300 BCE earned him the title of "Father of Geometry." Diophantus of Alexandria, around 250 CE, expanded the understanding of algebra. Aryabhata I of India [5th century CE] explained quadratic equations, assembled a table of sines, and explored spherical astronomy by means of plane trigonometry and spherical geometry—in verse couplets to aid memorization, no less.

Around 800 CE, the efforts of Muḥammad ibn Mūsā al-Khwārizmī helped summarize these centuries of mathematical developments. Two seminal works by this polymath, who lived in Baghdad, clarified, expanded, and fostered the spread of new ideas in mathematics. His Latinized name and the title of one of his works subsequently gave rise to the terms algorithm and algebra.

Up to this time, mathematics in Europe had lagged behind the centers of learning in Asia, the Middle East, and parts of the Mediterranean. A few Latin translations of al-Khwārizmī had introduced the key concepts of the Hindu-Arabic numerals, place value, and zero. This trickle of new mathematical ideas turned into a spring with the 1202 publication of *Book of the Abacus* by Italian Leonardo Pisano, also known as Fibonacci. It was the first European text to present the breadth of Indian and Arabic mathematics. This jolt of sophistication accelerated the development of mathematics and science.

A new "universal language" of mathematics had now found general acceptance throughout much of the Old World. The innovation of the movable-type printing press in the mid-1400s added to the explosive spread of mathematical and scientific knowledge. The demand for more accurate calculations and measurements for navigation and the physical sciences helped drive mathematical innovation. For example, Scotsman John Napier (1550–1617) originated the concept of logarithms as an invaluable device for managing large, complex computations.

The exploration of numbers and mathematics has always tended toward the esoteric and at its cutting edge has grown increasingly intricate in the last 400 years. The study of numbers moved into a new phase when Pierre de Fermat (1601–1605) founded modern number theory, a field concerned with properties of the positive integers such as 1, 2, and 3. Number theory is sometimes called "higher arithmetic" because of its emphasis on pure idea rather than practical applications. Fermat posed questions and identified issues that have shaped number theory ever since, but he wrote little and often did not publish proofs of his own ideas. Without the interest of other mathematicians, who were more concerned with the exciting new discoveries in astronomy and geometry at that time, number theory languished until the prolific and influential Swiss mathematician Leonhard Euler (1707–83) reignited interest in it. Euler published more than 1,000 pages of research on the subject, much of it proofs of Fermat, bringing number theory into the mainstream. A number of thinkers continued to develop the field through the 19th century. The once esoteric world of number theory, which seemed to have no practical applications 400 years ago, now reaches into virtually every human activity and endeavor today. It seems to inch closer to a Pythagorean vision, as described by Aristotle more than two millennia ago: "The so-called Pythagoreans, who were the first to take up mathematics . . . fancied that the principles of mathematics were the principles of all things."

The history of measurement follows a similar path to that of numbers and mathematics. Its value in commerce, engineering, construction, manufacturing, and science, as well as in personal and domestic activities is very difficult to overstate.

Measurement, at its base, is a process of comparing the known and the unknown. A tape measure provides a known measurement for length, useful for comparing with the unknown height of a toddler, for example. An accurate stopwatch ticks out a known quantity of time that can be compared to the unknown time it takes a sprinter to run 100 metres.

Archeologists have found evidence of measuring practices from Mesopotamia but generally recognize the Egyptian cubit, developed around 3000 BCE, as the most common linear measurement in the ancient world. The cubit and other measuring standards began to work their way west from the Middle East and spread through trade and conquest, until they were ubiquitous in the ancient world. Originally, techniques encompassed four main measurements: mass (or weight), distance (or length), area, and volume. The variety of phenomena that we measure today has expanded beyond these original four, of course. They now include time, temperature, light, pressure, electricity, energy, and magnetism, as well as hybrids measurements such as acceleration (distance over time) and force (mass times acceleration).

Like the relationship between numbers and fingers, early measurement tools and units were usually based on the body. The Egyptian cubit, for example, was originally based on the length between the elbow and outstretched fingertips. This rule of thumb was at some point standardized into the royal cubit of 524 millimetres (20.62 inches). The remarkable symmetry of the Pyramids of Giza stands as proof of the accuracy of this measurement device, as well as a testament to the talents of its builders.

As trade and other interactions brought differing communities and cultures into contact, it benefited them to reach agreements on weights and measures. Such standards sought to guarantee a certain level of portability and reliability in commerce and technology, so that an amphora of wine (about 34 litres) in one Roman village met the expectations in another, at least in terms of volume. For this reason, societies and governments have long placed a premium on standardizing weights and measures. The role of the federal government in fixing the standard of weights and measures is even enshrined in the U.S.

Constitution and merited mention in the first inaugural address of President George Washington.

An effective system of weights and measures depends on three principles. First, the system must have uniformity, that is, accurate and reliable standards of such measures as mass and length, for example, based on agreed-to units. Second, the system needs units, or recognized and accepted quantities with a shared terminology. Finally, the system must have standards, that is, physical embodiments of these units, such as the block of black granite—a royal cubit long—against which the ancient Egyptian craftsmen regularly checked their royal cubit sticks.

Historically, establishing a standardized system of weights and measures has been more easily proposed than instituted. People by nature are conservative when it comes to day-to-day practices, and planned measurement systems have always struggled with tradition and existing infrastructure that may have evolved over centuries. In early China, for instance, units of land area and other measurements varied from region to region and even from profession to profession. It took China's first emperor, Shihuangdi, to impose regulations that set empire-wide standards for basic units in the 200s BCE.

Often, major shifts in measurement systems require social and political upheaval to gain traction. That was the case with the metric system. The concept of a decimal-based system of measurement had been imagined as early as the 17th century, due in part to the commercial and trade needs of an increasingly integrated Europe. Academics in Revolutionary France fleshed out the metric system in the late 1700s, and in 1799 it was officially adopted under the motto "For all people, for all time." Napoleon's subsequent conquests facilitated its rapid introduction across Europe. It took root and over the next 150 years spread to most of the rest of the world.

Today, the metric system—like the unified system of numbers and mathematics—provides the uniformity necessary for a global economy and the scientific community's broad collaborations across international and cultural boundaries. Only three countries—Myanmar (Burma), Liberia, and the United States—have not adopted the standard metric system, known as the International System of Units, as their official system of measurement. Still, metres, litres, and grams are the terms used in the vast majority of labs, factories, and classrooms in the world—a universal language indeed.

CHAPTER I

NUMBERS

The notions of numbers and measurement appeared thousands of years ago. Early herders needed to know how many goats they had in their flocks. Early farmers needed to understand how much grain they had stored for the winter. When bartering, people needed to keep track of how many items or how much of a substance was traded. This volume presents the history and principles of these subjects.

Just as the first attempts at writing came long after the development of speech, so the first efforts at the graphical representation of numbers came long after people had learned how to count. Probably the earliest way of keeping record of a count was by some tally system involving physical objects such as pebbles or sticks. Judging by the habits of indigenous peoples today as well as by the oldest remaining traces of written or sculptured records, the earliest numerals were simple notches in a stick, scratches on a stone, marks on a piece of pottery, and the like. Having no fixed units of measure, no coins, no commerce beyond the rudest barter, no system of taxation, and no needs beyond those to sustain life, people had no necessity for written numerals until the beginning of what are called historical times. Vocal sounds were probably used to designate the number of objects in a small group long before there were separate symbols for the small numbers, and it seems likely that the sounds differed according to the kind of object being counted. The abstract notion of two, signified orally by a sound independent of any particular objects, probably appeared very late.

NUMERALS AND NUMERAL SYSTEMS

NUMBER BASES

When it became necessary to count frequently to numbers larger than 10 or so, the numeration had to be systematized and simplified; this was commonly done through use of a group unit or base, just as might be done today counting 43 eggs as three dozen and seven. In fact, the earliest numerals of which there is a definite record were simple straight marks for the small numbers with some special form for 10. These symbols appeared in Egypt as early as 3400 BCE and in Mesopotamia as early as 3000 BCE, long preceding the first known inscriptions containing numerals in China (c. 1600 BCE), Crete (c. 1200 BCE), and India (c. 300 BCE). Some ancient symbols for 1 and 10 are given in the figure.

Ancient number symbols

Egyptian hieroglyphic, c. 3400 BCE

Egyptian hieratic, c. 3400 BCE

Sumerian, c. 3000 BCE

Cretan, c. 1200 BCE

Some ancient symbols for 1 and 10. Encyclopædia Britannica, Inc.

The special position occupied by 10 stems from the number of human fingers, of course, and it is still evident in modern usage not only in the logical structure of the decimal number system but in the English names for the numbers. Thus, *eleven* comes from Old English *endleofan*, literally meaning "[ten and] one left [over]," and *twelve* from *twelf*, meaning "two left;" the endings *-teen* and *-ty* both refer to ten, and *hundred* comes originally from a pre-Greek term meaning "ten times [ten]."

It should not be inferred, however, that 10 is either the only possible base or the only one actually used. The pair system, in which the counting goes "one, two, two and one, two twos, two and two and one," and so on, is found among the ethnologically oldest tribes of Australia, in many Papuan languages of the Torres Strait and the adjacent coast of New Guinea, among some African Pygmies, and in various South American tribes. The indigenous peoples of Tierra del Fuego and the South American continent use number systems with bases three and four. The quinary scale, or number system with base five, is very old, but in pure form it seems to be used at present only by speakers of Saraveca, a South American Arawakan language; elsewhere it is combined with the decimal or the vigesimal system, where the base is 20. Similarly, the pure base six scale seems to occur only sparsely in northwest Africa and is otherwise combined with the duodecimal, or base 12, system.

In the course of history, the decimal system finally over-shadowed all others. Nevertheless, there are still many vestiges of other systems, chiefly in commercial and domestic units, where change always meets the resistance of tradition. Thus, 12 occurs as the number of inches in a foot, months in a year, ounces in a pound (troy weight or apothecaries' weight), and twice 12 hours in a day, and both the dozen and the gross measure by twelves. In English the base 20 occurs chiefly in the score ("Four score and seven years ago . . ."); in French it survives in the word *quatre-vingts* ("four twenties"), for 80; other traces are found in ancient Celtic, Gaelic, Danish, and Welsh. The base 60 still occurs in measurement of time and angles.

NUMERAL SYSTEMS

It appears that the primitive numerals were |, ||, |||, and so on, as found in Egypt and the Grecian lands, or -, =, ≡, and so on, as found in early records in East Asia, each going as far as the simple needs of people required. As life became more complicated, the need for group numbers became apparent, and it was only a small step from the simple system with names only for one and ten to the further naming of other special numbers. Sometimes this happened in a very unsystematic fashion; for example, the Yukaghirs of Siberia counted, "one, two, three, three and one, five, two threes, two threes and one, two fours, ten with one missing, ten." Usually, however, a more regular system resulted, and most of these systems can be classified, at least roughly, according to the logical principles underlying them.

SIMPLE GROUPING SYSTEMS

In its pure form a simple grouping system is an assignment of special names to the small numbers, the base b, and its powers b^2, b^3, and so on, up to a power bk large enough to represent all numbers actually required in use. The intermediate numbers are then formed by addition, each symbol being repeated the required number of times, just as 23 is written XXIII in Roman numerals.

Ancient Egyptian hieroglyphic numeral system

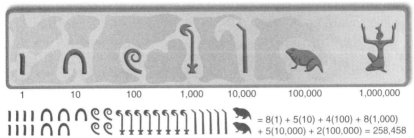

Ancient Egyptians customarily wrote from right to left. Because they did not have a positional system, they needed separate symbols for each power of 10. Encyclopædia Britannica, Inc.

The earliest example of this kind of system is the scheme encountered in hieroglyphs, which the Egyptians used for writing on stone. (Two later Egyptian systems, the hieratic and demotic, which were used for writing on clay or papyrus, will be considered below; they are not simple grouping systems.) The number 258,458 written in hieroglyphics appears in the figure.

Numbers of this size actually occur in extant records concerning royal estates and may have been commonplace in the logistics and engineering of the great pyramids.

Cuneiform Numerals

Around Babylon, clay was abundant, and the people impressed their symbols in damp clay tablets before drying them in the sun or in a kiln, thus forming documents that were practically as permanent as stone. Because the pressure of the stylus gave a wedge-shaped symbol, the inscriptions are known as cuneiform, from the Latin *cuneus* ("wedge") and *forma* ("shape"). The symbols could be made either with the pointed or the circular end (hence curvilinear writing) of the stylus, and for numbers up to 60 these symbols were used in the same way as the hieroglyphs, except that a subtractive symbol was also used. The figure

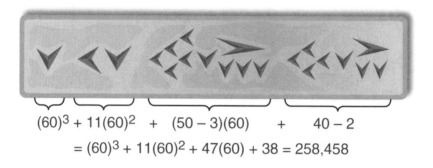

$(60)^3 + 11(60)^2 \quad + \quad (50-3)(60) \quad + \quad 40-2$

$= (60)^3 + 11(60)^2 + 47(60) + 38 = 258{,}458$

The number 258,458 expressed in the sexagesimal (base 60) system of the Babylonians and in cuneiform. Encyclopædia Britannica, Inc.

shows the number 258,458 in cuneiform.

The cuneiform and the curvilinear numerals occur together in some documents from about 3000 BCE. There seem to have been some conventions regarding their use: cuneiform was always used for the number of the year or the age of an animal, while wages already paid were written in curvilinear and wages due in cuneiform. For numbers larger than 60, the Babylonians used a mixed system, described below.

Greek Numerals

The Greeks had two important systems of numerals, besides the primitive plan of repeating single strokes, as in ||| ||| for six, and one of these was again a simple grouping system. Their predecessors in culture—the Babylonians, Egyptians, and Phoenicians—had generally repeated the units up to 9, with a special symbol for 10, and so on. The early Greeks also repeated the units to 9 and probably had various symbols for 10. In Crete, where the early civilization was so much influenced by those of Phoenicia and Egypt, the symbol for 10 was -, a circle was used for 100, and a rhombus for 1,000. Cyprus also used the horizontal bar for 10, but the precise forms are of less importance than the fact that the grouping by tens, with special symbols for certain powers of 10, was characteristic of the early number systems of the Middle East.

The Greeks, who entered the field much later and were influenced in their alphabet by the Phoenicians, based their first elaborate system chiefly on the initial letters of the numeral names. This was a natural thing for all early civilizations, since the custom of writing out the names for large numbers was at first quite general, and the use of an initial by way of abbreviation of a word is universal. The Greek system of abbreviations, known today as Attic numerals, appears in the records of the 5th century BCE but was probably used much earlier.

Roman Numerals

The direct influence of Rome for such a long period, the superiority of its numeral system over any other simple one that had been known in Europe before about the 10th century, and the compelling force of tradition explain the strong position that the system maintained for nearly 2,000 years in commerce, in scientific and theological literature, and in belles lettres. It had the great advantage that, for the mass of users, memorizing the values of only four letters was necessary—V, X, L, and C. Moreover, it was easier to see three in III than in 3 and to see nine in VIIII than in 9, and it was correspondingly easier to add numbers—the most basic arithmetic operation.

As in all such matters, the origin of these numerals is obscure, although the changes in their forms since the 3rd century BCE are well known. The theory of German historian Theodor Mommsen (1850) has had wide acceptance.

Momson argued that the use of V for five is due to the fact that it is a kind of hieroglyph representing the open hand with its five fingers. Two of these V symbols, one inverted on the top of the other, would form an X, which eventually became the symbol for 10. Three of the other symbols, he asserted, were modifications of Greek letters not needed in the Etruscan and early Latin alphabet. These were X (chi) for 50, which later became the L; θ (theta) for 100, which later changed to C under the influence of the Latin word *centum* ("hundred"); and Φ (phi) for 1,000, which finally took the forms I and M. The last of these, the symbol M, was most likely chosen because the word *mille* means "a thousand."

The oldest noteworthy inscription containing numerals representing very large numbers is on the Columna Rostrata, a monument erected in the Roman Forum to commemorate a victory in 260 BCE over Carthage during the First Punic War. In this column a symbol for 100,000, which was an early form of (((I))), was repeated 23 times, making 2,300,000. This illustrates not only the early Roman use of repeated symbols but also a custom that extended to modern times—that of using (I) for 1,000, ((I)) for 10,000, and (((I))) for 100,000, and ((((I)))) for 1,000,000. The symbol (I) for 1,000 frequently appears in various other forms, including the cursive ∞. All these symbols persisted until long after printing became common. In the Middle Ages a bar (known as the *vinculum* or *titulus*) was placed over a number to multiply it by 1,000, but this use is not found in the Roman inscriptions. When the bar appeared in early manuscripts, it was merely for the purpose of distinguishing numerals from words. Also used in the Middle Ages were such forms as |X| or |X| for 1,000,000 and |M| for 100,000,000.

Of the later use of the numerals, a few of the special types are as follows:

1. c·lxiiij·ccc·l·i for 164,351, Adelard of Bath (*c.* 1120)
2. II.DCCC.XIIII for 2,814, Jordanus Nemorarius (*c.* 1125)
3. MƆCLVI for 1,656, in San Marco, Venice
4. cIɔ.Iɔ.Ic for 1,599, Leiden edition of the work of Martianus Capella (1599)
5. IIIIxx et huit for 88, a Paris treaty of 1388
6. four Cli.M for 451,000, Humphrey Baker's *The Well Spryng of Sciences Whiche Teacheth the Perfecte Woorke and Practise of Arithmeticke* (1568)
7. vj.C for 600 and CCC.M for 300,000, Robert Recorde (*c.* 1542)

Item (1) represents the use of the *vinculum*; (2) represents the place value as it occasionally appears in Roman numerals (D represents 500); (3) illustrates the not infrequent use of Ɑ, like D, originally half of (I), the symbol for 1,000; (4) illustrates the persistence of the old Roman form for 1,000 and 500 and the subtractive principle so rarely used by the Romans for a number like 99; (5) shows the use of *quatrevingts* for 80, commonly found in French manuscripts until the 17th century and occasionally later, the numbers often being written like iiij^{xx}, vij^{xx}, and so on; and (6) represents the coefficient method, "four C" meaning 400, a method often leading to forms like ijM or IIM for 2,000, as shown in (7).

The subtractive principle is seen in Hebrew number names, as well as in the occasional use of IV for 4 and IX for 9 in Roman inscriptions. The Romans also used *unus de viginti* ("one from twenty") for 19 and *duo de viginti* ("two from twenty") for 18, occasionally writing these numbers as XIX (or IXX) and IIXX, respectively. On the whole, however, the subtractive principle was little used in the numerals of the Classical period.

MULTIPLICATIVE GROUPING SYSTEMS

In multiplicative systems, special names are given not only to 1, b, b^2, and so on but also to the numbers 2, 3, . . ., b - 1; the symbols of this second set are then used in place of repetitions of the first set. Thus, if 1, 2, 3, . . ., 9 are designated in the usual way but 10, 100, and $1,000$ are replaced by X, C, and M, respectively, then in a multiplicative grouping system one should write $7,392$ as $7M3C9X2$.

The principal example of this kind of notation is the Chinese numeral system, three variants of which are shown in the figure below.

Chinese numeral systems

Encyclopædia Britannica, Inc.

The modern national and mercantile systems are positional systems, as described below, and use a circle for zero.

CIPHERED NUMERAL SYSTEMS

In ciphered systems, names are given not only to 1 and the powers of the base b but also to the multiples of these powers. Thus, starting from the artificial example given above for a multiplicative grouping system, one can obtain a ciphered system if unrelated names are given to the numbers 1, 2, . . ., 9; X, $2X$, . . ., $9X$; C, $2C$, . . ., $9C$; M, $2M$, . . ., $9M$.

This requires memorizing many different symbols, but it results in a very compact notation.

The first ciphered system seems to have been the Egyptian hieratic (literally "priestly") numerals, so called because the priests were presumably the ones who had the time and learning required to develop this shorthand outgrowth of the earlier hieroglyphic numerals. An Egyptian arithmetical work on papyrus, employing hieratic numerals, was found in Egypt about 1855; known after the name of its purchaser as the Rhind papyrus, it provides the chief source of information about this numeral system. There was a still later Egyptian system, the demotic, which was also a ciphered system.

As early as the 3rd century BCE, a second system of numerals, paralleling the Attic numerals, came into use in Greece that was better adapted to the theory of numbers, though it was more difficult for the trading classes to comprehend. These Ionic, or alphabetical, numerals, were simply a cipher system in which nine Greek letters were assigned to the numbers 1–9, nine more to the numbers 10, . . ., 90, and nine more to 100, . . ., 900. Thousands were often indicated by placing a bar at the left of the corresponding numeral.

Such numeral forms were not particularly difficult for computing purposes once the operator was able automatically to recall the meaning of each. Only the capital letters were used in this ancient numeral system, the lowercase letters being a relatively modern invention.

Other ciphered numeral systems include Coptic, Hindu Brahmin, Hebrew, Syrian, and early Arabic. The last three, like the Ionic, are alphabetic ciphered numeral systems.

POSITIONAL NUMERAL SYSTEMS

The decimal number system is an example of a positional system, in which, after the base b has been adopted, the digits 1, 2, . . ., b - 1 are given special names, and all larger numbers are written as sequences of these digits. It is the only one of the systems that can be used for describing large numbers, since each of the other kinds gives special names to various numbers larger than b, and an infinite number of names would be required for all the numbers. The success of the positional system depends on the fact that, for an arbitrary base b, every number N can be written in a unique fashion in the form

$$N = a_n b^n + a_{n-1} b^{n-1} + \cdots + a_1 b + a_0$$

where $a_n, a_{n-1}, \ldots, a_0$ are digits; i.e., numbers from the group 0, 1, . . ., b - 1. Then N to the base b can be represented by the sequence of symbols $a_n a_{n-1} \ldots a_1 a_0$. It was this principle which was used in the multiplicative grouping systems, and the relation between the two kinds of systems is immediately seen from the earlier noted equivalence between 7,392 and 7M3C9X2; the positional system derives from the multiplicative simply by omitting the names of the powers b, b^2, and so on and by depending on the position of the digits to supply this information. It is then necessary, however, to use some symbol for zero to indicate any missing powers of the base; otherwise 792 could mean, for example, either 7M9X2 (i.e., 7,092) or 7C9X2 (792).

The Babylonians developed (c. 3000–2000 BCE) a positional system with base 60—a sexagesimal system. With such a large base, it would have been awkward to have unrelated names for the digits 0, 1, . . ., 59, so a simple grouping system to base 10 was used for these numbers, as shown in the figure on page 24.

In addition to being somewhat cumbersome because of the large base chosen, the Babylonian system suffered until very late from the lack of a zero symbol; the resulting ambiguities may well have bothered the Babylonians as much as later translators.

In the course of early Spanish expeditions into Yucatan, it was discovered that the Maya, at an early but still undated time, had a well-developed positional system, complete with zero. It seems to have been used primarily for the calendar rather than for commercial or other computation; this is reflected in the fact that, although the base is 20, the third digit from the end signifies multiples not of 20^2 but of 18×20, thus giving their year a simple number of days. The digits $0, 1, \ldots, 19$ are, as in the Babylonian, formed by a simple grouping system, in this case to base 5 (*see* figure); the groups were written vertically.

Mayan numeral system

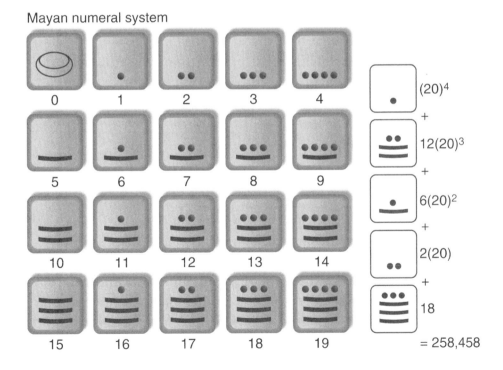

The Mayan number system, which is base 20 with simple grouping to base 5. Encyclopædia Britannica, Inc.

Neither the Mayan nor the Babylonian system was ideally suited to arithmetical computations, because the digits—the numbers less than 20 or 60—were not represented by single symbols. The complete development of this idea must be attributed to the Hindus, who also were the first to use zero in the modern way. As was mentioned earlier, some symbol is required in positional number systems to mark the place of a power of the base not actually occurring. This was indicated by the Hindus by a dot or small circle, which was given the name *sunya*, the Sanskrit word for "vacant." This was translated into the Arabic *ṣifr* about 800 CE with the meaning kept intact, and the latter was transliterated into Latin about 1200, the sound being retained but the meaning ignored. Subsequent changes have led to the modern *cipher* and *zero*.

A symbol for zero appeared in the Babylonian system about the 3rd century BCE. However, it was not used consistently and apparently served to hold only interior places, never final places, so that it was impossible to distinguish between 77 and 7,700, except by the context.

DEVELOPMENT OF MODERN NUMERALS AND NUMERAL SYSTEMS

THE HINDU-ARABIC SYSTEM

Several different claims, each having a certain amount of justification, have been made with respect to the origin of modern Western numerals, commonly spoken of as Arabic but preferably as Hindu-Arabic. These include the assertion that the origin is to be found among the Arabs, Persians, Egyptians, and Hindus. It is not improbable that the intercourse among traders served to carry such symbols from country to country, so that modern Western numerals may be a conglomeration from different sources. However, as far as is known, the country that first used the largest number of these numeral forms is India. The 1, 4, and 6 are found in the Ashoka inscriptions (3rd century BCE); the 2, 4, 6, 7, and 9 appear in the Nana Ghat inscriptions about a century later; and the 2, 3, 4, 5, 6, 7, and 9 in the Nasik caves of the 1st or 2nd century CE—all in forms that have considerable resemblance to today's, 2 and 3 being well-recognized cursive derivations from the ancient = and ≡. None of these early Indian inscriptions gives evidence of place value or of a zero that would make modern place value possible. Hindu literature gives evidence that the zero may have been known earlier, but there is no inscription with such a symbol before the 9th century.

The first definite external reference to the Hindu numerals is a note by Severus Sebokht, a bishop who lived in Mesopotamia about 650. Since he speaks of "nine signs," the zero seems to have been unknown to him. By the close of the 8th century, however, some astronomical tables of India are said to have been translated into Arabic at Baghdad, and in any case the numeral became known to Arabian scholars about this time. About 825 the mathematician Muḥammad ibn Mūsā al-Khwārizmī wrote a small book on the subject, and this was translated into Latin by Adelard of Bath (c. 1120) under the title of *Liber Algorismi de numero Indorum*. The earliest European manuscript known to contain Hindu numerals was written in Spain in 976.

The advantages enjoyed by the perfected positional system are so numerous and so manifest that the Hindu-Arabic numerals and the base 10 have been adopted almost everywhere. These might be said to be the nearest approach to a universal human language yet devised; they are found in Chinese, Japanese, and Russian scientific journals and in every Western language.

The Binary System

There is one area, however, in which the familiar decimal system is no longer supreme: the electronic computer. Here the binary positional system has been found to have great advantages over the decimal. In the binary system, in which the base is 2, there are just two digits, 0 and 1; the number two must be represented here as 10, since it plays the same role as does 10 in the decimal system. The first few binary numbers are displayed in the table.

DECIMAL NUMERALS REPRESENTED BY DIGITS

DECIMAL	BINARY	CONVERSION
0 =	0	$0\,(2^0)$
1 =	1	$1\,(2^0)$
2 =	10	$1\,(2^1)+0\,(2^0)$
3 =	11	$1\,(2^1)+1\,(2^0)$
4 =	100	$1\,(2^2)+0\,(2^1)+0\,(2^0)$
5 =	101	$1\,(2^2)+0\,(2^1)+1\,(2^0)$
6 =	110	$1\,(2^2)+1\,(2^1)+0\,(2^0)$
7 =	111	$1\,(2^2)+1\,(2^1)+1\,(2^0)$
8 =	1000	$1\,(2^3)+0\,(2^2)+0\,(2^1)+0\,(2^0)$
9 =	1001	$1\,(2^3)+0\,(2^2)+0\,(2^1)+1\,(2^0)$
10 =	1010	$1\,(2^3)+0\,(2^2)+1\,(2^1)+0\,(2^0)$

A binary number is generally much longer than its corresponding decimal number; for example, 256,058 has the binary representation 111 11010 00001 11010. The reason for the greater length of the binary number is that a binary digit distinguishes between only two possibilities, 0 or 1, whereas a decimal digit distinguishes among 10 possibilities; in other words, a binary digit carries less information than a decimal digit. Because of this, its name has been shortened to *bit*; a bit of information is thus transmitted whenever one of two alternatives is realized in the machine. It is of course much easier to construct a machine to distinguish between two possibilities than among 10, and this is another advantage for the base 2; but a more important point is that bits serve simultaneously to carry numerical information and the logic of the problem. That is, the dichotomies of yes and no, and of true and false, are preserved in the machine in the same way as 1 and 0, so in the end everything reduces to a sequence of those two characters.

ARITHMETIC

Arithmetic (a term derived from the Greek word *arithmos*, "number") refers generally to the elementary aspects of the theory of numbers, arts of mensuration (measurement), and numerical computation (that is, the processes of addition, subtraction, multiplication, division, raising to powers, and extraction of roots). Its meaning, however, has not been uniform in mathematical usage. An eminent German mathematician, Carl Friedrich Gauss, in *Disquisitiones Arithmeticae* (1801), and certain modern-day mathematicians have used the term to include more advanced topics. The reader interested in the latter is referred to the section on number theory.

FUNDAMENTAL DEFINITIONS AND LAWS

NATURAL NUMBERS

In a collection (or set) of objects (or elements), the act of determining the number of objects present is called counting. The numbers thus obtained are called the counting numbers or natural numbers (1, 2, 3, . . .). For an empty set, no object is present, and the count yields the number 0, which, appended to the natural numbers, produces what are known as the whole numbers.

If objects from two sets can be matched in such a way that every element from each set is uniquely paired with an element from the other set, the sets are said to be equal or equivalent. The concept of equivalent sets is basic to the foundations of modern mathematics and has been introduced into primary education, notably as part of the "new math" that has been alternately acclaimed and decried since it appeared in the 1960s.

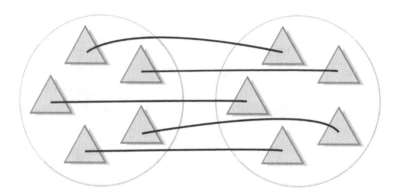

A page from a first-grade workbook typical of "new math" might state: "Draw connecting lines from triangles in the first set to triangles in the second set. Are the two sets equivalent in number?" © Encyclopædia Britannica, Inc.

ADDITION AND MULTIPLICATION

Combining two sets of objects together, which contain a and b elements, a new set is formed that contains $a + b = c$ objects. The number c is called the sum of a and b; and each of the latter is called a summand. The operation of forming the sum is called addition, the symbol + being read as "plus." This is the simplest binary operation, where *binary* refers to the process of combining two objects.

From the definition of counting it is evident that the order of the summands can be changed and the order of the operation of addition can be changed, when applied to three summands, without affecting the sum. These are called the commutative law of addition and the associative law of addition, respectively (*see* table).

FUNDAMENTAL LAWS OF ARITHMETIC
Commutative law of addition: $a + b = b + a$
Associative law of addition: $a + (b + c) = (a + b) + c$
Commutative law of multiplication: $a\,b = b\,a$
Associative law of multiplication: $a\,(b\,c) = (a\,b)\,c$
Distributive law: $a\,(b + c) = a\,b + a\,c$

If there exists a natural number k such that $a = b + k$, it is said that a is greater than b (written $a > b$) and that b is less than a (written $b < a$). If a and b are any two natural numbers, then it is the case that either $a = b$ or $a > b$ or $a < b$ (the trichotomy law).

From the above laws, it is evident that a repeated sum such as $5 + 5 + 5$ is independent of the way in which the summands are grouped; it can be written 3×5. Thus, a second binary operation called multiplication is defined. The number 5 is called the multiplicand; the number 3, which denotes the number of summands, is called the multiplier; and the result 3×5 is called the product. The symbol $\times$ of this operation is read "times." If such letters as a and b are used to denote the numbers, the product $a \times b$ is often written $a \cdot b$ or simply ab. If three rows of five dots each are written, as illustrated below,

$$
\begin{array}{ccccc}
\cdot & \cdot & \cdot & \cdot & \cdot \\
\cdot & \cdot & \cdot & \cdot & \cdot \\
\cdot & \cdot & \cdot & \cdot & \cdot
\end{array}
$$

it is clear that the total number of dots in the array is 3 × 5, or 15. This same number of dots can evidently be written in five rows of three dots each, whence 5 × 3 = 15. The argument is general, leading to the law that the order of the multiplicands does not affect the product, called the commutative law of multiplication. But it is notable that this law does not apply to all mathematical entities. Indeed, much of the mathematical formulation of modern physics, for example, depends crucially on the fact that some entities do not commute.

By the use of a three-dimensional array of dots, it becomes evident that the order of multiplication when applied to three numbers does not affect the product. Such a law is called the associative law of multiplication. If the 15 dots written above are separated into two sets, as shown,

· · · · ·

· · · · ·

· · · · ·

then the first set consists of three columns of three dots each, or 3 × 3 dots; the second set consists of two columns of three dots each, or 2 × 3 dots; the sum (3 × 3) + (2 × 3) consists of 3 + 2 = 5 columns of three dots each, or (3 + 2) × 3 dots. In general, one may prove that the multiplication of a sum by a number is the same as the sum of two appropriate products. Such a law is called the distributive law.

INTEGERS

Subtraction has not been introduced for the simple reason that it can be defined as the inverse of addition. Thus, the difference $a - b$ of two numbers a and b is defined as a solution x of the equation $b + x = a$. If a number system is restricted to the natural numbers, differences need not always exist, but, if they do, the five basic laws of arithmetic, as already discussed, can be used to prove that they are unique. Furthermore, the laws of operations of addition and multiplication can be extended to apply to differences. The whole numbers (including zero) can be extended to include the solution of $1 + x = 0$, that is, the number -1, as well as all products of the form $-1 \times n$, in which n is a whole number. The extended collection of numbers is called the integers, of which the positive integers are the same as the natural numbers. The numbers that are newly introduced in this way are called negative integers.

EXPONENTS

Just as a repeated sum $a + a + \cdots + a$ of k summands is written ka, so a repeated product $a \times a \times \cdots \times a$ of k factors is written a^k. The number k is called the exponent, and a the base of the power a^k.

The fundamental laws of exponents follow easily from the definitions, and other laws are immediate consequences of the fundamental ones.

THEORY OF DIVISORS

At this point an interesting development occurs, for, so long as only additions and multiplications are performed with integers, the resulting numbers are invariably themselves integers—that is, numbers of the same kind as their antecedents. This characteristic changes drastically, however, as soon as division is introduced. Performing division (its symbol $\div$, read "divided by") leads to results, called quotients or fractions, which surprisingly include numbers of a new kind—namely, rationals—that are not integers. These, though arising from the combination of integers, patently constitute a distinct extension of the natural-number and integer concepts as defined above. By means of the application of the division operation, the domain of the natural numbers becomes extended and enriched immeasurably beyond the integers.

The preceding illustrates one of the proclivities that are often associated with mathematical thought: relatively simple concepts (such as integers), initially based on very concrete operations (for example, counting), are found to be capable of assuming novel meanings and potential uses, extending far beyond the limits of the concept as originally defined. A similar extension of basic concepts, with even more powerful results, will be found with the introduction of irrationals.

A second example of this pattern is presented by the following: Under the primitive definition of exponents, with k equal to either zero or a fraction, a^k would, at first sight, appear to be utterly devoid of meaning. Clarification is needed before writing a repeated product of either zero factors or a fractional number of factors. Considering the case $k = 0$, a little reflection shows that a^0 can, in fact, assume a perfectly precise meaning, coupled with an additional and quite extraordinary property. Since the result of dividing any (nonzero) number by itself is 1, or unity, it follows that

$$a^m \div a^m = a^{m-m} = a^0 = 1.$$

Not only can the definition of a^k be extended to include the case $k = 0$, but the ensuing result also possesses the noteworthy property that it is independent of the particular (nonzero) value of the base a. A similar argument may be given to show that a^k is a meaningful expression even when k is negative, namely,

$$a^{-k} = 1/a^k.$$

The original concept of exponent is thus broadened to a great extent.

FUNDAMENTAL THEORY

If three positive integers a, b, and c are in the relation $ab = c$, it is said that a and b are divisors or factors of c, or that a divides c (written $a|c$), and b divides c. The number c is said to be a multiple of a and a multiple of b.

The number 1 is called the unit, and it is clear that 1 is a divisor of every positive integer. If c can be expressed as a product ab in which a and b are positive integers each greater than 1, then c is called composite. A positive integer neither 1 nor composite is called a prime number. Thus, 2, 3, 5, 7, 11, 13, 17, 19, . . . are prime numbers. The ancient Greek mathematician Euclid proved in his *Elements* (c. 300 BCE) that there are infinitely many prime numbers.

The fundamental theorem of arithmetic was proved by Gauss in his *Disquisitiones Arithmeticae*. It states that every composite number can be expressed as a product of prime numbers and that, save for the order in which the factors are written, this representation is unique. Gauss's theorem follows rather directly from another theorem of Euclid to the effect that if a prime divides a product, then it also divides one of the factors in the product; for this reason the fundamental theorem is sometimes credited to Euclid.

For every finite set a_1, a_2, . . ., a_k of positive integers, there exists a largest integer that divides each of these numbers, called their greatest common divisor (GCD). If the GCD = 1, the numbers are said to be relatively prime. There also exists a smallest positive integer that is a multiple of each of the numbers, called their least common multiple (LCM).

A systematic method for obtaining the GCD and LCM starts by factoring each a_i (where i = 1, 2, . . ., k) into a product of primes $p_1, p_2, \ldots, p_h$, with the number of times that each distinct prime occurs indicated by q_i; thus,

$$a_i = p_1^{q_1} p_2^{q_2} \ldots p_h^{q_h}.$$

Then the GCD is obtained by multiplying together each prime that occurs in every a_i as many times as it occurs the fewest (smallest power) among all of the a_i. The LCM is obtained by multiplying together each prime that occurs in any of the a_i as many times as it occurs the most (largest power) among all of the a_i. An example is easily constructed. Given $a_1 = 3{,}000 = 2^3 \times 3^1 \times 5^3$ and $a_2 = 2{,}646 = 2^1 \times 3^3 \times 7^2$, the GCD $= 2^1 \times 3^1 = 6$ and the LCM $= 2^3 \times 3^3 \times 5^3 \times 7^2 = 1{,}323{,}000$. When only two numbers are involved, the product of the GCD and the LCM equals the product of the original numbers. (*See* the table for useful divisibility tests.)

SOME DIVISIBILITY RULES	
DIVISOR	CONDITION
2	The number is even.
3	The sum of the digits in the number is divisible by 3.
4	The last two digits in the number form a number that is divisible by 4.
5	The number ends in 0 or 5.
6	The number is even and the sum of its digits is divisible by 3.
8	The last three digits in the number form a number that is divisible by 8.
9	The sum of the digits in the number is divisible by 9.
10	The number ends in 0.
11	The difference between the sum of the number's digits in the odd places and that of the digits in the even places is either 0 or divisible by 11.

If a and b are two positive integers, with $a > b$, two whole numbers q and r exist such that $a = qb + r$, with r less than b. The number q is called the partial quotient (the quotient if $r = 0$), and r is called the remainder. Using a process known as the Euclidean algorithm, which works because the GCD of a and b is equal to the GCD of b and r, the GCD can be obtained without first factoring the numbers a and b into prime factors. The Euclidean algorithm begins by determining the values of q and r, after which b and r assume the role of a and b and the process repeats until finally the remainder is zero; the last positive remainder is the GCD of the original two numbers. For example, starting with 544 and 119:

- 1. $544 = 4 \times 119 + 68$;
- 2. $119 = 1 \times 68 + 51$;
- 3. $68 = 1 \times 51 + 17$;
- 4. $51 = 3 \times 17$.

Thus, the GCD of 544 and 119 is 17.

RATIONAL NUMBERS

From a less abstract point of view, the notion of division, or of fraction, may also be considered to arise as follows: if the duration of a given process is required to be known to an accuracy of better than one hour, the number of minutes may be specified; or, if the hour is to be retained as the fundamental unit, each minute may be represented by 1/60 or by

$$\frac{1}{60}.$$

In general, the fractional unit $1/d$ is defined by the property $d \times 1/d = 1$. The number $n \times 1/d$ is written n/d and is called a common fraction. It may be considered as the quotient of n divided by d. The number d is called the denominator (it determines the fractional unit or denomination), and *n* is called the numerator (it enumerates the number of fractional units that are taken). The numerator and denominator together are called the terms of the fraction. A positive fraction *n/d* is said to be proper if *n* < *d*; otherwise it is improper.

The numerator and denominator of a fraction are not unique, since for every positive integer *k*, the numerator and denominator of a fraction can each simultaneously be multiplied by the integer *k* without altering the fractional value. Every fraction can be written as the quotient of two relatively prime integers, however. In this form it is said to be in lowest terms.

The integers and fractions constitute what are called the rational numbers. The five fundamental laws stated earlier with regard to the positive integers can be generalized to apply to all rational numbers.

Adding and Subtracting Fractions

From the definition of fraction it follows that the sum (or difference) of two fractions having the same denominator is another fraction with this denominator, the numerator of which is the sum (or difference) of the numerators of the given fractions. Two fractions having different denominators may be added or subtracted by first reducing them to fractions with the same denominator. Thus, to add *a/b* and *c/d*, the LCM of *b* and *d*, often called the least common denominator of the fractions, must be determined. It follows that there exist numbers *k* and *l* such that *kb* = *ld*, and both fractions can be written with this common denominator, so that the sum or difference of the fractions is obtained by the simple operation of adding or subtracting the new numerators and placing the value over the new denominator.

Multiplying and Dividing Fractions

In order to multiply two fractions—in case one of the numbers is a whole number, it is placed over the number 1 to create a fraction—the numerators and denominators are multiplied separately to produce the new fraction's numerator and denominator: $a/b \times c/d = ac/bd$. In order to divide by a fraction, it must be inverted—that is, the numerator and denominator interchanged—after which it becomes a multiplication problem: $a/b \div c/d = a/b \times d/c = ad/bc$.

Theory of Rationals

A method of introducing the positive rational numbers that is free from intuition (that is, with all logical steps included) was given in 1910 by the German mathematician Ernst Steinitz. In considering the set of all number pairs (a, b), (c, d), . . . in which $a, b, c, d,$ . . . are positive integers, the equals relation $(a, b) = (c, d)$ is defined to mean that $ad = bc$, and the two operations + and × are defined so that the sum of a pair $(a, b) + (c, d) = (ad + bc, bd)$ is a pair and the product of a pair $(a, b) \times (c, d) = (ac, bd)$ is a pair. It can be proved that, if these sums and products are properly specified, the fundamental laws of arithmetic hold for these pairs and that the pairs of the type $(a, 1)$ are abstractly identical with the positive integers a. Moreover, $b \times (a, b) = a$, so that the pair (a, b) is abstractly identical with the fraction a/b.

IRRATIONAL NUMBERS

It was known to the Pythagoreans (followers of the ancient Greek mathematician Pythagoras) that, given a straight line segment a and a unit segment u, it is not always possible to find a fractional unit such that both a and u are multiples of it (*see* incommensurables). For instance, if the sides of an isosceles right triangle have length 1, then by the Pythagorean theorem the hypotenuse has a length the square of which must be 2. But there exists no rational number the square of which is 2.

Eudoxus of Cnidus, a contemporary of Plato, established the technique necessary to extend numbers beyond the rationals. His contribution, one of the most important in the history of mathematics, was included in Euclid's *Elements* and elsewhere, and then it lay dormant until the modern period of growth in mathematical analysis in Germany in the 19th century.

It is customary to assume on an intuitive basis that, corresponding to every line segment and every unit length, there exists a number (called a positive real number) that represents the length of the line segment. Not all such numbers are rational, but every one can be approximated arbitrarily closely by a rational number. That is, if x is a positive real number and ε is any positive rational number— no matter how small—it is possible to find two positive rational numbers a and b within ε distance from each other such that x is between them; in symbols, given any $\varepsilon > 0$, there exist positive rational numbers a and b such that $b - a < \varepsilon$ and $a < x < b$. In problems in mensuration, irrational numbers are usually replaced by suitable rational approximations.

A rigorous development of the irrational numbers is beyond the scope of arithmetic. They are most satisfactorily introduced by means of Dedekind cuts, as introduced by the German mathematician Richard Dedekind, or sequences of rationals, as introduced by Eudoxus and developed by the German mathematician Georg Cantor. These methods are discussed in analysis.

The employment of irrational numbers greatly increases the scope and usefulness of arithmetic. For instance, if n is any whole number and a is any positive real number, there exists a unique positive real number $\sqrt[n]{a}$, called the nth root of a, whose nth power is a. The root symbol $\sqrt{}$ is a conventionalized r for *radix*, or "root." The term *evolution* is sometimes applied to the process of finding a rational approximation to an nth root.

MODULAR ARITHMETIC

Modular arithmetic, sometimes referred to as clock arithmetic in its most elementary form, is arithmetic done with a count that resets itself to zero every time a certain whole number N greater than one, known as the modulus (mod), has been reached. Examples are a digital clock in the 24-hour system, which resets itself to 0 at midnight ($N = 24$), and a circular protractor marked in 360 degrees ($N = 360$). Modular arithmetic is important in number theory, where it is a fundamental tool in the solution of Diophantine equations (particularly those restricted to integer solutions). Generalizations of the subject led to important 19th-century attempts to prove Fermat's last theorem and the development of significant parts of modern algebra.

Under modular arithmetic (with mod N), the only numbers are $0, 1, 2, \ldots, N - 1$, and they are known as residues modulo N. Residues are added by taking the usual arithmetic sum, then subtracting the modulus from the sum as many times as is necessary to reduce the sum to a number M between 0 and $N - 1$ inclusive. M is called the sum of the numbers modulo N. Using notation introduced by the German mathematician Carl Friedrich Gauss in 1801, one writes, for example, $2 + 4 + 3 + 7 \equiv 6 \pmod{10}$, where the symbol $\equiv$ is read "is congruent to."

Examples of the use of modular arithmetic occur in ancient Chinese, Indian, and Islamic cultures. In particular, they occur in calendrical and astronomical problems since these involve cycles (man-made or natural), but one also finds modular arithmetic in purely mathematical problems. An example from a 3rd-century-CE Chinese book, Sun Zi's *Sunzi suanjing* (*Master Sun's Mathematical Manual*), asks

We have a number of things, but we do not know exactly how many. If we count them by threes we have two left over. If we count by fives we have three left over. If we count by sevens there are two left over. How many things are there?

This is equivalent to asking for the solution of the simultaneous congruences $X \equiv 2 \pmod 3$, $X \equiv 3 \pmod 5$, and $X \equiv 2 \pmod 7$, one solution of which is 23. The general solution of such problems came to be known as the Chinese remainder theorem.

The Swiss mathematician Leonhard Euler pioneered the modern approach to congruence about 1750, when he explicitly introduced the idea of congruence modulo a number N and showed that this concept partitions the integers into N congruence classes, or residue classes. Two integers are in the same congruence class modulo N if their difference is divisible by N. For example, if N is 5, then -6 and 4 are members of the same congruence class {. . ., -6, -1, 4, 9, . . .}. Since each congruence class may be represented by any of its members, this particular class may be called, for example, "the congruence class of -6 modulo 5" or "the congruence class of 4 modulo 5."

In Euler's system any N numbers that leave different remainders on division by N may represent the congruence classes modulo N. Thus, one possible system for arithmetic modulo 5 would be -2, -1, 0, 1, 2. Addition of congruence classes modulo N is defined by choosing any element from each class, adding the elements together, and then taking the congruence class modulo N that the sum belongs to as the answer. Euler similarly defined subtraction and multiplication of residue classes. For example, to multiply -3 by 4 (mod 5), first multiply -3 × 4 = -12; since -12 ≡ 3 (mod 5), the solution is -3 × 4 ≡ 3 (mod 5). Euler showed that one would get the same result with any two elements from the corresponding congruence classes.

Note that when the modulus N is not prime, division is not always possible. For example, 1 ÷ 2 ≡ 3 (mod 5), since 2 × 3 ≡ 1 (mod 5). However, the equation 1 ÷ 2 ≡ X (mod 4) does not have a solution, since there is no X such that 2 × X ≡ 1 (mod 4). When the modulus N is not prime, it is possible to divide a class represented by r by a class represented by s if and only if s and N are relatively prime (that is, if their only common factor is the number 1). For example, 7 ÷ 4 ≡ 4 (mod 9) since 4 × 4 ≡ 7 (mod 9)—in this case, 7 and 9 are relatively prime.

LOGARITHMS

A logarithm is the exponent or power to which a base must be raised to yield a given number. Expressed mathematically, x is the logarithm of n to the base b if $b^x = n$, in which case one writes $x = \log_b n$. For example, $2^3 = 8$; therefore, 3 is the logarithm of 8 to base 2, or $3 = \log_2 8$. In the same fashion, since $10^2 = 100$, then $2 = \log_{10} 100$. Logarithms of the latter sort (that is, logarithms with base 10) are called common, or Briggsian, logarithms and are written simply $\log n$.

Invented in the 17th century to speed up calculations, logarithms vastly reduced the time required for multiplying numbers with many digits. They were basic in numerical work for more than 300 years, until the perfection of mechanical calculating machines in the late 19th century and computers in the 20th century rendered them obsolete for large-scale computations. The natural, or Napierian, logarithm (with base $e \cong 2.71828$ and written $\ln n$), however, continues to be one of the most useful functions in mathematics, with applications to mathematical models throughout the physical and biological sciences.

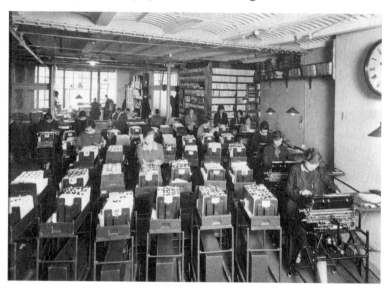

Adding machines, like those seen in use above, were developed by William Seward Burroughs in the late 19th century to facilitate the solving of arithmetical problems. SSPL/Getty Images

PROPERTIES OF LOGARITHMS

Logarithms were quickly adopted by scientists because of various useful properties that simplified long, tedious calculations. In particular, scientists could find the product of two numbers m and n by looking up each number's logarithm in a special table, adding the logarithms together, and then consulting the table again to find the number with that calculated logarithm (known as its antilogarithm). Expressed in terms of common logarithms, this relationship is given by log mn = log m + log n. For example, 100 × 1,000 can be calculated by looking up the logarithms of 100 (2) and 1,000 (3), adding the logarithms together (5), and then finding its antilogarithm (100,000) in the table. Similarly, division problems are converted into subtraction problems with logarithms: $\log m/n = \log m - \log n$. This is not all; the calculation of powers and roots can be simplified with the use of logarithms. Logarithms can also be converted between any positive bases (except that 1 cannot be used as the base since all of its powers are equal to 1).

Only logarithms for numbers between 0 and 10 are typically included in logarithm tables. To obtain the logarithm of some number outside of this range, the number must first be written in scientific notation as the product of its significant digits and its exponential power—for example, 358 would be written as 3.58×10^2, and 0.0046 would be written as 4.6×10^{-3}. Then the logarithm of the significant digits—a decimal fraction between 0 and 1, known as the mantissa—can be found in a table. Finally, the integer exponential power, known as the characteristic of the logarithm, is appended before the decimal point to give the logarithm of the original number. However, when this integer is negative, the minus sign is omitted and a bar is placed over it to distinguish it from the positive mantissa. For example, to find the logarithm of 0.0046, one would look up $\log 4.6 \cong 0.6628$ and then write $\log 0.0046 \cong \bar{3}.6628$.

HISTORY OF LOGARITHMS

The invention of logarithms was foreshadowed by the comparison of arithmetic and geometric sequences. In a geometric sequence each term forms a constant ratio with its successor; for example,

$$\ldots 1/1{,}000, \; 1/100, \; 1/10, \; 1, \; 10, \; 100, \; 1{,}000 \ldots$$

has a common ratio of 10. In an arithmetic sequence each successive term differs by a constant, known as the common difference; for example,

$$\ldots -3, -2, -1, 0, 1, 2, 3 \ldots$$

has a common difference of 1. Note that a geometric sequence can be written in terms of its common ratio; for the example geometric sequence given above:

$$\ldots 10^{-3}, 10^{-2}, 10^{-1}, 10^{0}, 10^{1}, 10^{2}, 10^{3} \ldots$$

Multiplying two numbers in the geometric sequence, say 1/10 and 100, is equal to adding the corresponding exponents of the common ratio, -1 and 2, to obtain $10^1 = 10$. Thus, multiplication is transformed into addition. The original comparison between the two series, however, was not based on any explicit use of the exponential notation; this was a later development. In 1620 the first table based on the concept of relating geometric and arithmetic sequences was published in Prague by the Swiss mathematician Joost Bürgi.

The Scottish mathematician John Napier published his discovery of logarithms in 1614. His purpose was to assist in the multiplication of quantities that were then called sines. The whole sine was the value of the side of a right-angled triangle with a large hypotenuse. (Napier's original hypotenuse was 10^7.) His definition was given in terms of relative rates.

The logarithme, therefore, of any sine is a number very neerely expressing the line which increased equally in the meene time whiles the line of the whole sine decreased proportionally into that sine, both motions being equal timed and the beginning equally shift.

In cooperation with the English mathematician Henry Briggs, Napier adjusted his logarithm into its modern form. For the Naperian, or natural, logarithm the comparison would be between points moving on a graduated straight line, the L point (for the logarithm) moving uniformly from minus infinity to plus infinity, the X point (for the sine) moving from zero to infinity at a speed proportional to its distance from zero. Furthermore, L is zero when X is one and their speed is equal at this point. The essence of Napier's discovery is that this constitutes a generalization of the relation between the arithmetic and geometric series; i.e., multiplication and raising to a power of the values of the X point correspond to addition and multiplication of the values of the L point, respectively. In practice it is convenient to limit the L and X motion by the requirement that $L = 1$ at $X = 10$ in addition to the condition that $X = 1$ at $L = 0$. This change produced the Briggsian, or common, logarithm.

Napier died in 1617 and Briggs continued alone, publishing in 1624 a table of logarithms calculated to 14 decimal places for numbers from 1 to 20,000 and from 90,000 to 100,000. In 1628 the Dutch publisher Adriaan Vlacq brought out a 10-place table for values from 1 to 100,000, adding the missing 70,000 values. Both Briggs and Vlacq engaged in setting up log trigonometric tables. Such early tables were either to one-hundreth of a degree or to one minute of arc. In the 18th century, tables were published for 10-second intervals, which were convenient for seven-decimal-place tables. In general, finer intervals are required for calculating logarithmic functions of smaller numbers—for example, in the calculation of the functions log sin x and log tan x.

The availability of logarithms greatly influenced the form of plane and spherical trigonometry. The procedures of trigonometry were recast to produce formulas in which the operations that depend on logarithms are done all at once. The recourse to the tables then consisted of only two steps, obtaining logarithms and, after performing computations with the logarithms, obtaining antilogarithms.

NUMBER THEORY

Number theory is concerned with properties of the positive integers (1, 2, 3, . . .). Sometimes called "higher arithmetic," it is among the oldest and most natural of mathematical pursuits.

Number theory has always fascinated amateurs as well as professional mathematicians. In contrast to other branches of mathematics, many of the problems and theorems of number theory can be understood by laypersons, although solutions to the problems and proofs of the theorems often require a sophisticated mathematical background.

Until the mid-20th century, number theory was considered the purest branch of mathematics, with no direct applications to the real world. The advent of digital computers and digital communications revealed that number theory could provide unexpected answers to real-world problems. At the same time, improvements in computer technology enabled number theorists to make remarkable advances in factoring large numbers, determining primes, testing conjectures, and solving numerical problems once considered out of reach.

Modern number theory is a broad subject that is classified into subheadings such as elementary number theory, algebraic number theory, analytic number theory, geometric number theory, and probabilistic number theory. These categories reflect the methods used to address problems concerning the integers.

From Prehistory Through Classical Greece

The ability to count dates back to prehistoric times. This is evident from archaeological artifacts, such as a 10,000-year-old bone from the Congo region of Africa with tally marks scratched upon it—signs of an unknown ancestor counting something. Very near the dawn of civilization, people had grasped the idea of "multiplicity" and thereby had taken the first steps toward a study of numbers.

It is certain that an understanding of numbers existed in ancient Mesopotamia, Egypt, China, and India, for tablets, papyri, and temple carvings from these early cultures have survived. A Babylonian tablet known as Plimpton 322 (c. 1700 BCE) is a case in point. In modern notation, it displays number triples x, y, and z with the property that $x^2 + y^2 = z^2$. One such triple is 2,291, 2,700, and 3,541, where $2,291^2 + 2,700^2 = 3,541^2$. This certainly reveals a degree of number theoretic sophistication in ancient Babylon.

Despite such isolated results, a general theory of numbers was nonexistent. For this—as with so much of theoretical mathematics—one must look to the Classical Greeks, whose groundbreaking achievements displayed an odd fusion of the mystical tendencies of the Pythagoreans and the severe logic of Euclid's *Elements* (c. 300 BCE).

Pythagoras

According to tradition, Pythagoras (c. 580–500 BCE) worked in southern Italy amid devoted followers. His philosophy enshrined number as the unifying concept necessary for understanding everything from planetary motion to musical harmony. Given this viewpoint, it is not surprising that the Pythagoreans attributed quasi-rational properties to certain numbers.

For instance, they attached significance to perfect numbers—i.e., those that equal the sum of their proper divisors. Examples are 6 (whose proper divisors 1, 2, and 3 sum to 6) and 28 (1 + 2 + 4 + 7 + 14). The Greek philosopher Nicomachus of Gerasa (flourished *c.* 100 CE), writing centuries after Pythagoras but clearly in his philosophical debt, stated that perfect numbers represented "virtues, wealth, moderation, propriety, and beauty." (Some modern writers label this kind of thinking numerical theology.)

In a similar vein, the Greeks called a pair of integers amicable ("friendly") if each was the sum of the proper divisors of the other. They knew only a single amicable pair: 220 and 284. One can easily check that the sum of the proper divisors of 284 is 1 + 2 + 4 + 71 + 142 = 220 and the sum of the proper divisors of 220 is 1 + 2 + 4 + 5 + 10 + 11 + 20 + 22 + 44 + 55 + 110 = 284. For those prone to number mysticism, such a phenomenon must have seemed like magic.

EUCLID

By contrast, Euclid presented number theory without the flourishes. He began Book VII of his *Elements* by defining a number as "a multitude composed of units." The plural here excluded 1; for Euclid, 2 was the smallest "number." He later defined a prime as a number "measured by a unit alone" (i.e., whose only proper divisor is 1), a composite as a number that is not prime, and a perfect number as one that equals the sum of its "parts" (i.e., its proper divisors).

From there, Euclid proved a sequence of theorems that marks the beginning of number theory as a mathematical (as opposed to a numerological) enterprise. Four Euclidean propositions deserve special mention.

The first, Proposition 2 of Book VII, is a procedure for finding the greatest common divisor of two whole numbers. This fundamental result is now called the Euclidean algorithm in his honour.

Second, Euclid gave a version of what is known as the unique factorization theorem or the fundamental theorem of arithmetic. This says that any whole number can be factored into the product of primes in one and only one way. For example, $1,960 = 2 \times 2 \times 2 \times 5 \times 7 \times 7$ is a decomposition into prime factors, and no other such decomposition exists. Euclid's discussion of unique factorization is not satisfactory by modern standards, but its essence can be found in Proposition 32 of Book VII and Proposition 14 of Book IX.

Third, Euclid showed that no finite collection of primes contains them all. His argument, Proposition 20 of Book IX, remains one of the most elegant proofs in all of mathematics. Beginning with any finite collection of primes — say, $a, b, c, \ldots, n$ — Euclid considered the number formed by adding one to their product: $N = (abc \cdots n) + 1$. He then examined the two alternatives:(1) If N is prime, then it is a new prime not among $a, b, c, \ldots, n$ because it is larger than all of these. For example, if the original primes were 2, 3, and 7, then $N = (2 \times 3 \times 7) + 1 = 43$ is a larger prime. (2) Alternately, if N is composite, it must have a prime factor which, as Euclid demonstrated, cannot be one of the originals. To illustrate, begin with primes 2, 7, and 11, so that $N = (2 \times 7 \times 11) + 1 = 155$. This is composite, but its prime factors 5 and 31 do not appear among the originals. Either way, a finite set of primes can always be augmented. It follows, by this beautiful piece of logic, that the collection of primes is infinite.

Fourth, Euclid ended Book IX with a blockbuster: if the series $1 + 2 + 4 + 8 + \ldots + 2k$ sums to a prime, then the number $N = 2^k(1 + 2 + 4 + \ldots + 2^k)$ must be perfect. For example, $1 + 2 + 4 = 7$, a prime, so $4(1 + 2 + 4) = 28$ is perfect.

Euclid's "recipe" for perfect numbers was a most impressive achievement for its day.

DIOPHANTUS

Of later Greek mathematicians, especially noteworthy is Diophantus of Alexandria (flourished *c.* 250), author of *Arithmetica*. This book features a host of problems, the most significant of which have come to be called Diophantine equations. These are equations whose solutions must be whole numbers. For example, Diophantus asked for two numbers, one a square and the other a cube, such that the sum of their squares is itself a square. In modern symbols, he sought integers x, y, and z such that $(x^2)^2 + (y^3)^2 = z^2$. It is easy to find real numbers satisfying this relationship (e.g., $x = \sqrt{2}$, $y = 1$, and $z = \sqrt{5}$), but the requirement that solutions be integers makes the problem more difficult. (One answer is $x = 6$, $y = 3$, and $z = 45$.) Diophantus's work strongly influenced later mathematics.

NUMBER THEORY IN THE EAST

The millennium following the decline of Rome saw no significant European advances, but Chinese and Indian scholars were making their own contributions to the theory of numbers. Motivated by questions of astronomy and the calendar, the Chinese mathematician Sun Zi (Sun Tzu; flourished *c.* 250 CE) tackled multiple Diophantine equations. As one example, he asked for a whole number that when divided by 3 leaves a remainder of 2, when divided by 5 leaves a remainder of 3, and when divided by 7 leaves a remainder of 2 (his answer: 23). Almost a thousand years later, Qin Jiushao (1202–61) gave a general procedure, now known as the Chinese remainder theorem, for solving problems of this sort.

Meanwhile, Indian mathematicians were hard at work. In the 7th century Brahmagupta took up what is now (erroneously) called the Pell equation. He posed the challenge to find a perfect square that, when multiplied by 92 and increased by 1, yields another perfect square. That is, he sought whole numbers x and y such that $92x^2 + 1 = y^2$—a Diophantine equation with quadratic terms. Brahmagupta suggested that anyone who could solve this problem within a year earned the right to be called a mathematician. His solution was $x = 120$ and $y = 1{,}151$.

In addition, Indian scholars developed the so-called Hindu-Arabic numerals—the base-10 notation subsequently adopted by the world's mathematical and civil communities. Although more number representation than number theory, these numerals have prevailed due to their simplicity and ease of use. The Indians employed this system—including the zero—as early as 800 CE.

At about this time, the Islamic world became a mathematical powerhouse. Situated on trade routes between East and West, Islamic scholars absorbed the works of other civilizations and augmented these with homegrown achievements. For example, Thabit ibn Qurrah (active in Baghdad in the 9th century) returned to the Greek problem of amicable numbers and discovered a second pair: 17,296 and 18,416.

MODERN NUMBER THEORY

As mathematics filtered from the Islamic world to Renaissance Europe, number theory received little serious attention. The period from 1400 to 1650 saw important advances in geometry, algebra, and probability, not to mention the discovery of both logarithms and analytic geometry. But number theory was regarded as a minor subject, largely of recreational interest.

PIERRE DE FERMAT

Credit for changing this perception goes to Pierre de Fermat (1601–65), a French magistrate with time on his hands and a passion for numbers. Although he published little, Fermat posed the questions and identified the issues that have shaped number theory ever since. Here are a few examples:

- In 1640 he stated what is known as Fermat's little theorem—namely, that if p is prime and a is any whole number, then p divides evenly into $a^p - a$. Thus, if $p = 7$ and $a = 12$, the far-from-obvious conclusion is that 7 is a divisor of $12^7 - 12 = 35,831,796$. This theorem is one of the great tools of modern number theory.
- Fermat investigated the two types of odd primes: those that are one more than a multiple of 4 and those that are one less. These are designated as the $4k + 1$ primes and the $4k - 1$ primes, respectively. Among the former are $5 = 4 \times 1 + 1$ and $97 = 4 \times 24 + 1$; among the latter are $3 = 4 \times 1 - 1$ and $79 = 4 \times 20 - 1$. Fermat asserted that any prime of the form $4k + 1$ can be written as the sum of two squares in one and only one way, whereas a prime of the form $4k - 1$ cannot be written as the sum of two squares in any manner whatever. Thus, $5 = 2^2 + 1^2$ and $97 = 9^2 + 4^2$, and these have no alternative decompositions into sums of squares. On the other hand, 3 and 79 cannot be so decomposed. This dichotomy among primes ranks as one of the landmarks of number theory.

- In 1638 Fermat asserted that every whole number can be expressed as the sum of four or fewer squares. He claimed to have a proof but did not share it.
- Fermat stated that there cannot be a right triangle with sides of integer length whose area is a perfect square. This amounts to saying that there do not exist integers x, y, z, and w such that $x^2 + y^2 = z^2$ (the Pythagorean relationship) and that $w^2 = \frac{1}{2}$ (base) (height) = $xy/2$.

Uncharacteristically, Fermat provided a proof of this last result. He used a technique called infinite descent that was ideal for demonstrating impossibility. The logical strategy assumes that there are whole numbers satisfying the condition in question and then generates smaller whole numbers satisfying it as well. Reapplying the argument over and over, Fermat produced an endless sequence of decreasing whole numbers. But this is impossible, for any set of positive integers must contain a smallest member. By this contradiction, Fermat concluded that no such numbers can exist in the first place.

Two other assertions of Fermat should be mentioned. One was that any number of the form $2^{2^n} + 1$ must be prime. He was correct if $n = 0, 1, 2, 3$, and 4, for the formula yields primes $2^{2^0} + 1 = 3$, $2^{2^1} + 1 = 5$, $2^{2^2} + 1 = 17$, $2^{2^3} + 1 = 257$, and $2^{2^4} + 1 = 65{,}537$. These are now called Fermat primes. Unfortunately for his reputation, the next such number $2^{2^5} + 1 = 2^{32} + 1 = 4{,}294{,}967{,}297$ is not a prime (more about that later). Even Fermat was not invincible.

The second assertion is one of the most famous statements from the history of mathematics. While reading Diophantus's *Arithmetica*, Fermat wrote in the book's margin: "To divide a cube into two cubes, a fourth power, or in general any power whatever into two powers of the same denomination above the second is impossible." He added that "I have assuredly found an admirable proof of this, but the margin is too narrow to contain it."

In symbols, he was claiming that if $n > 2$, there are no whole numbers x, y, z such that $x^n + y^n = z^n$, a statement that came to be known as Fermat's last theorem. For three and a half centuries, it defeated all who attacked it, earning a reputation as the most famous unsolved problem in mathematics.

Despite Fermat's genius, number theory still was relatively neglected. His reluctance to supply proofs was partly to blame, but perhaps more detrimental was the appearance of calculus in the last decades of the 17th century. Calculus is the most useful mathematical tool of all, and scholars eagerly applied its ideas to a range of real-world problems. By contrast, number theory seemed too "pure," too divorced from the concerns of physicists, astronomers, and engineers.

NUMBER THEORY IN THE 18TH CENTURY

Credit for bringing number theory into the mainstream, for finally realizing Fermat's dream, is due to the 18th century's dominant mathematical figure, the Swiss Leonhard Euler (1707–83). Euler was the most prolific mathematician ever—and one of the most influential—and when he turned his attention to number theory, the subject could no longer be ignored.

Initially, Euler shared the widespread indifference of his colleagues, but he was in correspondence with Christian Goldbach (1690–1764), a number theory enthusiast acquainted with Fermat's work. Like an insistent salesman, Goldbach tried to interest Euler in the theory of numbers, and eventually his insistence paid off.

It was a letter of Dec. 1, 1729, in which Goldbach asked Euler, "Is Fermat's observation known to you, that all numbers $2^{2^n} + 1$ are primes?" This caught Euler's attention. Indeed, he showed that Fermat's assertion was wrong by splitting the number $2^{2^5} + 1$ into the product of 641 and 6,700,417.

Through the next five decades, Euler published over a thousand pages of research on number theory, much of it furnishing proofs of Fermat's assertions. In 1736 he proved Fermat's little theorem. By midcentury he had established Fermat's theorem that primes of the form $4k + 1$ can be uniquely expressed as the sum of two squares. He later took up the matter of perfect numbers, demonstrating that any even perfect number must assume the form discovered by Euclid 20 centuries earlier. And when he turned his attention to amicable numbers—of which, by this time, only three pairs were known—Euler vastly increased the world's supply by finding 58 new ones!

Of course, even Euler could not solve every problem. He gave proofs, or near-proofs, of Fermat's last theorem for exponents $n = 3$ and $n = 4$ but despaired of finding a general solution. And he was completely stumped by Goldbach's assertion that any even number greater than 2 can be written as the sum of two primes. Euler endorsed the result—today known as the Goldbach conjecture—but acknowledged his inability to prove it.

Euler gave number theory a mathematical legitimacy, and thereafter progress was rapid. In 1770, for instance, Joseph-Louis Lagrange (1736–1813) proved Fermat's assertion that every whole number can be written as the sum of four or fewer squares. Soon thereafter, he established a beautiful result known as Wilson's theorem: p is prime if and only if p divides evenly into

$$[(p\text{-}1) \times (p\text{-}2) \times \cdots \times 3 \times 2 \times 1] + 1.$$

NUMBER THEORY IN THE 19TH CENTURY

Disquisitiones Arithmeticae

Of immense significance was the 1801 publication of *Disquisitiones Arithmeticae* by Carl Friedrich Gauss (1777–1855). This became, in a sense, the holy writ of number theory. In it Gauss organized and summarized much of the work of his predecessors before moving boldly to the frontier of research. Observing that the problem of resolving composite numbers into prime factors is "one of the most important and useful in arithmetic," Gauss provided the first modern proof of the unique factorization theorem. He also gave the first proof of the law of quadratic reciprocity, a deep result previously glimpsed by Euler. To expedite his work, Gauss introduced the idea of congruence among numbers—i.e., he defined a and b to be congruent modulo m (written $a \equiv b \bmod m$) if m divides evenly into the difference $a - b$. For instance, $39 \equiv 4 \bmod 7$. This innovation, when combined with results like Fermat's little theorem, has become an indispensable fixture of number theory.

From Classical to Analytic Number Theory

Inspired by Gauss, other 19th-century mathematicians took up the challenge. Sophie Germain (1776–1831), who once stated, "I have never ceased thinking about the theory of numbers," made important contributions to Fermat's last theorem, and Adrien-Marie Legendre (1752–1833) and Peter Gustav Lejeune Dirichlet (1805–59) confirmed the theorem for $n = 5$—i.e., they showed that the sum of two fifth powers cannot be a fifth power. In 1847 Ernst Kummer (1810–93) went further, demonstrating that Fermat's last theorem was true for a large class of exponents; unfortunately, he could not rule out the possibility that it was false for a large class of exponents, so the problem remained unresolved.

The same Dirichlet (who reportedly kept a copy of Gauss's *Disquisitiones Arithmeticae* by his bedside for evening reading) made a profound contribution by proving that, if a and b have no common factor, then the arithmetic progression $a, a + b, a + 2b, a + 3b, \ldots$ must contain infinitely many primes. Among other things, this established that there are infinitely many $4k + 1$ primes and infinitely many $4k - 1$ primes as well. But what made this theorem so exceptional was Dirichlet's method of proof: he employed the techniques of calculus to establish a result in number theory. This surprising but ingenious strategy marked the beginning of a new branch of the subject: analytic number theory.

Prime Number Theorem

One of the supreme achievements of 19th-century mathematics was the prime number theorem, and it is worth a brief digression. To begin, designate the number of primes less than or equal to n by $\pi(n)$. Thus $\pi(10) = 4$ because 2, 3, 5, and 7 are the four primes not exceeding 10. Similarly $\pi(25) = 9$ and $\pi(100) = 25$. Next, consider the proportion of numbers less than or equal to n that are prime—i.e., $\pi(n)/n$. Clearly $\pi(10)/10 = 0.40$, meaning that 40 percent of the numbers not exceeding 10 are prime.

A pattern is anything but clear, but the prime number theorem identifies one, at least approximately, and thereby provides a rule for the distribution of primes among the whole numbers. The theorem says that, for large n, the proportion $\pi(n)/n$ is roughly $1/\log n$, where $\log n$ is the natural logarithm of n. This link between primes and logs is nothing short of extraordinary.

One of the first to perceive this was the young Gauss, whose examination of log tables and prime numbers suggested it to his fertile mind. Following Dirichlet's exploitation of analytic techniques in number theory, Bernhard Riemann (1826–66) and Pafnuty Chebyshev (1821–94) made substantial progress before the prime number theorem was proved in 1896 by Jacques Hadamard (1865–1963) and Charles Jean de la Vallée-Poussin (1866–1962). This brought the 19th century to a triumphant close.

NUMBER THEORY IN THE 20TH CENTURY

The next century saw an explosion in number theoretic research. Along with classical and analytic number theory, scholars now explored specialized subfields such as algebraic number theory, geometric number theory, and combinatorial number theory. The concepts became more abstract and the techniques more sophisticated. Unquestionably, the subject had grown beyond Fermat's wildest dreams.

One of the great contributors from early in the 20th century was the incandescent genius Srinivasa Ramanujan (1887–1920). Ramanujan, whose formal training was as limited as his life was short, burst upon the mathematical scene with a series of brilliant discoveries. Analytic number theory was among his specialties, and his publications carried titles such as "Highly composite numbers" and "Proof that almost all numbers n are composed of about $\log(\log n)$ prime factors."

A legendary figure in 20th-century number theory was Paul Erdös (1913–96), a Hungarian genius known for his deep insights, his vast circle of collaborators, and his personal eccentricities. At age 18, Erdös published a much-simplified proof of a theorem of Chebyshev stating that, if $n \geq 2$, then there must be a prime between n and $2n$. This was the first in a string of number theoretic results that would span most of the century. In the process, Erdös—who also worked in combinatorics, graph theory, and dimension theory—published over 1,500 papers with more than 500 collaborators from around the world. He achieved this astonishing output while living more or less out of a suitcase, traveling constantly from one university to another in pursuit of new mathematics. It was not uncommon for him to arrive, unannounced, with the declaration that "My brain is open" and then to plunge into the latest problem with gusto.

Two later developments deserve mention. One was the invention of the electronic computer, whose speed has been advantageously applied to number theoretic questions. As an example, Euler once speculated that at least four fourth powers must be added together for the sum to be a fourth power. But in 1988, using a combination of mathematical insight and computer muscle, the American Noam Elkies discovered that $2,682,440^4 + 15,36$ $5,639^4 + 18,796,760^4 = 20,615,673^4$—a stupendous counter-example that destroyed Euler's conjecture. (The number on the right contains 30 digits, so there is little wonder that Euler missed it.)

Second, number theory acquired an applied flavour, for it became instrumental in designing encryption schemes widely used in government and business. These rely upon the factorization of gigantic numbers into primes—a factorization that the code's user knows and the potential code-breaker does not. This application runs counter to the long-held perception of number theory as beautiful but essentially useless.

Twentieth-century number theory reached a much-publicized climax in 1995, when Fermat's last theorem was proved by the Englishman Andrew Wiles, with timely assistance from his British colleague Richard Taylor. Wiles succeeded where so many had failed with a 130-page proof of incredible complexity, one that certainly would not fit into any margin.

UNSOLVED PROBLEMS

This triumph notwithstanding, number theory remains the source of many unsolved problems, some of the most perplexing of which sound innocent enough. For example:

- Do any odd perfect numbers exist?
- Are there infinitely many primes of the form $n^2 + 1$ (i.e., one more than a perfect square)?
- Are there infinitely many pairs of twin primes (i.e., primes that differ by 2, like 5 and 7 or 41 and 43)?
- Is Goldbach's conjecture true? (Euler failed to prove it; so has everyone since.)

Although there has been no lack of effort, these questions remain open. Perhaps, like Fermat's last theorem, they will eventually be resolved. Or perhaps they will remain as challenges into the indefinite future. In order to spur research efforts across a wide range of mathematical disciplines, the privately funded Clay Mathematics Institute of Cambridge, Massachusetts, named seven "Millennium Prize Problems" in 2000, each with a million-dollar award for a correct solution. In any case, these mysteries justify Eric Temple Bell's characterization of number theory as "the last great uncivilized continent of mathematics."

The theory of numbers, then, is a vast and challenging subject as old as mathematics and as fresh as today's news. Its problems retain their fascination because of an apparent (often deceptive) simplicity and an irresistible beauty. With such a rich and colorful history, number theory surely deserves to be called, in the famous words of Gauss, "the queen of mathematics."

SET THEORY

Set theory is the branch of mathematics that deals with the properties of well-defined collections of objects, which may or may not be of a mathematical nature, such as numbers or functions. The theory is less valuable in direct application to ordinary experience than as a basis for precise and adaptable terminology for the definition of complex and sophisticated mathematical concepts.

Between the years 1874 and 1897, the German mathematician and logician Georg Cantor created a theory of abstract sets of entities and made it into a mathematical discipline. This theory grew out of his investigations of some concrete problems regarding certain types of infinite sets of real numbers. A set, wrote Cantor, is a collection of definite, distinguishable objects of perception or thought conceived as a whole. The objects are called elements or members of the set.

The theory had the revolutionary aspect of treating infinite sets as mathematical objects that are on an equal footing with those that can be constructed in a finite number of steps. Since antiquity, a majority of mathematicians had carefully avoided the introduction into their arguments of the actual infinite (i.e., of sets containing an infinity of objects conceived as existing simultaneously, at least in thought). Since this attitude persisted until almost the end of the 19th century, Cantor's work was the subject of much criticism to the effect that it dealt with fictions — indeed, that it encroached on the domain of philosophers and violated the principles of religion. Once applications to analysis began to be found, however, attitudes began to change, and by the 1890s Cantor's ideas and results were gaining acceptance. By 1900, set theory was recognized as a distinct branch of mathematics.

At just that time, however, several contradictions in so-called naive set theory were discovered. In order to eliminate such problems, an axiomatic basis was developed for the theory of sets analogous to that developed for elementary geometry. The degree of success that has been achieved in this development, as well as the present stature of set theory, has been well expressed in the Nicolas Bourbaki *Éléments de mathématique* (begun 1939; "Elements of Mathematics"): "Nowadays it is known to be possible, logically speaking, to derive practically the whole of known mathematics from a single source, The Theory of Sets."

INTRODUCTION TO NAIVE SET THEORY

FUNDAMENTAL SET CONCEPTS

In naive set theory, a set is a collection of objects (called members or elements) that is regarded as being a single object. To indicate that an object x is a member of a set A one writes $x \in A$, while $x \notin A$ indicates that x is not a member of A. A set may be defined by a membership rule (formula) or by listing its members within braces. For example, the set given by the rule "prime numbers less than 10" can also be given by {2, 3, 5, 7}. In principle, any finite set can be defined by an explicit list of its members, but specifying infinite sets requires a rule or pattern to indicate membership; for example, the ellipsis in {0, 1, 2, 3, 4, 5, 6, 7, . . .} indicates that the list of natural numbers null goes on forever. The empty (or void, or null) set, symbolized by {} or $\emptyset$, contains no elements at all. Nonetheless, it has the status of being a set.

A set A is called a subset of a set B (symbolized by $A \subseteq B$) if all the members of A are also members of B. For example, any set is a subset of itself, and $\emptyset$ is a subset of any set. If both $A \subseteq B$ and $B \subseteq A$, then A and B have exactly the same members. Part of the set concept is that in this case $A = B$; that is, A and B are the same set.

Operations on Sets

The symbol $\cup$ is employed to denote the union of two sets. Thus, the set $A \cup B$—read "A union B" or "the union of A and B"—is defined as the set that consists of all elements belonging to either set A or set B (or both). For example, suppose that Committee A, consisting of the 5 members Jones, Blanshard, Nelson, Smith, and Hixon, meets with Committee B, consisting of the 5 members Blanshard, Morton, Hixon, Young, and Peters. Clearly, the union of Committees A and B must then consist of 8 members rather than 10 — namely, Jones, Blanshard, Nelson, Smith, Morton, Hixon, Young, and Peters.

The intersection operation is denoted by the symbol $\cap$. The set $A \cap B$—read "A intersection B" or "the intersection of A and B"—is defined as the set composed of all elements that belong to both A and B. Thus, the intersection of the two committees in the foregoing example is the set consisting of Blanshard and Hixon.

If E denotes the set of all positive even numbers and O denotes the set of all positive odd numbers, then their union yields the entire set of positive integers, and their intersection is the empty set. Any two sets whose intersection is the empty set are said to be disjoint.

When the admissible elements are restricted to some fixed class of objects U, U is called the universal set (or universe). Then for any subset A of U, the complement of A (symbolized by A' or $U - A$) is defined as the set of all elements in the universe U that are not in A. For example, if the universe consists of the 26 letters of the alphabet, the complement of the set of vowels is the set of consonants.

In analytic geometry, the points on a Cartesian grid are ordered pairs (x, y) of numbers. In general, $(x, y) \neq (y, x)$; ordered pairs are defined so that $(a, b) = (c, d)$ if and only if both $a = c$ and $b = d$. In contrast, the set $\{x, y\}$ is identical to the set $\{y, x\}$ because they have exactly the same members.

The Cartesian product of two sets A and B, denoted by $A \times B$, is defined as the set consisting of all ordered pairs (a, b) for which $a \in A$ and $b \in B$. For example, if $A = \{x, y\}$ and $B = \{3, 6, 9\}$, then $A \times B = \{(x, 3), (x, 6), (x, 9), (y, 3), (y, 6), (y, 9)\}$.

Relations in Set Theory

In mathematics, a relation is an association between, or property of, various objects. Relations can be represented by sets of ordered pairs (a, b) where a bears a relation to b. Sets of ordered pairs are commonly used to represent relations depicted on charts and graphs, on which, for example, calendar years may be paired with automobile production figures, weeks with stock market averages, and days with average temperatures.

A function f can be regarded as a relation between each object x in its domain and the value $f(x)$. A function f is a relation with a special property, however: each x is related by f to one and only one y. That is, two ordered pairs (x, y) and (x, z) in f imply that $y = z$.

A one-to-one correspondence between sets A and B is similarly a pairing of each object in A with one and only one object in B, with the dual property that each object in B has been thereby paired with one and only one object in A. For example, if $A = \{x, z, w\}$ and $B = \{4, 3, 9\}$, a one-to-one correspondence can be obtained by pairing x with 4, z with 3, and w with 9. This pairing can be represented by the set $\{(x, 4), (z, 3), (w, 9)\}$ of ordered pairs.

Many relations display identifiable properties. For example, in the relation "is the same colour as," each object bears the relation to itself as well as to some other objects. Such relations are said to be reflexive. The ordering relation "less than or equal to" (symbolized by ≤) is reflexive, but "less than" (symbolized by <) is not. The relation "is parallel to" (symbolized by //) has the property that, if an object bears the relation to a second object, then the second also bears that relation to the first. Relations with this property are said to be symmetric. (Note that the ordering relation is not symmetric.) These examples also have the property that whenever one object bears the relation to a second, which further bears the relation to a third, then the first bears that relation to the third—e.g., if $a < b$ and $b < c$, then $a < c$. Such relations are said to be transitive.

Relations that have all three of these properties—reflexivity, symmetry, and transitivity—are called equivalence relations. In an equivalence relation, all elements related to a particular element, say a, are also related to each other, and they form what is called the equivalence class of a. For example, the equivalence class of a line for the relation "is parallel to" consists of the set of all lines parallel to it.

ESSENTIAL FEATURES OF CANTORIAN SET THEORY

At best, the foregoing description presents only an intuitive concept of a set. Essential features of the concept as Cantor understood it include: (1) that a set is a grouping into a single entity of objects of any kind, and (2) that, given an object x and a set A, exactly one of the statements $x \in A$ and $x \notin A$ is true and the other is false. The definite relation that may or may not exist between an object and a set is called the membership relation.

A further intent of this description is conveyed by what is called the principle of extension—a set is determined by its members rather than by any particular way of describing the set. Thus, sets A and B are equal if and only if every element in A is also in B and every element in B is in A; symbolically, $x \in A$ implies $x \in B$ and vice versa. There exists, for example, exactly one set the members of which are 2, 3, 5, and 7. It does not matter whether its members are described as "prime numbers less than 10" or listed in some order (which order is immaterial) between small braces, possibly $\{5, 2, 7, 3\}$.

The positive integers $\{1, 2, 3, \ldots\}$ are typically used for counting the elements in a finite set. For example, the set $\{a, b, c\}$ can be put in one-to-one correspondence with the elements of the set $\{1, 2, 3\}$. The number 3 is called the cardinal number, or cardinality, of the set $\{1, 2, 3\}$ as well as any set that can be put into a one-to-one correspondence with it. (Because the empty set has no elements, its cardinality is defined as 0.) In general, a set A is finite and its cardinality is n if there exists a pairing of its elements with the set $\{1, 2, 3, \ldots, n\}$. A set for which there is no such correspondence is said to be infinite.

To define infinite sets, Cantor used predicate formulas. The phrase "x is a professor" is an example of a formula; if the symbol x in this phrase is replaced by the name of a person, there results a declarative sentence that is true or false. The notation $S(x)$ will be used to represent such a formula. The phrase "x is a professor at university y and x is a male" is a formula with two variables. If the occurrences of x and y are replaced by names of appropriate, specific objects, the result is a declarative sentence that is true or false. Given any formula $S(x)$ that contains the letter x (and possibly others), Cantor's principle of abstraction asserts the existence of a set A such that, for each object x, $x \in A$ if and only if $S(x)$ holds. (Mathematicians later formulated a restricted principle of abstraction, also known as the principle of comprehension, in which self-referencing predicates, or $S(A)$, are excluded in order to prevent certain paradoxes. Because of the principle of extension, the set A corresponding to $S(x)$ must be unique, and it is symbolized by $\{x \mid S(x)\}$, which is read "The set of all objects x such that $S(x)$." For instance, $\{x \mid x$ is blue$\}$ is the set of all blue objects. This illustrates the fact that the principle of abstraction implies the existence of sets the elements of which are all objects having a certain property. It is actually more comprehensive. For example, it asserts the existence of a set B corresponding to "Either x is an astronaut or x is a natural number." Astronauts have no particular property in common with numbers (other than both being members of B).

Equivalent Sets

Cantorian set theory is founded on the principles of extension and abstraction, described above. To describe some results based upon these principles, the notion of equivalence of sets will be defined. The idea is that two sets are equivalent if it is possible to pair off members of the first set with members of the second, with no leftover members on either side. To capture this idea in set-theoretic terms, the set A is defined as equivalent to the set B (symbolized by $A \equiv B$) if and only if there exists a third set the members of which are ordered pairs such that: (1) the first member of each pair is an element of A and the second is an element of B, and (2) each member of A occurs as a first member and each member of B occurs as a second member of exactly one pair. Thus, if A and B are finite and $A \equiv B$, then the third set that establishes this fact provides a pairing, or matching, of the elements of A with those of B. Conversely, if it is possible to match the elements of A with those of B, then $A \equiv B$, because a set of pairs meeting requirements (1) and (2) can be formed—i.e., if $a \in A$ is matched with $b \in B$, then the ordered pair (a, b) is one member of the set. By thus defining equivalence of sets in terms of the notion of matching, equivalence is formulated independently of finiteness. As an illustration involving infinite sets, null may be taken to denote the set of natural numbers 0, 1, 2, . . . (some authors exclude 0 from the natural numbers). Then $\{(n, n^2) \mid n \in \text{null}\}$ establishes the seemingly paradoxical equivalence of null and the subset of null formed by the squares of the natural numbers.

As stated previously, a set B is included in, or is a subset of, a set A (symbolized by $B \subseteq A$) if every element of B is an element of A. So defined, a subset may possibly include all of the elements of A, so that A can be a subset of itself. Furthermore, the empty set, because it by definition has no elements that are not included in other sets, is a subset of every set.

If every element of set B is an element of set A, but the converse is false (hence $B \neq A$), then B is said to be properly included in, or is a proper subset of, A (symbolized by $B \subset A$). Thus, if $A = \{3, 1, 0, 4, 2\}$, both $\{0, 1, 2\}$ and $\{0, 1, 2, 3, 4\}$ are subsets of A; but $\{0, 1, 2, 3, 4\}$ is not a proper subset. A finite set is nonequivalent to each of its proper subsets. This is not so, however, for infinite sets, as is illustrated with the set null in the earlier example. (The equivalence of null and its proper subset formed by the squares of its elements was noted by Galileo Galilei in 1638, who concluded that the notions of less than, equal to, and greater than did not apply to infinite sets.)

Cardinality and Transfinite Numbers

The application of the notion of equivalence to infinite sets was first systematically explored by Cantor. With null defined as the set of natural numbers, Cantor's initial significant finding was that the set of all rational numbers is equivalent to null but that the set of all real numbers is not equivalent to null. The existence of nonequivalent infinite sets justified Cantor's introduction of "transfinite" cardinal numbers as measures of size for such sets. Cantor defined the cardinal of an arbitrary set A as the concept that can be abstracted from A taken together with the totality of other equivalent sets. Gottlob Frege, in 1884, and Bertrand Russell, in 1902, both mathematical logicians, defined the cardinal number $\overline{\overline{A}}$ of a set A somewhat more explicitly, as the set of all sets that are equivalent to A. This definition thus provides a place for cardinal numbers as objects of a universe whose only members are sets.

The above definitions are consistent with the usage of natural numbers as cardinal numbers. Intuitively, a cardinal number, whether finite (i.e., a natural number) or transfinite (i.e., nonfinite), is a measure of the size of a set. Exactly how a cardinal number is defined is unimportant; what is important is that $\overline{\overline{A}} = \overline{\overline{B}}$ if and only if $A \equiv B$.

To compare cardinal numbers, an ordering relation (symbolized by <) may be introduced by means of the definition $\overline{\overline{A}} < \overline{\overline{B}}$ if A is equivalent to a subset of B and B is equivalent to no subset of A. Clearly, this relation is irreflexive $\overline{\overline{A}} \not< \overline{\overline{A}}$ and transitive: $\overline{\overline{A}} < \overline{\overline{B}}$ and $\overline{\overline{B}} < \overline{\overline{C}}$ imply $\overline{\overline{A}} < \overline{\overline{C}}$.

When applied to natural numbers used as cardinals, the relation < (less than) coincides with the familiar ordering relation for null, so that < is an extension of that relation.

The symbol $\aleph_0$ (aleph-null) is standard for the cardinal number of null (sets of this cardinality are called denumerable), and $\aleph$ (aleph) is sometimes used for that of the set of real numbers. Then $n < \aleph_0$ for each $n \in$ null and $\aleph_0 < \aleph$.

This, however, is not the end of the matter. If the power set of a set A—symbolized $P(A)$—is defined as the set of all subsets of A, then, as Cantor proved, $\overline{\overline{A}} < \overline{\overline{P(A)}}$

for every set A — a relation that is known as Cantor's theorem. It implies an unending hierarchy of transfinite cardinals: $\overline{\overline{N}} = \aleph_0, \overline{\overline{P(N)}}, \overline{\overline{P(P(N))}}, \ldots$. Cantor proved that $\aleph = \overline{\overline{P(N)}}$ and suggested that there are no cardinal numbers between $\aleph_0$ and $\aleph$, a conjecture known as the continuum hypothesis.

There is an arithmetic for cardinal numbers based on natural definitions of addition, multiplication, and exponentiation (squaring, cubing, and so on), but this arithmetic deviates from that of the natural numbers when transfinite cardinals are involved. For example, $\aleph_0 + \aleph_0 = \aleph_0$ (because the set of integers is equivalent to null), $\aleph_0 \cdot \aleph_0 = \aleph_0$ (because the set of ordered pairs of natural numbers is equivalent to null), and $c + \aleph_0 = c$ for every transfinite cardinal c (because every infinite set includes a subset equivalent to null).

The so-called Cantor paradox, discovered by Cantor himself in 1899, is the following. By the unrestricted principle of abstraction, the formula "x is a set" defines a set U; i.e., it is the set of all sets. Now $P(U)$ is a set of sets and so $P(U)$ is a subset of U. By the definition of $<$ for cardinals, however, if $A \subseteq B$, then it is not the case that $\overline{\overline{B}} < \overline{\overline{A}}$. Hence, by substitution, $\overline{\overline{U}} \not< \overline{\overline{P(U)}}$. But by Cantor's theorem, $\overline{\overline{U}} < \overline{\overline{P(U)}}$. This is a contradiction. In 1901 Russell devised another contradiction of a less technical nature that is now known as Russell's paradox. The formula "x is a set and $(x \notin x)$" defines a set R of all sets not members of themselves. Using proof by contradiction, however, it is easily shown that (1) $R \in R$. But then by the definition of R it follows that (2) $(R \notin R)$. Together, (1) and (2) form a contradiction.

AXIOMATIC SET THEORY

In contrast to naive set theory, the attitude adopted in an axiomatic development of set theory is that it is not necessary to know what the "things" are that are called "sets" or what the relation of membership means. Of sole concern are the properties assumed about sets and the membership relation. Thus, in an axiomatic theory of sets, *set* and the membership relation ϵ are undefined terms. The assumptions adopted about these notions are called the axioms of the theory. Axiomatic set theorems are the axioms together with statements that can be deduced from the axioms using the rules of inference provided by a system of logic. Criteria for the choice of axioms include: (1) consistency—it should be impossible to derive as theorems both a statement and its negation; (2) plausibility—axioms should be in accord with intuitive beliefs about sets; and (3) richness—desirable results of Cantorian set theory can be derived as theorems.

THE ZERMELO-FRAENKEL AXIOMS

The first axiomatization of set theory was given in 1908 by Ernst Zermelo, a German mathematician. From his analysis of the paradoxes described above in the section Cardinality and Transfinite Numbers, he concluded that they are associated with sets that are "too big," such as the set of all sets in Cantor's paradox. Thus, the axioms that Zermelo formulated are restrictive insofar as the asserting or implying of the existence of sets is concerned. As a consequence, there is no apparent way, in his system, to derive the known contradictions from them. On the other hand, the results of classical set theory short of the paradoxes can be derived. Zermelo's axiomatic theory is here discussed in a form that incorporates modifications and improvements suggested by later mathematicians, principally Thoralf Albert Skolem, a Norwegian pioneer in metalogic, and Abraham Adolf Fraenkel, an Israeli mathematician. In the literature on set theory, it is called Zermelo-Fraenkel set theory and abbreviated ZFC ("C" because of the inclusion of the axiom of choice).

Schemas for Generating Well-Formed Formulas

The ZFC "axiom of extension" conveys the idea that, as in naive set theory, a set is determined solely by its members. It should be noted that this is not merely a logically necessary property of equality but an assumption about the membership relation as well.

The set defined by the "axiom of the empty set" is the empty (or null) set Ø.

For an understanding of the "axiom schema of separation" considerable explanation is required. Zermelo's original system included the assumption that, if a formula $S(x)$ is "definite" for all elements of a set A, then there exists a set the elements of which are precisely those elements x of A for which $S(x)$ holds. This is a restricted version of the principle of abstraction, now known as the principle of comprehension, for it provides for the existence of sets corresponding to formulas. It restricts that principle, however, in two ways: (1) Instead of asserting the existence of sets unconditionally, it can be applied only in conjunction with preexisting sets, and (2) only "definite" formulas may be used. Zermelo offered only a vague description of "definite," but clarification was given by Skolem (1922) by way of a precise definition of what will be called simply a formula of ZFC. Using tools of modern logic, the definition may be made as follows:

- I. For any variables x and y, $x \in y$ and $x = y$ are formulas (such formulas are called atomic).
- II. If S and T are formulas and x is any variable, then each of the following is a formula: If S, then T; S if and only if T; S and T; S or T; not S; for all x, S; for some x, T.

Formulas are constructed recursively (in a finite number of systematic steps) beginning with the (atomic) formulas of (I) and proceeding via the constructions permitted in (II). "Not $(x \in y)$," for example, is a formula (which is abbreviated to $x \notin y$), and "There exists an x such that for every y, $y \notin x$" is a formula. A variable is free in a formula if it occurs at least once in the formula without being introduced by one of the phrases "for some x" or "for all x." Henceforth, a formula S in which x occurs as a free variable will be called "a condition on x" and symbolized $S(x)$. The formula "For every y, $x \in y$," for example, is a condition on x. It is to be understood that a formula is a formal expression—i.e., a term without meaning. Indeed, a computer can be programmed to generate atomic formulas and build up from them other formulas of ever-increasing complexity using logical connectives ("not," "and," etc.) and operators ("for all" and "for some"). A formula acquires meaning only when an interpretation of the theory is specified; i.e., when (1) a nonempty collection (called the domain of the interpretation) is specified as the range of values of the variables (thus the term set is assigned a meaning, viz., an object in the domain), (2) the membership relation is defined for these sets, (3) the logical connectives and operators are interpreted as in everyday language, and (4) the logical relation of equality is taken to be identity among the objects in the domain.

The phrase "a condition on x" for a formula in which x is free is merely suggestive; relative to an interpretation, such a formula does impose a condition on x. Thus, the intuitive interpretation of the "axiom schema of separation" is: given a set A and a condition on x, $S(x)$, those elements of A for which the condition holds form a set. It provides for the existence of sets by separating off certain elements of existing sets. Calling this the axiom schema of separation is appropriate, because it is actually a schema for generating axioms—one for each choice of $S(x)$.

Axioms for Compounding Sets

Although the axiom schema of separation has a constructive quality, further means of constructing sets from existing sets must be introduced if some of the desirable features of Cantorian set theory are to be established. Three axioms—axiom of pairing, axiom of union, and axiom of power set—are of this sort.

By using five of the axioms (2–6), a variety of basic concepts of naive set theory (e.g., the operations of union, intersection, and Cartesian product; the notions of relation, equivalence relation, ordering relation, and function) can be defined with ZFC. Further, the standard results about these concepts that were attainable in naive set theory can be proved as theorems of ZFC.

Axioms for Infinite and Ordered Sets

If I is an interpretation of an axiomatic theory of sets, the sentence that results from an axiom when a meaning has been assigned to "set" and "ϵ," as specified by I, is either true or false. If each axiom is true for I, then I is called a model of the theory. If the domain of a model is infinite, this fact does not imply that any object of the domain is an "infinite set." An infinite set in the latter sense is an object d of the domain D of I for which there is an infinity of distinct objects d' in D such that $d'Ed$ holds (E standing for the interpretation of ϵ). Though the domain of any model of the theory of which the axioms thus far discussed are axioms is clearly infinite, models in which every set is finite have been devised. For the full development of classical set theory, including the theories of real numbers and of infinite cardinal numbers, the existence of infinite sets is needed; thus the "axiom of infinity" is included.

The existence of a unique minimal set ω having properties expressed in the axiom of infinity can be proved; its distinct members are $\emptyset$, $\{\emptyset\}$, $\{\emptyset, \{\emptyset\}\}$, $\{\emptyset, \{\emptyset\}, \{\emptyset, \{\emptyset\}\}\}$, ... These elements are denoted by 0, 1, 2, 3, . . . and are called natural numbers. Justification for this terminology rests with the fact that the Peano postulates (five axioms published in 1889 by the Italian mathematician Giuseppe Peano), which can serve as a base for arithmetic, can be proved as theorems in set theory. Thereby the way is paved for the construction within ZFC of entities that have all the expected properties of the real numbers.

The origin of the axiom of choice was Cantor's recognition of the importance of being able to "well-order" arbitrary sets—i.e., to define an ordering relation for a given set such that each nonempty subset has a least element. The virtue of well-ordering a set is that it offers a means of proving that a property holds for each of its elements by a process (transfinite induction) similar to mathematical induction. Zermelo (1904) gave the first proof that any set can be well-ordered. His proof employed a set-theoretic principle that he called the "axiom of choice," which, shortly thereafter, was shown to be equivalent to the so-called well-ordering theorem.

Intuitively, the axiom of choice asserts the possibility of making a simultaneous choice of an element in every nonempty member of any set; this guarantee accounts for its name. The assumption is significant only when the set has infinitely many members. Zermelo was the first to state explicitly the axiom, although it had been used but essentially unnoticed earlier. It soon became the subject of vigorous controversy because of its nonconstructive nature. Some mathematicians rejected it totally on this ground. Others accepted it but avoided its use whenever possible. Some changed their minds about it when its equivalence with the well-ordering theorem was proved as well as the assertion that any two cardinal numbers c and d are comparable (i.e., that exactly one of $c < d$, $d < c$, $c = d$

holds). There are many other equivalent statements, though even today a few mathematicians feel that the use of the axiom of choice is improper. To the vast majority, however, it, or an equivalent assertion, has become an indispensable and commonplace tool. (Because of this controversy, ZFC was adopted as an acronym for the majority position with the axiom of choice and ZF for the minority position without the axiom of choice.)

Schema for Transfinite Induction and Ordinal Arithmetic

When Zermelo's axioms were found to be inadequate for a full-blown development of transfinite induction and ordinal arithmetic, Fraenkel and Skolem independently proposed an additional axiom schema to eliminate the difficulty. As modified by John von Neumann, a Hungarian-born American mathematician, it says, intuitively, that if with each element of a set there is associated exactly one set, then the collection of the associated sets is itself a set; i.e., it offers a way to "collect" existing sets to form sets. As an illustration, each of ω, $P(\omega)$, $P(P(\omega))$, . . ., formed by recursively taking power sets (sets formed of all the subsets of the preceding set), is a set in the theory based on Zermelo's original eight axioms. But there appears to be no way to establish the existence of the set having all these sets as its members. However, an instance of the "axiom schema of replacement" provides for its existence.

Intuitively, the axiom schema of replacement is the assertion that, if the domain of a function is a set, then so is its range. That this is a powerful schema (in respect to the further inferences that it yields) is suggested by the fact that the axiom schema of separation can be derived from it and that, when applied in conjunction with the axiom of the power set, the axiom of pairing can be deduced.

The axiom schema of replacement has played a significant role in developing a theory of ordinal numbers. In contrast to cardinal numbers, which serve to designate the size of a set, ordinal numbers are used to determine positions within a prescribed well-ordered sequence. Under an approach conceived by von Neumann, if A is a set, the successor A' of A is the set obtained by adjoining A to the elements of A ($A' = A \cup \{A\}$). In terms of this notion the natural numbers, as defined above, are simply the succession $0, 0', 0'', 0''', \ldots$; i.e., the natural numbers are the sets obtained starting with $\emptyset$ and iterating the prime operation a finite number of times. The natural numbers are well-ordered by the $\in$ relation, and with this ordering they constitute the finite ordinal numbers. The axiom of infinity secures the existence of the set of natural numbers, and the set ω is the first infinite ordinal. Greater ordinal numbers are obtained by iterating the prime operation beginning with ω. An instance of the axiom schema of replacement asserts that $\omega, \omega', \omega'', \ldots$ form a set. The union of this set and ω is the still greater ordinal that is denoted by $\omega 2$ (employing notation from ordinal arithmetic). A repetition of this process beginning with $\omega 2$ yields the ordinals $(\omega 2)', (\omega 2)'', \ldots$; next after all of those of this form is $\omega 3$. In this way the sequence of ordinals $\omega, \omega 2, \omega 3, \ldots$ is generated. An application of the axiom schema of replacement then yields the ordinal that follows all of these in the same sense in which ω follows the finite ordinals; in the notation from ordinal arithmetic, it is ω^2. At this point the iteration process can be repeated. In summary, the axiom schema of replacement together with the other axioms make possible the extension of the counting process as far beyond the natural numbers as one chooses.

In the ZFC system, cardinal numbers are defined as certain ordinals. From the well-ordering theorem (a consequence of the axiom of choice), it follows that every set A is equivalent to some ordinal number. Also, the totality of ordinals equivalent to A can be shown to form a set. Then a natural choice for the cardinal number of A is the least ordinal to which A is equivalent. This is the motivation for defining a cardinal number as an ordinal that is not equivalent to any smaller ordinal. The arithmetics of both cardinal and ordinal numbers have been fully developed. That of finite cardinals and ordinals coincides with the arithmetic of the natural numbers. For infinite cardinals, the arithmetic is uninteresting since, as a consequence of the axiom of choice, both the sum and product of two such cardinals are equal to the maximum of the two. In contrast, the arithmetic of infinite ordinals is interesting and presents a wide assortment of oddities.

In addition to the guidelines already mentioned for the choice of axioms of ZFC, another guideline is taken into account by some set theorists. For the purposes of foundational studies of mathematics, it is assumed that mathematics is consistent; otherwise, any foundation would fail. It may thus be reasoned that, if a precise account of the intuitive usages of sets by mathematicians is given, an adequate and correct foundation will result. Traditionally, mathematicians deal with the integers, with real numbers, and with functions. Thus, an intuitive hierarchy of sets in which these entities appear should be a model of ZFC. It is possible to construct such a hierarchy explicitly from the empty set by iterating the operations of forming power sets and unions in the following way.

The bottom of the hierarchy is composed of the sets $A_0 = \emptyset, A_1, \ldots, A_n, \ldots$, in which each A_{n+1} is the power set of the preceding A_n. Then one can form the union A_ω of all sets constructed thus far. This can be followed by iterating the power set operation as before: $A_{\omega'}$ is the power set of A_ω and so forth. This construction can be extended to arbitrarily high transfinite levels. There is no highest level of the hierarchy; at each level, the union of what has been constructed thus far can be taken and the power set operation applied to the elements. In general, for each ordinal number α one obtains a set A_α, each member of which is a subset of some A_β that is lower in the hierarchy. The hierarchy obtained in this way is called the iterative hierarchy. The domain of the intuitive model of ZFC is conceived as the union of all sets in the iterative hierarchy. In other words, a set is in the model if it is an element of some set A_α of the iterative hierarchy.

Axiom for Eliminating Infinite Descending Species

From the assumptions that this system of set theory is sufficiently comprehensive for mathematics and that it is the model to be "captured" by the axioms of ZFC, it may be argued that models of axioms that differ sharply from this system should be ruled out. The discovery of such a model led to the formulation by von Neumann of axiom 10, the axiom of restriction, or foundation axiom.

This axiom eliminates from the models of the first nine axioms those in which there exist infinite descending ∈-chains (i.e., sequences $x_1, x_2, x_3, \ldots$ such that $x_2 \in x_1, x_3 \in x_2$, . . .), a phenomenon that does not appear in the model based on an iterative hierarchy described above. (The existence of models having such chains was discovered by the Russian mathematician Dimitry Mirimanoff in 1917.) It also has other attractive consequences; e.g., a simpler definition of the notion of ordinal number is possible. Yet there is no unanimity among mathematicians whether there are sufficient grounds for adopting it as an additional axiom. On the one hand, the axiom is equivalent (in a theory that allows only sets) to the statement that every set appears in the iterative hierarchy informally described above—there are no other sets. So it formulates the view that this is what the universe of all sets is really like. On the other hand, there is no compelling need to rule out sets that might lie outside the hierarchy—the axiom has not been shown to have any mathematical applications.

THE NEUMANN-BERNAYS-GÖDEL AXIOMS

The second axiomatization of set theory originated with John von Neumann in the 1920s. His formulation differed considerably from ZFC because the notion of function, rather than that of set, was taken as undefined, or "primitive." In a series of papers beginning in 1937, however, the Swiss logician Paul Bernays, a collaborator with the German formalist David Hilbert, modified the von Neumann approach in a way that put it in much closer contact with ZFC. In 1940, the Austrian-born American logician Kurt Gödel, known for his undecidability proof, further simplified the theory. This axiomatic version of set theory is called NBG, after the Neumann-Bernays-Gödel axioms. As will be explained shortly, NBG is closely related to ZFC, but it allows explicit treatment of so-called classes: collections that might be too large to be sets, such as the class of all sets or the class of all ordinal numbers.

For expository purposes it is convenient to adopt two undefined notions for NBG: class and the binary relation ϵ of membership (though, as is also true in ZFC, ϵ suffices). For the intended interpretation, variables take classes—the totalities corresponding to certain properties— as values. A class is defined to be a set if it is a member of some class; those classes that are not sets are called proper classes. Intuitively, sets are intended to be those classes that are adequate for mathematics, and proper classes are thought of as those collections that are "so big" that, if they were permitted to be sets, contradictions would follow. In NBG, the classical paradoxes are avoided by proving in each case that the collection on which the paradox is based is a proper class—i.e., is not a set.

Comments about the axioms that follow are limited to features that distinguish them from their counterpart in ZFC. The axiom schema for class formation is presented in a form to facilitate a comparison with the axiom schema of separation of ZFC. In a detailed development of NBG, however, there appears instead a list of seven axioms (not schemas) that state that, for each of certain conditions, there exists a corresponding class of all those sets satisfying the condition. From this finite set of axioms, each an instance of the above schema, the schema (in a generalized form) can be obtained as a theorem. When obtained in this way, the axiom schema for class formation of NBG is called the class existence theorem.

In brief, axioms 4 through 8 of NBG are axioms of set existence. The same is true of the next axiom, which for technical reasons is usually phrased in a more general form. Finally, there may appear in a formulation of NBG an analog of the last axiom of ZFC (axiom of restriction).

A comparison of the two theories that have been formulated is in order. In contrast to the axiom schema of replacement of ZFC, the NBG version is not an axiom schema but an axiom. Thus, with the comments above about the ZFC axiom schema of separation in mind, it follows that NBG has only a finite number of axioms. On the other hand, since the axiom schema of replacement of ZFC provides an axiom for each formula, ZFC has infinitely many axioms—which is unavoidable because it is known that no finite subset yields the full system of axioms. The finiteness of the axioms for NBG makes the logical study of the system simpler. The relationship between the theories may be summarized by the statement that ZFC is essentially the part of NBG that refers only to sets. Indeed, it has been proved that every theorem of ZFC is a theorem of NBG and that any theorem of NBG that speaks only about sets is a theorem of ZFC. From this it follows that ZFC is consistent if and only if NBG is consistent.

LIMITATIONS OF AXIOMATIC SET THEORY

The fact that NBG avoids the classical paradoxes and that there is no apparent way to derive any one of them in ZFC does not settle the question of the consistency of either theory. One method for establishing the consistency of an axiomatic theory is to give a model—i.e., an interpretation of the undefined terms in another theory such that the axioms become theorems of the other theory. If this other theory is consistent, then that under investigation must be consistent. Such consistency proofs are thus relative: the theory for which a model is given is consistent if that from which the model is taken is consistent. The method of models, however, offers no hope for proving the consistency of an axiomatic theory of sets. In the case of set theory and, indeed, of axiomatic theories generally, the alternative is a direct approach to the problem.

If T is the theory of which the (absolute) consistency is under investigation, this alternative means that the proposition "There is no sentence of T such that both it and its negation are theorems of T" must be proved. The mathematical theory (developed by the formalists) to cope with proofs about an axiomatic theory T is called proof theory, or metamathematics. It is premised upon the formulation of T as a formal axiomatic theory—i.e., the theory of inference (as well as T) must be axiomatized. It is then possible to present T in a purely symbolic form—i.e., as a formal language based on an alphabet the symbols of which are those for the undefined terms of T and those for the logical operators and connectives. A sentence in this language is a formula composed from the alphabet according to pre-scribed rules. The hope for metamathematics was that, by using only intuitively convincing, weak number-theoretic arguments (called finitary methods), unimpeachable proofs of the consistency of such theories as axiomatic set theory could be given.

That hope suffered a severe blow in 1931 from a theorem proved by Kurt Gödel about any formal theory S that includes the usual vocabulary of elementary arithmetic. By coding the formulas of such a theory with natural numbers (now called Gödel numbers) and by talking about these numbers, Gödel was able to make the metamathematics of S become part of the arithmetic of S and hence expressible in S. The theorem in question asserts that the formula of S that expresses (via a coding) "S is consistent" in S is unprovable in S if S is consistent. Thus, if S is consistent, then the consistency of S cannot be proved within S; rather, methods beyond those that can be expressed or reflected in S must be employed. Because, in both ZFC and NBG, elementary arithmetic can be developed, Gödel's theorem applies to these two theories. Although there remains the theoretical possibility of a finitary proof of consistency that cannot be reflected in the foregoing systems of set theory, no hopeful, positive results have been obtained.

Other theorems of Gödel when applied to ZFC (and there are corresponding results for NBG) assert that, if the system is consistent, then (1) it contains a sentence such that neither it nor its negation is provable (such a sentence is called undecidable), (2) there is no algorithm (or iterative process) for deciding whether a sentence of ZFC is a theorem, and (3) these same statements hold for any consistent theory resulting from ZFC by the adjunction of further axioms or axiom schemas. Apparently ZFC can serve as a foundation for all of present-day mathematics because every mathematical theorem can be translated into and proved within ZFC or within extensions obtained by adding suitable axioms. Thus, the existence of undecidable sentences in each such theory points out an inevitable gap between the sentences that are true in mathematics and sentences that are provable within a single axiomatic theory. The fact that there is more to conceivable mathematics than can be captured by the axiomatic approach prompted the American logician Emil Post to comment in 1944 that "mathematical thinking is, and must remain, essentially creative."

Mathematician Kurt Gödel, left, walks with his close friend, Albert Einstein. Though most famous for his incompleteness theorem, Gödel made other significant contributions to the field of mathematics, including his work on axiomatic set theory. Leonard McCombe/Time & Life Pictures/Getty Images

PRESENT STATUS OF AXIOMATIC SET THEORY

The foundations of axiomatic set theory are in a state of significant change as a result of new discoveries. The situation with alternate (and conflicting) axiom systems for set theory is analogous to the 19th-century revolution in geometry that was set off by the discovery of non-Euclidean geometries. It is difficult to predict the ultimate consequences of these late 20th-century findings for set theory, but already they have had profound effects on attitudes about certain axioms and have forced the realization of a continuous search for additional axioms. These discoveries have focused attention on the concept of the independence of an axiom. If T is an axiomatic theory and S is a sentence (i.e., a formula) of T that is not an axiom, and if $T + S$ denotes the theory that results from T upon the adjunction of S to T as a further axiom, then S is said to be consistent with T if $T + S$ is consistent and independent of T whenever both S and ~S (the negation of S) are consistent with T. Thus, if S is independent of T, then the addition of S or ~S to T yields a consistent theory. The role of the axiom of restriction (AR) can be clarified in terms of the notion of independence. If ZF' denotes the theory obtained from ZF by deleting AR and either retaining or deleting the axiom of choice (AC), then it can be proved that, if ZF' is consistent, AR is independent of ZF'.

Of far greater significance for the foundations of set theory is the status of AC relative to the other axioms of ZF. The status in ZF of the continuum hypothesis (CH) and its extension, the generalized continuum hypothesis (GCH), are also of profound importance. In the following discussion of these questions, ZF denotes Zermelo-Fraenkel set theory without AC. The first finding was obtained by Kurt Gödel in 1939. He proved that AC and GCH are consistent relative to ZF (i.e., if ZF is consistent, then so is ZF + AC + GCH) by showing that a contradiction within ZF + AC + GCH can be transformed into a contradiction in ZF. In 1963 American mathematician Paul Cohen proved that (1) if ZF is consistent, then so is ZF + AC + ~CH, and (2) if ZF is consistent, then so is ZF + ~AC. Since in ZF + AC it can be demonstrated that GCH implies CH, Gödel's theorem together with Cohen's establishes the independence of AC and CH. For his proofs Cohen introduced a new method (called forcing) of constructing interpretations of ZF + AC. The method of forcing is applicable to many problems in set theory, and since 1963 it has been used to give independence proofs for a wide variety of highly technical propositions. Some of these results have opened new avenues for attacks on important foundational questions.

The current unsettled state of axiomatic set theory can be sensed by the responses that have been made to the question of how to regard CH in the light of its independence from ZF + AC. Someone who believes that set theory deals only with nonexistent fictions will have no concern about the question. But for most mathematicians sets actually exist; in particular, ω and $P(\omega)$ exist (the set of the natural numbers and its power set, respectively). Further, it should be the case that every nondenumerable subset of $P(\omega)$ either is or is not equivalent to $P(\omega)$; i.e., CH either is true or is false. Followers of this faith regard the axioms of set theory as describing some well-defined reality—one in which CH must be either true or false. Thus there is the inescapable conclusion that the present axioms do not provide a complete description of that reality. A search for new axioms is in progress. One who hopes to prove CH as a theorem must look for axioms that restrict the number of sets. There seems to be little hope for this restriction, however, without changing the intuitive notion of the set. Thus the expectations favour the view that CH will be disproved. This disproof requires an axiom that guarantees the existence of more sets—e.g., of sets having cardinalities greater than those that can be proved to exist in ZF + AC. So far, none of the axioms that have been proposed that are aimed in this direction (called "generalized axioms of infinity") serves to prove ~CH. Although there is little supporting evidence, the optimists hope that the status of the continuum hypothesis will eventually be settled.

CHAPTER 2
GREAT ARITHMETICIANS AND NUMBER THEORISTS

Mathematics is often called the universal language. Even many animals can recognize or count small numbers. It should therefore come as no surprise that the oldest known written records contain numbers, often in trade and tax receipts. Nevertheless, the study of numbers in their own right lagged behind the development of geometry, which dates back to at least 3000 BCE in the Fertile Crescent from the Nile valley to Mesopotamia. Although ancient mathematicians dabbled in their consideration, the real impetus for the study of numbers began with Diophantus of Alexandria in the 3rd century CE.

THE ANCIENT WORLD

ARYABHATA I
(b. 476, possibly Ashmaka or Kusumapura, India)

Aryabhata was an astronomer and the earliest Indian mathematician whose work and history are available to modern scholars. Known as Aryabhata I or Aryabhata the Elder to distinguish him from a 10th-century Indian mathematician of the same name, he flourished in Kusumapura—near Pataliputra (Patna), then the capital of the Gupta dynasty—where he composed at least two works, *Aryabhatiya* (c. 499) and the now lost *Aryabhatasiddhanta*. *Aryabhatasiddhanta* circulated mainly in the northwest of India and, through the Sa-sa-nian dynasty (224–651) of Iran, had a profound influence on the development of Islamic astronomy. Its contents are preserved to some extent in the works of Varahamihira

97

(flourished *c.* 550), Bhaskara I (flourished *c.* 629), Brahmagupta (598–*c.* 665), and others. It is one of the earliest astronomical works to assign the start of each day to midnight.

Aryabhatiya was particularly popular in South India, where numerous mathematicians over the ensuing millennium wrote commentaries. Written in verse couplets, this work deals with mathematics and astronomy. Following an introduction that contains astronomical tables and Aryabhata's system of phonemic number notation, the work is characteristically divided into three sections: *Ganita* ("Mathematics"), *Kala-kriya* ("Time Calculations"), and *Gola* ("Sphere").

In *Ganita* Aryabhata names the first 10 decimal places and gives algorithms for obtaining square and cubic roots, utilizing the decimal number system. Then he treats geometric measurements—employing 62,832/20,000 (= 3.1416) for π—and develops properties of similar right-angled triangles and of two intersecting circles. Utilizing the Pythagorean theorem, he obtained one of the two methods for constructing his table of sines. He also realized that second-order sine difference is proportional to sine. Mathematical series, quadratic equations, compound interest (involving a quadratic equation), proportions (ratios), and the solution of various linear equations are among the arithmetic and algebraic topics included. Aryabhata's general solution for linear indeterminate equations, which Bhaskara I called *kuttakara* ("pulverizer"), consisted of breaking the problem down into new problems with successively smaller coefficients—essentially the Euclidean algorithm and related to the method of continued fractions.

With *Kala-kriya* Aryabhata turned to astronomy—in particular, treating planetary motion along the ecliptic. The topics include definitions of various units of time, eccentric and epicyclic models of planetary motion, planetary longitude corrections for different terrestrial locations, and a theory of "lords of the hours and days" (an astrological concept used for determining propitious times for action).

Aryabhatiya ends with spherical astronomy in *Gola*, where he applied plane trigonometry to spherical geometry by projecting points and lines on the surface of a sphere onto appropriate planes. Topics include prediction of solar and lunar eclipses and an explicit statement that the apparent westward motion of the stars is due to the spherical Earth's rotation about its axis. Aryabhata also correctly ascribed the luminosity of the Moon and planets to reflected sunlight.

The Indian government named its first satellite Aryabhata (launched 1975) in his honour.

DIOPHANTUS OF ALEXANDRIA
(fl. *c.* 250 CE)

Diophantus was a Greek mathematician, famous for his work in algebra.

What little is known of Diophantus's life is circumstantial. From the appellation "of Alexandria" it seems that he worked in the main scientific centre of the ancient Greek world; and because he is not mentioned before the 4th century, it seems likely that he flourished during the 3rd century. An arithmetic epigram from the *Anthologia Graeca* of late antiquity, purported to retrace some landmarks of his life (marriage at 33, birth of his son at 38, death of his son four years before his own at 84), may well be contrived. Two works have come down to us under his name, both incomplete. The first is a small fragment on polygonal numbers (a number is polygonal if that same number of dots can be arranged in the form of a regular polygon). The second, a large and extremely influential treatise upon which all the ancient and modern fame of Diophantus reposes, is his *Arithmetica*. Its historical importance is twofold: it is the first known work to employ algebra in a modern style, and it inspired the rebirth of number theory.

The *Arithmetica* begins with an introduction addressed to Dionysius—arguably St. Dionysius of Alexandria. After some generalities about numbers, Diophantus explains his symbolism—he uses symbols for the unknown (corresponding to our x) and its powers, positive or negative, as well as for some arithmetic operations—most of these symbols are clearly scribal abbreviations. This is the first and only occurrence of algebraic symbolism before the 15th century. After teaching multiplication of the powers of the unknown, Diophantus explains the multiplication of positive and negative terms and then how to reduce an equation to one with only positive terms (the standard form preferred in antiquity). With these preliminaries out of the way, Diophantus proceeds to the problems. Indeed, the *Arithmetica* is essentially a collection of problems with solutions, about 260 in the part still extant.

The introduction also states that the work is divided into 13 books. Six of these books were known in Europe in the late 15th century, transmitted in Greek by Byzantine scholars and numbered from I to VI; four other books were discovered in 1968 in a 9th-century Arabic translation by Qusṭā ibn Lūqā. However, the Arabic text lacks mathematical symbolism, and it appears to be based on a later Greek commentary—perhaps that of Hypatia (c. 370–415)—that diluted Diophantus's exposition. We now know that the numbering of the Greek books must be modified: the *Arithmetica* thus consists of Books I to III in Greek, Books IV to VII in Arabic, and, presumably, Books VIII to X in Greek (the former Greek Books IV to VI). Further renumbering is unlikely; it is fairly certain that the Byzantines only knew the six books they transmitted and the Arabs no more than Books I to VII in the commented version.

The problems of Book I are not characteristic, being mostly simple problems used to illustrate algebraic reckoning. The distinctive features of Diophantus's problems appear in the later books: they are indeterminate (having more than one solution), are of the second degree or are reducible to the second degree (the highest power on variable terms is 2, i.e., x^2), and end with the determination of a positive rational value for the unknown that will make a given algebraic expression a numerical square or sometimes a cube. (Throughout his book Diophantus uses "number" to refer to what are now called positive, rational numbers; thus, a square number is the square of some positive, rational number.) Books II and III also teach general methods. In three problems of Book II it is explained how to represent: (1) any given square number as a sum of the squares of two rational numbers; (2) any given nonsquare number, which is the sum of two known squares, as a sum of two other squares; and (3) any given rational number as the difference of two squares. While the first and third problems are stated generally, the assumed knowledge of one solution in the second problem suggests that not every rational number is the sum of two squares. Diophantus later gives the condition for an integer: the given number must not contain any prime factor of the form $4n + 3$ raised to an odd power, where n is a non-negative integer. Such examples motivated the rebirth of number theory. Although Diophantus is typically satisfied to obtain one solution to a problem, he occasionally mentions in problems that an infinite number of solutions exists.

In Books IV to VII Diophantus extends basic methods such as those outlined above to problems of higher degrees that can be reduced to a binomial equation of the first or second degree. The prefaces to these books state that their purpose is to provide the reader with "experience and skill." While this recent discovery does not increase knowledge of Diophantus's mathematics, it does alter the appraisal of his pedagogical ability. Books VIII and IX (presumably Greek Books IV and V) solve more difficult problems, even if the basic methods remain the same. For instance, one problem involves decomposing a given integer into the sum of two squares that are arbitrarily close to one another. A similar problem involves decomposing a given integer into the sum of three squares; in it, Diophantus excludes the impossible case of integers of the form $8n + 7$ (again, n is a non-negative integer). Book X (presumably Greek Book VI) deals with right-angled triangles with rational sides and subject to various further conditions.

The contents of the three missing books of the *Arithmetica* can be surmised from the introduction, where, after saying that the reduction of a problem should "if possible" conclude with a binomial equation, Diophantus adds that he will "later on" treat the case of a trinomial equation—a promise not fulfilled in the extant part.

Although he had limited algebraic tools at his disposal, Diophantus managed to solve a great variety of problems, and the *Arithmetica* inspired Arabic mathematicians such as al-Karajī (c. 980–1030) to apply his methods. The most famous extension of Diophantus's work was by Pierre de Fermat (1601–65), the founder of modern number theory. In the margins of his copy of the *Arithmetica*, Fermat wrote various remarks, proposing new solutions, corrections, and generalizations of Diophantus's methods as well as some conjectures such as Fermat's last theorem, which occupied mathematicians for generations to come.

Indeterminate equations restricted to integral solutions have come to be known, though inappropriately, as Diophantine equations.

MUḤAMMAD IBN MŪSĀ AL-KHWĀRIZMĪ
(b. c. 780, Baghdad, Iraq — d. c. 850)

Al-Khwārizmī was a Muslim mathematician and astrono-mer whose major works introduced Hindu-Arabic numerals and the concepts of algebra into European mathematics. Latinized versions of his name and of his most famous book title live on in the terms *algorithm* and *algebra*.

Al-Khwārizmī lived in Baghdad, where he worked at the "House of Wisdom" (*Dār al-Ḥikma*) under the caliphate of al-Ma'mūn. (The House of Wisdom acquired and translated scientific and philosophic treatises, particularly Greek, as well as publishing original research.) Al-Kwārizmī's work on elementary algebra, *al-Kitāb al-mukhtaṣar fī Ḥisāb al-jabr wa'l-muqābala* ("The Compendious Book on Calculation by Completion and Balancing"), was trans-lated into Latin in the 12th century, from which the title and term *Algebra* derives. *Algebra* is a compilation of rules, together with demonstrations, for finding solutions of linear and quadratic equations based on intuitive geometric arguments, rather than the abstract notation now associated with the subject. Its systematic, demonstrative approach distinguishes it from earlier treatments of the subject. It also contains sections on calculating areas and volumes of geometric figures and on the use of algebra to solve inheri-tance problems according to proportions prescribed by Islamic law. Elements within the work can be traced from Babylonian mathematics of the early 2nd millennium BCE through Hellenistic, Hebrew, and Hindu treatises.

Detail from a 1983 commemorative stamp from the U.S.S.R. celebrates Muhammad ibn Mūsā al-Khwārizmī on the 1200th anniversary of his birth. Though nothing is known today about his actual appearance, the significance of his work on algebra and beyond has endured for centuries.

In the 12th century a second work by al-Khwārizmī introduced Hindu-Arabic numerals and their arithmetic to the West. It is preserved only in a Latin translation, *Algoritmi de numero Indorum* ("Al-Khwārizmī Concerning the Hindu Art of Reckoning"). From the name of the author, rendered in Latin as *algoritmi*, originated the term *algorithm*.

A third major book was his *Kitāb ṣūrat al-arḍ* ("The Image of the Earth"; translated as *Geography*), which presented the coordinates of localities in the known world based, ultimately, on those in the *Geography* of Ptolemy (fl. 127–145 CE) but with improved values for the length of the Mediterranean Sea and the location of cities in Asia and Africa. He also assisted in the construction of a world map for al-Ma'mūn and participated in a project to determine the circumference of the Earth, which had long been known to be spherical, by measuring the length of a degree of a meridian through the plain of Sinjār in Iraq.

Finally, al-Khwārizmī also compiled a set of astronomical tables (*Zīj*), based on a variety of Hindu and Greek sources. This work included a table of sines, evidently for a circle of radius 150 units. Like his treatises on algebra and Hindu-Arabic numerals, this astronomical work (or an Andalusian revision thereof) was translated into Latin.

NICOMACHUS OF GERASA
(fl. *c.* 100 CE, Gerasa, Roman Syria [now Jarash, Jordan])

Nicomachus was a neo-Pythagorean philosopher and mathematician who wrote *Arithmētikē eisagōgē* (*Introduction to Arithmetic*), an influential treatise on number theory. Considered a standard authority for 1,000 years, the book sets out the elementary theory and properties of numbers and contains the earliest-known Greek multiplication table.

Nicomachus was interested in philosophical questions dealing with whole numbers, the classification of even and odd numbers and their ratios, and wondrous or curious properties of numbers. For example, he was interested in the notion of "perfect numbers," such as 6, which equals the sum of its proper divisors, and "amicable numbers," pairs of numbers, such as 220 and 284, whose proper divisors sum to one another. He was not interested, however, in abstract theorems on whole numbers and their proofs, as found in Books VII–IX of Euclid's *Elements*; contrary to Euclid's approach, Nicomachus would merely give specific numerical examples. A Latin translation of the *Arithme̅tike̅* by Lucius Apuleius (*c.* 124–170) is lost, but a version by Ancius Boethius (*c.* 470–524) survived and was used in schools up to the Renaissance. Nicomachus also wrote *Encheiridion Harmonikēs* ("Handbook of Harmony") on the Pythagorean theory of music and the two-volume *Theologoumena arithmetikēs* ("The Theology of Numbers") on the mystic properties of numbers; only fragments of the latter survive.

LEONARDO PISANO
(b. *c.* 1170, Pisa? — d. after 1240)

Leonardo Pisano, also known as Fibonacci, was a medieval Italian mathematician and author of *Liber abaci* (1202;

"Book of the Abacus"), the first European work on Indian and Arabian mathematics.

Little is known about Leonardo's life beyond the few facts given in his mathematical writings. During his boyhood his father, Guglielmo, a Pisan merchant, was appointed consul over the community of Pisan merchants in the North African port of Bugia (now Bejaïa, Alg.). Leonardo was sent to study calculation with an Arab master. He later went to Egypt, Syria, Greece, Sicily, and Provence, where he studied different numerical systems and methods of calculation.

When Leonardo's *Liber abaci* first appeared, Hindu-Arabic numerals were known to only a few European intellectuals through translations of the writings of the 9th-century Arab mathematician Muhammad ibn Mūsā al-Khwārizmī. The first seven chapters dealt with the notation, explaining the principle of place value, by which the position of a figure determines whether it is a unit, 10, 100, and so forth, and demonstrating the use of the numerals in arithmetical operations. The techniques were then applied to such practical problems as profit margin, barter, money changing, conversion of weights and measures, partnerships, and interest. Most of the work was devoted to speculative mathematics—proportion (represented by such popular medieval techniques as the Rule of Three and the Rule of Five, which are rule-of-thumb methods of finding proportions), the Rule of False Position (a method by which a problem is worked out by a false assumption, then corrected by proportion), extraction of roots, and the properties of numbers, concluding with some geometry and algebra. In 1220 Leonardo produced a brief work, the *Practica geometriae* ("Practice of Geometry"), which included eight chapters of theorems based on Euclid's *Elements* and *On Divisions*.

The *Liber abaci*, which was widely copied and imitated, drew the attention of the Holy Roman emperor Frederick II. In the 1220s Leonardo was invited to appear before the emperor at Pisa, and there John of Palermo, a member of Frederick's scientific entourage, propounded a series of problems, three of which Leonardo presented in his books. The first two belonged to a favourite Arabic type, the indeterminate, which had been developed by the 3rd-century Greek mathematician Diophantus. This was an equation with two or more unknowns for which the solution must be in rational numbers (whole numbers or common fractions). The third problem was a third-degree equation (i.e., containing a cube), $x^3 + 2x^2 + 10x = 20$ (expressed in modern algebraic notation), which Leonardo solved by a trial-and-error method known as approximation; he arrived at the answer

$$1^0 22' 7'' 42''' 33^{IV} 4^V 40^{VI}$$

$$\left(1 + \frac{22}{60} + \frac{7}{3,600} + \frac{42}{216,000} + ...\right)$$

in sexagesimal fractions (a fraction using the Babylonian number system that had a base of 60), which, when translated into modern decimals (1.3688081075), is correct to nine decimal places.

For several years Leonardo corresponded with Frederick II and his scholars, exchanging problems with them. He dedicated his *Liber quadratorum* (1225; "Book of Square Numbers") to Frederick. Devoted entirely to Diophantine equations of the second degree (i.e., containing squares), the *Liber quadratorum* is considered Leonardo's masterpiece. It is a systematically arranged collection of theorems, many invented by the author, who used his own proofs to work out general solutions. Probably his most creative work was in congruent numbers—numbers that give the same remainder when divided by a given number. He worked out an original solution for finding a number that, when added to or subtracted from a square number, leaves a square number. His statement that $x^2 + y^2$ and $x^2 - y^2$ could not both be squares was of great importance to the determination of the area of rational right triangles. Although the *Liber abaci* was more influential and broader in scope, the *Liber quadratorum* alone ranks Leonardo as the major contributor to number theory between Diophantus and the 17th-century French mathematician Pierre de Fermat.

Except for his role in spreading the use of the Hindu-Arabic numerals, Leonardo's contribution to mathematics has been largely overlooked. His name is known to modern mathematicians mainly because of the Fibonacci sequence derived from a problem in the *Liber abaci:*

A certain man put a pair of rabbits in a place surrounded on all sides by a wall. How many pairs of rabbits can be produced from that pair in a year if it is supposed that every month each pair begets a new pair which from the second month on becomes productive?

The resulting number sequence, 1, 1, 2, 3, 5, 8, 13, 21, 34, 55 (Leonardo himself omitted the first term), in which each number is the sum of the two preceding numbers, is the first recursive number sequence (in which the relation between two or more successive terms can be expressed by a formula) known in Europe. Terms in the sequence were stated in a formula by the French-born mathematician Albert Girard in 1634: $u_{n+2} = u_{n+1} + u_n$, in which u represents the term and the subscript its rank in the sequence. The mathematician Robert Simson at the University of Glasgow in 1753 noted that, as the numbers increased in magnitude, the ratio between succeeding numbers approached the number α, the golden ratio, whose value is 1.6180..., or (1 + 5)/2. In the 19th century the term Fibonacci sequence was coined by the French mathematician Edouard Lucas, and scientists began to discover such sequences in nature; for example, in the spirals of sunflower heads, in pine cones, in the regular descent (genealogy) of the male bee, in the related logarithmic (equiangular) spiral in snail shells, in the arrangement of leaf buds on a stem, and in animal horns.

Leonardo Pisano ("Fibonacci"), statue by Giovanni Paganucci, 1863; in the camposanto *in Pisa, Italy.* © www.istockphoto.com/ Roberto A. Sanchez

QIN JIUSHAO

(b. *c.* 1202, Puzhou [modern Anyue, Sichuan province], China—d. *c.* 1261, Meizhou [modern Meixian, Guangdong province])

Chinese mathematician Qin Jiushao developed a method of solving simultaneous linear congruences.

In 1219 Qin joined the army as captain of a territorial volunteer unit and helped quash a local rebellion. In 1224–25 Qin studied astronomy and mathematics in the capital Lin'an (modern Hangzhou) with functionaries of the

Imperial Astronomical Bureau and with an unidentified hermit. In 1233 Qin began his official mandarin (government) service. He interrupted his government career for three years beginning in 1244 because of his mother's death; during the mourning period he wrote his only mathematical book, now known as *Shushu jiuzhang* (1247; "Mathematical Writings in Nine Sections"). He later rose to the position of provincial governor of Qiongzhou (in modern Hainan), but charges of corruption and bribery brought his dismissal in 1258. Contemporary authors mention his ambitious and cruel personality.

His book is divided into nine "categories," each containing nine problems related to calendrical computations, meteorology, surveying of fields, surveying of remote objects, taxation, fortification works, construction works, military affairs, and commercial affairs. Categories concern indeterminate analysis, calculation of the areas and volumes of plane and solid figures, proportions, calculation of interest, simultaneous linear equations, progressions, and solution of higher-degree polynomial equations in one unknown. Every problem is followed by a numerical answer, a general solution, and a description of the calculations performed with counting rods.

The two most important methods found in Qin's book are for the solution of simultaneous linear congruences $N \equiv r_1 \pmod{m_1} \equiv r_2 \pmod{m_2} \equiv \ldots \equiv r_n \pmod{m_n}$ and an algorithm for obtaining a numerical solution of higher-degree polynomial equations based on a process of successively better approximations. This method was rediscovered in Europe about 1802 and was known as the Ruffini-Horner method. Although Qin's is the earliest surviving description of this algorithm, most scholars believe that it was widely known in China before this time.

RENAISSANCE EUROPE

HENRY BRIGGS
(b. February 1561, Warleywood, Yorkshire, Eng. — d. Jan. 26, 1630, Oxford)

Henry Briggs was an English mathematician and inventor of the common, or Briggsian, logarithm. His writings were mainly responsible for the widespread acceptance of logarithms throughout Europe. His innovation was instrumental in easing the burden of mathematicians, astronomers, and other scientists who must make long and tedious calculations.

About 1577 Briggs entered St. John's College, Cambridge, where he received a bachelor's degree in 1581 and a master's degree in 1585. He was elected a fellow of St. John's in 1589 and a lecturer in mathematics and medicine there in 1592. While at St. John's, Briggs began research in astronomy and navigation with the mathematician Edward Wright. In 1596 Briggs was appointed the first professor of geometry at the newly opened Gresham College in London, and for more than two decades he was instrumental in establishing it as a major centre for scientific research and advanced mathematical instruction. Briggs also took an active part in bridging the gap between mathematical theory and practice. He instructed mariners in navigation, advised explorers on various proposed expeditions, and invested in the London Company (responsible for founding Jamestown, Virginia, in 1607). His publications from this period include *A Table to find the Height of the Pole, the Magnetic Declination being given* (1602) and *Tables for the Improvement of Navigation* (1610); he returned to the subject of exploration later with *A Treatise of the Northwest Passage to the South Sea, Through the*

Continent of Virginia and by Fretum Hudson (1622). In addition, Briggs's advice was avidly sought on surveying, shipbuilding, mining, and drainage.

Briggs's early research focused primarily on astronomy and its applications to navigation, and he was among the first to disseminate the ideas of the astronomer Johannes Kepler (1571–1630) in England. However, with the publication of John Napier's *Mirifici Logarithmorum Canonis Descriptio* (1614; "Description of the Marvelous Canon of Logarithms"), Briggs immediately realized the logarithm's potential to ease astronomical and navigational calculations and so turned his attention and energy to improving the idea. During 1615 and 1616 Briggs paid two long visits to Edinburgh, Scotland, to collaborate with Napier on his new invention, during which time he convinced Napier of the benefit of modifying his logarithms to use base 10, now known as common logarithms, or Briggsian logarithms in his honour. (Napier had used a base approximately equal to $1/e$, where $e \cong 2.718$, and logarithms with base e are now called natural logarithms, or Napierian logarithms.) In 1617, shortly after Napier's death, Briggs published *Logarithmorum Chilias Prima* ("Introduction to Logarithms"), wherein he offered a brief explanation of the new invention together with the logarithms of numbers from 1 to 1,000, calculated to 14 decimal places. For the next several years, Briggs devoted himself to the time-consuming and laborious task of constructing a larger table of logarithms. *The Arithmetica Logarithmica* ("Common Logarithms"), published in 1624, advertised the utility of logarithms in expediting calculations. In addition to tables of logarithms from 1 to 20,000 and from 90,000 to 100,000 calculated to 14 decimal places, an extended preface provided ample testimony of Briggs's originality. The preface contained an important discussion of the nature and construction of logarithms that anticipated by nearly half a century the foundational work of James Gregory (1638–1675) and Isaac Newton (1643–1727), among others. Furthermore, Briggs's lengthy immersion in the practical interpolation of logarithmic functions resulted in his anticipating Newton in the discovery of the binomial theorem.

By the time the *Arithmetica Logarithmica* was published, Briggs no longer resided in London, as he was elected Savilian Professor of Astronomy at the University of Oxford in 1619. The following year he published an edition of the first six books of Euclid's *Elements* but, unfortunately, did not live long enough to complete a revised and full edition of the text. His final publication, the *Trigonometria Britannica* (1633; "Trigonometry in Britain"), covering the application of logarithms to trigonometric functions, appeared posthumously.

Joost Bürgi

(b. Feb. 28, 1552, Lichtensteig, Switz.—d. Jan. 31, 1632, Kassel, Hesse-Kassel)

Joost Bürgi was a Swiss mathematician who invented logarithms independently of the Scottish mathematician John Napier.

Bürgi served as court watchmaker to Duke Wilhelm IV of Hesse-Kassel from 1579 to 1592 and worked in the royal observatory at Kassel, where he developed geometrical and astronomical instruments. Word of his exceptional instruments reached Prague, where Holy Roman Emperor Rudolf II was trying to establish a science centre, and in about 1603 Bürgi journeyed to Prague to take up the post of imperial clockmaker. Later he also became assistant to the German astronomer Johannes Kepler.

Bürgi was a major contributor to the development of decimal fractions and exponential notation, but his most notable contribution was published in 1620 as a table of antilogarithms. He may have developed the idea for logarithms as early as 1588, but he certainly had compiled his table before his journey to Prague, more than 10 years before Napier published his own logarithm table in 1614.

PIERRE DE FERMAT

(b. Aug. 17, 1601, Beaumont-de-Lomagne, France—d. Jan. 12, 1665, Castres)

Pierre de Fermat is often called the founder of the modern theory of numbers. Together with fellow Frenchman René Descartes, Fermat was one of the two leading mathematicians of the first half of the 17th century. Independently of Descartes, Fermat discovered the fundamental principle

Fermat, portrait by Roland Lefèvre; in the Narbonne City Museums, France. Courtesy of the Musée de la Ville de Narbonne, France

of analytic geometry. His methods for finding tangents to curves and their maximum and minimum points led him to be regarded as the inventor of the differential calculus. Through his correspondence with Blaise Pascal he was a cofounder of the theory of probability.

Fermat vainly sought to persuade Pascal to join him in research in number theory. Inspired by an edition in 1621 of the *Arithmetica* of Diophantus, the Greek mathematician of the 3rd century CE, Fermat had discovered new results in the so-called higher arithmetic, many of which concerned properties of prime numbers (those positive integers that have no factors other than 1 and themselves). One of the most elegant of these had been the theorem that every prime of the form $4n + 1$ is uniquely expressible as the sum of two squares. A more important result, now known as Fermat's lesser theorem, asserts that if p is a prime number and if a is any positive integer, then $a^p - a$ is divisible by p. Fermat seldom gave demonstrations of his results, and in this case proofs were provided by Gottfried Leibniz, the 17th-century German mathematician and philosopher, and Leonhard Euler, the 18th-century Swiss mathematician. For occasional demonstrations of his theorems Fermat used a device that he called his method of "infinite descent," an inverted form of reasoning by recurrence or mathematical induction. One unproved conjecture by Fermat turned out to be false. In 1640, in letters to mathematicians and to other knowledgeable thinkers of the day, including Blaise Pascal, he announced his belief that numbers of the form $2^{2n} + 1$, known since as "numbers of Fermat," are necessarily prime; but a century later Euler showed that $2^{25} + 1$ has 641 as a factor. It is not known if there are any primes among the Fermat numbers for $n > 5$. Carl Friedrich Gauss in 1796 in Germany found an unexpected application for Fermat numbers when he showed that a regular polygon of N sides is constructible in a Euclidean sense if N is a prime Fermat number or a product of distinct Fermat primes. By far the best known of Fermat's many theorems is a problem known as his "great," or "last," theorem. This appeared in the margin of his copy of Diophantus's *Arithmetica* and states that the equation $x^n + y^n = z^n$, where x, y, z, and n are positive integers, has no solution if n is greater than 2. This theorem remained unsolved until the late 20th century.

Fermat was the most productive mathematician of his day. But his influence was circumscribed by his reluctance to publish.

Carl Friedrich Gauss

(b. April 30, 1777, Brunswick [Germany]—d. Feb. 23, 1855, Göttingen, Hanover)

German Carl Friedrich Gauss is generally regarded as one of the greatest mathematicians of all time for his contributions to number theory, geometry, probability theory, geodesy, planetary astronomy, the theory of functions, and potential theory (including electromagnetism).

Gauss's first significant discovery, in 1792, was that a regular polygon of 17 sides can be constructed by ruler and compass alone. Its significance lies not in the result but in the proof, which rested on a profound analysis of the factorization of polynomial equations and opened the door to later ideas of Galois theory. His doctoral thesis of 1797 gave a proof of the fundamental theorem of algebra: every polynomial equation with real or complex coefficients has as many roots (solutions) as its degree (the highest power of the variable). Gauss's proof, though not wholly convincing, was remarkable for its critique of earlier attempts. Gauss later gave three more proofs of this major result, the last on the 50th anniversary of the first, which shows the importance he attached to the topic.

Gauss's recognition as a truly remarkable talent, though, resulted from two major publications in 1801. Foremost was his publication of the first systematic textbook on algebraic number theory, *Disquisitiones Arithmeticae*. This book begins with the first account of modular arithmetic, gives a thorough account of the solutions of quadratic polynomials in two variables in integers, and ends with the theory of factorization mentioned above. This choice of topics and its natural generalizations set the agenda in number theory for much of the 19th century, and Gauss's continuing interest in the subject spurred much research, especially in German universities.

The second publication was his rediscovery of the asteroid Ceres. Its original discovery, by the Italian astronomer Giuseppe Piazzi in 1800, had caused a sensation, but it vanished behind the Sun before enough observations could be taken to calculate its orbit with sufficient accuracy to know where it would reappear. Many astronomers competed for the honour of finding it again, but Gauss won. His success rested on a novel method for dealing with errors in observations, today called the method of least squares. Thereafter Gauss worked for many years as an astronomer and published a major work on the computation of orbits—the numerical side of such work was much less onerous for him than for most people. As an intensely loyal subject of the duke of Brunswick and, after 1807 when he returned to Göttingen as an astronomer, of the duke of Hanover, Gauss felt that the work was socially valuable.

Similar motives led Gauss to accept the challenge of surveying the territory of Hanover, and he was often out in the field in charge of the observations. The project, which lasted from 1818 to 1832, encountered numerous difficulties, but it led to a number of advancements. One was Gauss's invention of the heliotrope (an instrument that reflects the Sun's rays in a focused beam that can be observed from several miles away), which improved the accuracy of the observations. Another was his discovery of a way of formulating the concept of the curvature of a surface. Gauss showed that there is an intrinsic measure of curvature that is not altered if the surface is bent without being stretched. For example, a circular cylinder and a flat sheet of paper have the same intrinsic curvature, which is why exact copies of figures on the cylinder can be made on the paper (as, for example, in printing). But a sphere and a plane have different curvatures, which is why no completely accurate flat map of the Earth can be made.

Gauss published works on number theory, the mathematical theory of map construction, and many other subjects. In the 1830s he became interested in terrestrial magnetism and participated in the first worldwide survey of the Earth's magnetic field (to measure it, he invented the magnetometer). With his Göttingen colleague, the physicist Wilhelm Weber, he made the first electric telegraph, but a certain parochialism prevented him from pursuing the invention energetically. Instead, he drew important mathematical consequences from this work for what is today called potential theory, an important branch of mathematical physics arising in the study of electromagnetism and gravitation.

Gauss also wrote on cartography, the theory of map projections. For his study of angle-preserving maps, he was awarded the prize of the Danish Academy of Sciences in 1823. This work came close to suggesting that complex functions of a complex variable are generally angle preserving, but Gauss stopped short of making that fundamental insight explicit, leaving it for Bernhard Riemann, who had a deep appreciation of Gauss's work. Gauss also had other unpublished insights into the nature of complex functions and their integrals, some of which he divulged to friends.

CHRISTIAN GOLDBACH
(b. March 18, 1690, Königsberg, Prussia [now Kaliningrad, Russia] — d. Nov. 20, 1764, Moscow, Russia)

The Russian mathematician Christian Goldbach is primarily remembered today for his contributions to number theory, including Goldbach's conjecture.

In 1725 Goldbach became professor of mathematics and historian of the Imperial Academy at St. Petersburg. Three years later he went to Moscow as tutor to Tsar

Peter II, and from 1742 he served as a staff member of the Russian Ministry of Foreign Affairs.

Goldbach first proposed the conjecture that bears his name in a letter to the Swiss mathematician Leonhard Euler in 1742. He claimed that "every number greater than 2 is an aggregate of three prime numbers." Because mathematicians in Goldbach's day considered 1 a prime number (prime numbers are now defined as those positive integers greater than 1 that are divisible only by 1 and themselves), Goldbach's conjecture is usually restated in modern terms as: Every even natural number greater than 2 is equal to the sum of two prime numbers.

The first breakthrough in the effort to prove Goldbach's conjecture occurred in 1930, when the Soviet mathematician Lev Genrikhovich Shnirelman proved that every natural number can be expressed as the sum of not more than 20 prime numbers. In 1937 the Soviet mathematician Ivan Matveyevich Vinogradov went on to prove that every "sufficiently large" (without stating exactly how large) odd natural number can be expressed as the sum of not more than three prime numbers. The latest refinement came in 1973, when the Chinese mathematician Chen Jing Run proved that every sufficiently large even natural number is the sum of a prime and a product of at most two primes.

Goldbach also made notable contributions to the theory of curves, to infinite series, and to the integration of differential equations.

MARIN MERSENNE
(b. Sept. 8, 1588, near Oizé, Maine, France—d. Sept. 1, 1648, Paris)

Marin Mersenne was a French theologian, natural philosopher, and mathematician. While best remembered by mathematicians for his search for a formula to generate prime numbers based on what are now known as "Mersenne numbers," his wider significance stems from his role as correspondent, publicizing and disseminating the work of some of the greatest thinkers of his age.

Mersenne was educated at the Jesuit college of La Flèche soon after its founding in 1604. He left La Flèche about 1609 to study theology in Paris at both the Sorbonne and the Collège de France. In 1611 he entered the austere Roman Catholic Order of Minims, spending his novitiate at Nigeon and Meaux. From 1614 to 1618 he taught philosophy and theology at Nevers. He resided in Paris, except for frequent trips abroad, from 1619 until his death in 1648.

Mersenne's earliest publications, such as *Quaestiones celeberrime in Genesim* (1623; "Frequent Questions Concerning Genesis") and *La vérité des sciences* (1625; "The Truth of Science"), defended orthodox theology by distinguishing between the ultimate nature, or essence, of things (knowable only by God) and the contingent facts observable by man. He disagreed, however, with the views of skepticism that the world is completely unknowable. He asserted that knowledge should freely advance through experiment and observation—frequently chiding scholars for not including accurate experimental data in their papers—while insisting that hypotheses are, at best, probable explanations. He also distinguished between a rational, indeed mechanistic, natural world populated by living automatons and a sentient humanity. From 1626 Mersenne's publications concentrated on applied mathematical sciences, such as astronomy and optics.

In 1635 Mersenne formed the informal, private Académie Parisienne (the precursor to the French Academy of Sciences), where many of the leading mathematicians and natural philosophers of France shared their research. He used this forum to disseminate the ideas of

René Descartes, who had moved to the Netherlands in 1629. He also assisted in the publication of Descartes's *Discours de la méthode* (1637; "Discourse on Method") and took charge of soliciting the "Objections" appended to Descartes's *Meditationes* (1641; "Meditations"). Other luminaries that Mersenne corresponded with, promulgated the ideas of, and mediated disputes among include Galileo Galilei, Blaise Pascal, Christiaan Huygens, and Pierre de Fermat. During the 1630s Mersenne was particularly important in promoting the work of Galileo. Through two small books and discussions of Galileo's work in his correspondence, Mersenne disseminated Galileo's ideas beyond Italy and greatly facilitated the acceptance of mechanical explanations against remnants of scholasticism.

In 1644 Mersenne communicated some research of his on numbers of the form $2^n - 1$, now known as Mersenne numbers. He observed that if $2^n - 1$ is prime, then n must be prime, but that the converse is not necessarily true. Although he failed to find a formula for primes (it is not certain that one even exists), Mersenne numbers continue to interest mathematicians, and his formula is still useful in testing large numbers to determine if they are prime.

Mersenne made several lengthy trips to the Netherlands, provincial France, and Italy. From the latter excursion he brought back news to France in 1645 of the barometric experiment of Evangelista Torricelli, which led to the famous work of Pascal on the weight of the air.

JOHN NAPIER

(b. 1550, Merchiston Castle, near Edinburgh, Scot.—d. April 4, 1617, Merchiston Castle)

John Napier was a Scottish mathematician and theological writer who originated the concept of logarithms as a mathematical device to aid in calculations.

John Napier, detail of an oil painting, 1616; in the collection of the University of Edinburgh. Courtesy of the University of Edinburgh; photograph, the Scottish National Portrait Gallery

Napier devoted most of his leisure to the study of mathematics, particularly to devising methods of facilitating computation, and it is with the greatest of these, logarithms, that his name is associated. He began working on logarithms probably as early as 1594, gradually elaborating his computational system whereby roots, products, and quotients could be quickly determined from tables showing powers of a fixed number used as a base.

His contributions to this powerful mathematical invention are contained in two treatises: *Mirifici Logarithmorum Canonis Descriptio* (*Description of the Marvelous Canon of Logarithms*), which was published in 1614, and *Mirifici Logarithmorum Canonis Constructio* (*Construction of the Marvelous Canon of Logarithms*), which was published two years after his death. In the former, he outlined the steps that had led to his invention.

Logarithms were meant to simplify calculations, especially multiplication, such as those needed in astronomy. Napier discovered that the basis for this computation was a relationship between an arithmetical progression—a sequence of numbers in which each number is obtained, following a geometric progression, from the one immediately preceding it by multiplying by a constant factor, which may be greater than unity (e.g., the sequence 2, 4, 8, 16 . . .) or less than unity (e.g., 8, 4, 2, 1, ½ . . .).

In the *Descriptio,* besides giving an account of the nature of logarithms, Napier confined himself to an account of the use to which they might be put. He promised to explain the method of their construction in a later work. This was the *Constructio,* which claims attention because of the systematic use in its pages of the decimal point to separate the fractional from the integral part of a number. Decimal fractions had already been introduced by the Flemish mathematician Simon Stevin in 1586, but his notation was unwieldy. The use of a point as the separator occurs frequently in the *Constructio.* Joost Bürgi, the Swiss mathematician, between 1603 and 1611 independently invented a system of logarithms, which he published in 1620. But Napier worked on logarithms earlier than Bürgi and has the priority due to his prior date of publication in 1614.

Although Napier's invention of logarithms overshadows all his other mathematical work, he made other mathematical contributions. In 1617 he published his *Rabdologiae, seu Numerationis per Virgulas Libri Duo (Study of Divining Rods, or Two Books of Numbering by Means of Rods,* 1667); in this he described ingenious methods of multiplying and dividing of small rods known as Napier's bones, a device that was the forerunner of the slide rule. He also made important contributions to spherical trigonometry, particularly by reducing the number of equations used to express trigonometrical relationships from 10 to 2 general statements. He is also credited with certain trigonometrical relations—Napier's analogies—but it seems likely that the English mathematician Henry Briggs had a share in these.

THE MODERN ERA

PAUL ISAAK BERNAYS

(b. Oct. 17, 1888, London, Eng.—d. Sept. 18, 1977, Zürich, Switz.)

Paul Bernays is best known for his work in proof theory and axiomatic set theory, which helped create the new discipline of mathematical logic.

After obtaining his doctorate from the University of Göttingen in Germany under Edmund Landau in 1912, Bernays taught for five years at the University of Zürich before returning to Göttingen. There he collaborated closely with the prominent mathematician David Hilbert, who in the twilight of his career sought to overcome the challenges to classical mathematics posed by L.E.J. Brouwer's intuitionism. Bernays's own philosophical views remained in the background during the "foundations crisis" of the 1920s. Nevertheless, he served as a strong pillar of support for Hilbert's program to formalize mathematics. Taking Hilbert's name as coauthor, he wrote the classic study *Grundlagen der Mathematik*, 2 vol. (1934–39; reissued 1968–70; "Foundations of Mathematics"). In 1956 Bernays also revised Hilbert's *Grundlagen der Geometrie* (1899; *The Foundations of Geometry*), which went through several editions.

After the Nazi takeover in 1933, Bernays was compelled to give up his post and moved to Switzerland. In Zürich he delved into the realm of set theory, trying to streamline the Zermelo-Fraenkel system of axioms. This work appeared in a series of articles under the title "A System of Axiomatic Set Theory" (1937–54), from which the principal theses were published as *Axiomatic Set Theory* (1958). In it Bernays simplified and refined the work of John von Neumann on logic and set theory; these modifications were further developed by the logician Kurt Gödel.

GEORG CANTOR
(b. March 3, 1845, St. Petersburg, Russia—d. Jan. 6, 1918, Halle, Ger.)

Georg Cantor founded set theory and introduced the mathematically meaningful concept of transfinite numbers, indefinitely large but distinct from one another.

An important exchange of letters with Richard Dedekind, mathematician at the Brunswick Technical Institute, who was his lifelong friend and colleague, marked the beginning of Cantor's ideas on the theory of sets. Both agreed that a set, whether finite or infinite, is a collection of objects (e.g., the integers, {0, ±1, ±2 . . .}) that share a particular property while each object retains its own individuality. But when Cantor applied the device of the one-to-one correspondence (e.g., {a, b, c} to {1, 2, 3}) to study the characteristics of sets, he quickly saw that they differed in the extent of their membership, even among infinite sets. (A set is infinite if one of its parts, or subsets, has as many objects as itself.) His method soon produced surprising results.

In 1873 Cantor demonstrated that the rational numbers, though infinite, are countable (or denumerable) because they may be placed in a one-to-one correspondence with the natural numbers (i.e., the integers, as 1, 2, 3, . . .). He showed that the set (or aggregate) of real numbers (composed of irrational and rational numbers) was infinite and uncountable. Even more paradoxically, he proved that the set of all algebraic numbers contains as many components as the set of all integers and that transcendental numbers (those that are not algebraic, as π), which are a subset of the irrationals, are uncountable and are therefore more numerous than integers, which must be conceived as infinite.

But Cantor's paper, in which he first put forward these results, was refused for publication in *Crelle's Journal* by one of its referees, Leopold Kronecker, who henceforth vehemently opposed his work. On Dedekind's intervention, however, it was published in 1874 as "Über eine Eigenschaft des Inbegriffes aller reellen algebraischen Zahlen" ("On a Characteristic Property of All Real Algebraic Numbers").

While honeymooning the same year with his bride, Vally Guttman, at Interlaken, Switz., Cantor met Dedekind, who gave a sympathetic hearing to his new theory. Cantor's salary was low, but the estate of his father, who died in 1863, enabled him to build a house for his wife and five children. Many of his papers were published in Sweden in the new journal *Acta Mathematica*, edited and founded by Gösta Mittag-Leffler, one of the first persons to recognize his ability.

Cantor's theory became a whole new subject of research concerning the mathematics of the infinite (e.g., an endless series, as 1, 2, 3, . . ., and even more complicated sets), and his theory was heavily dependent on the device of the one-to-one correspondence. In thus developing new ways of asking questions concerning continuity and infinity, Cantor quickly became controversial. When he argued that infinite numbers had an actual existence, he drew on ancient and medieval philosophy concerning the "actual" and "potential" infinite and also on the early religious training given him by his parents. In his book on sets, *Grundlagen einer allgemeinen Mannigfaltigkeitslehre* ("Foundations of a General Theory of Aggregates"), Cantor in 1883 allied his theory with Platonic metaphysics. By contrast, Kronecker, who held that only the integers "exist" ("God made the integers, and all the rest is the work of man"), for many years heatedly rejected his reasoning and blocked his appointment to the faculty at the University of Berlin.

In 1895–97 Cantor fully propounded his view of continuity and the infinite, including infinite ordinals and cardinals, in his best known work, *Beiträge zur Begründung der transfiniten Mengelehre* (published in English under the title *Contributions to the Founding of the Theory of Transfinite Numbers,* 1915). This work contains his conception of transfinite numbers, to which he was led by his demonstration that an infinite set may be placed in a one-to-one correspondence with one of its subsets. By the smallest transfinite cardinal number he meant the cardinal number of any set that can be placed in one-to-one correspondence with the positive integers. This transfinite number he referred to as aleph-null. Larger transfinite cardinal numbers were denoted by aleph-one, aleph-two, ... He then developed an arithmetic of transfinite numbers that was analogous to finite arithmetic. Thus, he further enriched the concept of infinity. The opposition he faced and the length of time before his ideas were fully assimilated represented in part the difficulties of mathematicians in reassessing the ancient question: "What is a number?" Cantor demonstrated that the set of points on a line possessed a higher cardinal number than aleph-null. This led to the famous problem of the continuum hypothesis, namely, that there are no cardinal numbers between aleph-null and the cardinal number of the points on a line. This problem has, in the first and second halves of the 20th century, been of great interest to the mathematical world and was studied by many mathematicians, including the Czech-Austrian-American Kurt Gödel and the American Paul J. Cohen.

PAUL JOSEPH COHEN

(b. April 2, 1934, Long Branch, N.J., U.S. — d. March 23, 2007, Stanford, Calif.)

Paul Cohen was awarded the Fields Medal in 1966 for his proof of the independence of the continuum hypothesis from the other axioms of set theory.

Cohen attended the University of Chicago (M.S., 1954; Ph.D., 1958). He held appointments at the University of Rochester, N.Y. (1957–58), and the Massachusetts Institute of Technology (1958–59) before joining the Institute for Advanced Study, Princeton, N.J. (1959–61). In 1961 he moved to Stanford University in California; he became professor emeritus in 2004.

Cohen was awarded the Fields Medal at the International Congress of Mathematicians in Moscow in 1966. Cohen solved a problem (first on David Hilbert's influential 1900 list of important unsolved problems) concerning the truth of the continuum hypothesis. Georg Cantor's continuum hypothesis states that there is no cardinal number between $\aleph_0$ and $2^{\aleph_0}$. In 1940 Kurt Gödel had shown that, if one accepts the Zermelo-Fraenkel system of axioms for set theory, then the continuum hypothesis is not disprovable. Cohen, in 1963, showed that it is not provable under these hypotheses and hence is independent of the other axioms. To do this he introduced a new technique known as forcing, a technique that has since had significant applications throughout set theory. The question still remains whether, with some axiom system for set theory, the continuum hypothesis is true. Alonzo Church, in his comments to the Congress in Moscow, suggested that the "Gödel-Cohen results and subsequent extensions of them have the consequence that there is not one set theory but many, with the difference arising in connection with a problem which intuition still seems to tell us must 'really' have only one true solution." After proving his startling result about the continuum hypothesis, Cohen returned to research in analysis.

Cohen's publications include *Set Theory and the Continuum Hypothesis* (1966).

RICHARD DEDEKIND

(b. Oct. 6, 1831, Braunschweig, duchy of Braunschweig
[Germany]—d. Feb. 12, 1916, Braunschweig)

Richard Dedekind developed a major redefinition of irrational numbers in terms of arithmetic concepts. Although not fully recognized in his lifetime, his treatment of the ideas of the infinite and of what constitutes a real number continues to influence modern mathematics.

Dedekind was the son of a lawyer. While attending the Gymnasium Martino-Catharineum in 1838–47 in Braunschweig, he was at first interested primarily in chemistry and physics. At the Caroline College in 1848–50, however, he turned to calculus, algebra, and analytic geometry, which helped qualify him to study advanced mathematics at the University of Göttingen under the mathematician Carl Friedrich Gauss.

After two years of independent study of algebra, geometry, and elliptic functions, Dedekind served as *Privatdozent* ("unsalaried lecturer") in 1854–58 at the University of Göttingen, where, in his lectures, he introduced, probably for the first time, the Galois theory of equations and attended the lectures of the mathematician Peter Gustav Lejeune Dirichlet. These experiences led

Richard Dedekind. Courtesy of the Library of the Swiss Federal Institute of Technology, Zurich

Dedekind to see the need for a redefinition of irrational numbers in terms of arithmetic properties. The geometric approach had led Eudoxus in the 4th century BCE to define them as approximations by rational numbers (e.g., a series of nonrepeating decimals, as 2 = 1.414213 . . .).

In 1858 Dedekind joined the faculty of the Zürich Polytechnic, where he remained for five years. In 1862 he accepted a position in the Technical High School in Braunschweig, where he remained in comparative isolation for the rest of his life.

While teaching there, Dedekind developed the idea that both rational and irrational numbers could form a continuum (with no gaps) of real numbers, provided that the real numbers have a one-to-one relationship with points on a line. He said that an irrational number would then be that boundary value that separates two especially constructed collections of rational numbers.

Dedekind perceived that the character of the continuum need not depend on the quantity of points on a line segment (or continuum) but rather on how the line submits to being divided. His method, now called the Dedekind cut, consisted in separating all the real numbers in a series into two parts such that each real number in one part is less than every real number in the other. Such a cut, which corresponds to a given value, defines an irrational number if no largest or no smallest is present in either part; whereas a rational is defined as a cut in which one part contains a smallest or a largest. Dedekind would therefore define the square root of 2 as the unique number dividing the continuum into two collections of numbers such that all the members of one collection are greater than those of the other, or that cut, or division, separating a series of numbers into two parts such that one collection contains all the numbers whose squares are larger than 2 and the other contains all the numbers whose squares are less than 2.

Dedekind developed his arithmetical rendering of irrational numbers in 1872 in his *Stetigkeit und Irrationale Zahlen* (Eng. trans., "Continuity and Irrational Numbers," published in *Essays on the Theory of Numbers*). He also proposed, as did the German mathematician Georg Cantor, two years later, that a set—a collection of objects or components—is infinite if its components may be arranged in a one-to-one relationship with the components of one of its subsets. By supplementing the geometric method in analysis, Dedekind contributed substantially to the modern treatment of the infinitely large and the infinitely small.

While vacationing in Interlaken, Switz., in 1874, Dedekind met Cantor. Dedekind gave a sympathetic hearing to an exposition of the revolutionary idea of sets that Cantor had just published, which later became prominent in the teaching of modern mathematics. Because both mathematicians were developing highly original concepts, such as in number theory and analysis, which were not readily accepted by their contemporaries, and because both lacked adequate professional recognition, a lasting friendship developed.

Continuing his investigations into the properties and relationships of integers—that is, the idea of number—Dedekind published *Über die Theorie der ganzen algebraischen Zahlen* (1879; "On the Theory of Algebraic Whole Numbers"). There he proposed the "ideal" as a collection of numbers that may be separated out of a larger collection, composed of algebraic integers that satisfy polynomial equations with ordinary integers as coefficients. The ideal is a collection of all algebraic integer multiples of a given algebraic integer. For example, the notation (2) represents such a particular collection, as . . . -8, -6, -4, -2, 0, 2, 4, 6, 8 . . .. The sum of two ideals is an ideal that is composed of all the sums of all their individual members. The product of two ideals is similarly defined. Ideals, considered as integers, can then be added, multiplied, and hence factored. By means of this theory of ideals, he allowed the process of unique factorization—that is, expressing a number as the product of only one set of primes, or 1 and itself—to be applied to many algebraic structures that hitherto had eluded analysis.

PETER GUSTAV LEJEUNE DIRICHLET

(b. Feb. 13, 1805, Düren, French Empire [now in Germany]—d. May 5, 1859, Göttingen, Hanover)

Peter Dirichlet made valuable contributions to number theory, analysis, and mechanics. He taught at the universities of Breslau (1827) and Berlin (1828–55) and in 1855 succeeded Carl Friedrich Gauss at the University of Göttingen.

Dirichlet made notable contributions still associated with his name in many fields of mathematics. In number theory he proved the existence of an infinite number of primes in any arithmetic series $a + b$, $2a + b$, $3a + b$, . . ., $na + b$, in which a and b are not divisible by one another. He developed the general theory of units in algebraic number theory. His *Vorlesungen über Zahlentheorie* (1863; "Lectures Concerning Number Theory"), with later addenda, contains some material important to the theory of ideals.

In 1837 Dirichlet proposed the modern concept of a function $y = f(x)$ in which for every x, there is associated with it a unique y. In mechanics he investigated the equilibrium of systems and potential theory, which led him to the Dirichlet problem concerning harmonic functions with prescribed boundary values. His *Gesammelte Werke* (1889, 1897; "Collected Works") was published in two volumes.

GOTTLOB FREGE
(b. Nov. 8, 1848, Wismar, Mecklenburg-Schwerin [now in Germany] — d. July 26, 1925, Bad Kleinen, Ger.)

Gottlob Frege founded modern mathematical logic. Working on the borderline between philosophy and mathematics — viz., in the philosophy of mathematics and mathematical logic (in which no intellectual precedents existed) — Frege discovered, on his own, the fundamental ideas that have made possible the whole modern development of logic and thereby invented an entire discipline.

In 1879 Frege published his *Begriffsschrift* ("Concept-script"), in which, for the first time, a system of mathematical logic in the modern sense was presented. No one at the time, however — philosopher or mathematician — comprehended clearly what Frege had done, and when, some decades later, the subject began to get under way, his ideas reached others mostly as filtered through the minds of other men, such as Peano; in his lifetime there were very few — one was Bertrand Russell — to give Frege the credit due to him. He was not yet too downcast by the failure of the learned world to appreciate the *Begriffsschrift,* which, after all, discourages the reader by the use of a complex and unfamiliar symbolism to express unfamiliar ideas.

Gottlob Frege. Courtesy of the Universitatsbibliothek, Jena, Ger.

He resolved, however, to compose his next book without the use of any symbols at all.

There followed a period of intensive work on the philosophy of logic and of mathematics, embodied initially in his first book, *Die Grundlagen der Arithmetik* (1884; *The Foundations of Arithmetic*). The *Grundlagen* was a work that must on any count stand as a masterpiece of philosophical writing. The only review that the book received, however, was a devastatingly hostile one by Georg Cantor, the mathematician whose ideas were the closest to Frege's, who had not bothered to understand Frege's book before subjecting it to totally unmerited scorn.

Wounded by the reception of his second book, Frege nevertheless devoted the next decade to producing a series of brilliant philosophical articles in which he elaborated his philosophy of logic. These articles contain many deep insights, although, as Frege systematized his theories, there appeared a certain hardening into a kind of scholasticism. There followed a return to the philosophy of mathematics with the first volume of *Grundgesetze der Arithmetik* (1893; partial Eng. trans., *Basic Laws of Arithmetic*), in which Frege presented, in a modified version of the symbolic system of the *Begriffsschrift,* a rigorous development of the theory of *Grundlagen.* This, too, received only a single review (by Peano). The neglect of what was to have been his chef d'oeuvre finally embittered Frege, who had complained, in the preface, of the apparent ignorance of his work on the part of writers working in allied fields. The resulting bitterness shows in the style of Frege's controversial writing. Seldom has criticism of previous writers been more deadly than in his *Grundlagen;* but it is expressed with a lightness of touch and is never unfair. In volume 2 of the *Grundgesetze* (1903), however, the attacks became heavyhanded and abusive—a means of getting back at the world that had ignored him.

A worse disaster than neglect, however, was in store for him. While volume 2 of the *Grundgesetze* was at the printer's, he received on June 16, 1902, a letter from one of the few contemporaries who had read and admired his works—Bertrand Russell. The latter pointed out, modestly but correctly, the possibility of deriving a contradiction in Frege's logical system—the celebrated Russell paradox. The two exchanged many letters; and, before the book was published, Frege had devised a modification of one of his axioms intended to restore consistency to the system. This he explained in an appendix to the book. After Frege's death, it would be shown by a Polish logician, Stanisław Leśniewski, that Frege's modified axiom still leads to contradiction. Probably Frege never discovered this. Even a brief inspection, however, of the proofs of the theorems in volume 1 would have revealed that several crucial proofs would no longer go through, and this Frege must have found out.

In any case, 1903 effectively marks the end of Frege's productive life. He never published the projected third volume of the *Grundgesetze,* and he took no part in the development of the subject, mathematical logic, that he had founded, though it had progressed considerably by the time of his death.

Kurt Gödel

(b. April 28, 1906, Brünn, Austria-Hungary [now Brno, Czech Rep.]—d. Jan. 14, 1978, Princeton, N.J., U.S.)

Kurt Gödel obtained what may be the most important mathematical result of the 20th century: his famous incompleteness theorem, which states that within any axiomatic mathematical system there are propositions that cannot be proved or disproved on the basis of the axioms within that system; thus, such a system cannot be simultaneously complete and consistent. This proof established Gödel as one of the greatest logicians since Aristotle, and its repercussions continue to be felt and debated today.

As a German-speaking Austrian, Gödel suddenly found himself living in the newly formed country of Czechoslovakia when the Austro-Hungarian Empire was broken up at the end of World War I in 1918. Six years later, though, he went to study in Austria, at the University of Vienna, where he earned his doctorate in mathematics in 1929. He joined the faculty at the University of Vienna the next year.

During that period, Vienna was one of the intellectual hubs of the world. It was home to the famed Vienna Circle, a group of scientists, mathematicians, and philosophers who endorsed the naturalistic, strongly empiricist, and antimetaphysical view known as logical positivism. Gödel's dissertation adviser, Hans Hahn, was one of the leaders of the Vienna Circle, and he introduced his star student to the group. However, Gödel's own philosophical views could not have been more different from those of the positivists. He subscribed to Platonism, theism, and mind-body dualism. In addition, he was also somewhat mentally unstable and subject to paranoia—a problem that grew worse as he aged. Thus, his contact with the members of the Vienna Circle left him with the feeling that the 20th century was hostile to his ideas.

In his doctoral thesis, "Über die Vollständigkeit des Logikkalküls" ("On the Completeness of the Calculus of Logic"), published in a slightly shortened form in 1930, Gödel proved one of the most important logical results of the century—indeed, of all time—namely, the completeness theorem, which established that classical first-order logic, or predicate calculus, is complete in the sense that all of the first-order logical truths can be proved in standard first-order proof systems.

This, however, was nothing compared with what Gödel published in 1931—namely, the incompleteness theorem: "Über formal unentscheidbare Sätze der *Principia Mathematica* und verwandter Systeme" ("On Formally Undecidable Propositions of *Principia Mathematica* and Related Systems"). Roughly speaking, this theorem established the result that it is impossible to use the axiomatic method to construct a mathematical theory, in any branch of mathematics, that entails all of the truths in that branch of mathematics. (In England, Alfred North Whitehead and Bertrand Russell had spent years on such a program, which they published as *Principia Mathematica* in three volumes in 1910, 1912, and 1913.) For instance, it is impossible to come up with an axiomatic mathematical theory that captures even all of the truths about the natural numbers (0, 1, 2, 3, . . .). This was an extremely important negative result, as before 1931 many mathematicians were trying to do precisely that—construct axiom systems that could be used to prove all mathematical truths. Indeed, several well-known logicians and mathematicians (e.g., Whitehead, Russell, Gottlob Frege, David Hilbert) spent significant portions of their careers on this project. Unfortunately for them, Gödel's theorem destroyed this entire axiomatic research program.

After the publication of the incompleteness theorem, Gödel became an internationally known intellectual figure. He traveled to the United States several times and lectured extensively at Princeton University in New Jersey, where he met Albert Einstein. This was the beginning of a close friendship that would last until Einstein's death in 1955.

After Nazi Germany annexed Austria on March 12, 1938, Gödel found himself in a rather awkward situation, partly because he had a long history of close associations with various Jewish members of the Vienna Circle (indeed, he had been attacked on the streets of Vienna by youths who thought that he was Jewish) and partly because he was suddenly in danger of being conscripted into the German army. On Sept. 20, 1938, Gödel married Adele Nimbursky (née Porkert), and, when World War II broke out a year later, he fled Europe with his wife, taking the trans-Siberian railway across Asia, sailing across the Pacific Ocean, and then taking another train across the United States to Princeton, N.J., where, with the help of Einstein, he took up a position at the newly formed Institute for Advanced Studies (IAS). He spent the remainder of his life working and teaching at the IAS, from which he retired in 1976. Gödel became a U.S. citizen in 1948.

In 1940, only months after he arrived in Princeton, Gödel published another classic mathematical paper, "Consistency of the Axiom of Choice and of the Generalized Continuum-Hypothesis with the Axioms of Set Theory," which proved that the axiom of choice and the continuum hypothesis are consistent with the standard axioms (such as the Zermelo-Fraenkel axioms) of set theory. This established half of a conjecture of Gödel's— namely, that the continuum hypothesis could not be proven true or false in standard set theories. Gödel's proof showed that it could not be proven false in those theories. In 1963 American mathematician Paul Cohen demonstrated that it could not be proven true in those theories either, vindicating Gödel's conjecture.

BERTRAND RUSSELL

(b. May 18, 1872, Trelleck, Monmouthshire, Wales—d. Feb. 2, 1970, Penrhyndeudraeth, Merioneth, Wales)

Bertrand Russell was a founding figure in the analytic movement in Anglo-American philosophy and recipient of the Nobel Prize for Literature in 1950. Russell's contributions to logic, epistemology, and the philosophy of mathematics established him as one of the foremost philosophers of the 20th century. To the general public, however, he was best known as a campaigner for peace and as a popular writer on social, political, and moral subjects. During a long, productive, and often turbulent life, he published more than 70 books and about 2,000 articles, married four times, became involved in innumerable public controversies, and was honoured and reviled in almost equal measure throughout the world.

Inspired by the work of the mathematicians whom he so greatly admired, Russell conceived the idea of demonstrating that mathematics not only had logically rigorous foundations but also that it was in its entirety nothing but logic. The philosophical case for this point of view—subsequently known as logicism—was stated at length in *The Principles of Mathematics* (1903). There Russell argued that the whole of mathematics could be derived from a few simple axioms that made no use of specifically mathematical notions, such as number and square root, but were rather confined to purely logical notions, such as proposition and class. In this way not only could the truths of mathematics be shown to be immune from doubt, they could also be freed from any taint of subjectivity, such as the subjectivity involved in Russell's earlier Kantian view that geometry describes the structure of spatial intuition. Near the end of his work on *The Principles of Mathematics*, Russell discovered that he had been anticipated in his logicist philosophy of mathematics by the German mathematician Gottlob Frege, whose book *The Foundations of Arithmetic* (1884) contained, as Russell put it, "many things . . . which I believed I had invented." Russell quickly added an appendix to his book that discussed Frege's work, acknowledged Frege's earlier discoveries, and explained the differences in their respective understandings of the nature of logic.

The tragedy of Russell's intellectual life is that the deeper he thought about logic, the more his exalted conception of its significance came under threat. He himself described his philosophical development after *The Principles of Mathematics* as a "retreat from Pythagoras." The first step in this retreat was his discovery of a contradiction—now known as Russell's Paradox—at the very heart of the system of logic upon which he had hoped to build the whole of mathematics. The contradiction arises from the following considerations: Some classes are members of themselves (e.g., the class of all classes), and some are not (e.g., the class of all men), so we ought to be able to construct the class of all classes that are not members of themselves. But now, if we ask of this class "Is it a member of itself?" we become enmeshed in a contradiction. If it is, then it is not, and if it is not, then it is. This is rather like defining the village barber as "the man who shaves all those who do not shave themselves" and then asking whether the barber shaves himself or not.

At first this paradox seemed trivial, but the more Russell reflected upon it, the deeper the problem seemed, and eventually he was persuaded that there was something fundamentally wrong with the notion of class as he had understood it in *The Principles of Mathematics*. Frege saw the depth of the problem immediately. When Russell wrote to him to tell him of the paradox, Frege replied, "arithmetic totters." The foundation upon which Frege and Russell had hoped to build mathematics had, it seemed, collapsed. Whereas Frege sank into a deep depression, Russell set about repairing the damage by attempting to construct a theory of logic immune to the paradox. Like a malignant cancerous growth, however, the contradiction reappeared in different guises whenever Russell thought that he had eliminated it.

Eventually, Russell's attempts to overcome the paradox resulted in a complete transformation of his scheme of logic, as he added one refinement after another to the basic theory. In the process, important elements of his "Pythagorean" view of logic were abandoned. In particular, Russell came to the conclusion that there were no such things as classes and propositions and that therefore, whatever logic was, it was not the study of them. In their place he substituted a bewilderingly complex theory known as the ramified theory of types, which, though it successfully avoided contradictions such as Russell's Paradox, was (and remains) extraordinarily difficult to understand. By the time he and his collaborator, Alfred North Whitehead, had finished the three volumes of *Principia Mathematica* (1910–13), the theory of types and other innovations to the basic logical system had made it unmanageably complicated. Very few people, whether philosophers or mathematicians, have made the gargantuan effort required to master the details of this monumental work. It is nevertheless rightly regarded as one of the great intellectual achievements of the 20th century.

Principia Mathematica is a herculean attempt to demonstrate mathematically what *The Principles of Mathematics* had argued for philosophically, namely that mathematics is a branch of logic. The validity of the individual formal proofs that make up the bulk of its three volumes has gone largely unchallenged, but the philosophical significance of the work as a whole is still a matter of debate. Does it demonstrate that mathematics is logic? Only if one regards the theory of types as a logical truth, and about that there is much more room for doubt than there was about the trivial truisms upon which Russell had originally intended to build mathematics. Moreover, Kurt Gödel's first incompleteness theorem (1931) proves that there cannot be a single logical theory from which the whole of mathematics is derivable: all consistent theories of arithmetic are necessarily incomplete. *Principia Mathematica* cannot, however, be dismissed as nothing more than a heroic failure. Its influence on the development of mathematical logic and the philosophy of mathematics has been immense.

ALAN MATHISON TURING

(b. June 23, 1912, London, Eng.—d. June 7, 1954, Wilmslow, Cheshire)

Alan Turing made major contributions to mathematics, cryptanalysis, logic, philosophy, and biology and to the new areas later named computer science, cognitive science, artificial intelligence, and artificial life.

In 1936 Turing's seminal paper *On Computable Numbers*, with an application to the *Entscheidungsproblem* [Decision Problem] was recommended for publication by the American mathematician-logician Alonzo Church, who had himself just published a paper that reached the same conclusion as Turing's. Later that year, Turing moved to Princeton University to study for a Ph.D. in mathematical logic under Church's direction (completed in 1938).

The *Entscheidungsproblem* seeks an effective method for deciding which mathematical statements are provable within a given formal mathematical system and which are not. In 1936 Turing and Church independently showed that in general this problem has no solution, proving that no consistent formal system of arithmetic is decidable. This result and others—notably the mathematician-logician Kurt Gödel's incompleteness theorems—ended the dream of a system that could banish ignorance from mathematics forever. (In fact, Turing and Church showed that even some purely logical systems, considerably weaker than arithmetic, are undecidable.) An important argument of Turing's and Church's was that the class of lambda-definable functions (functions on the positive integers whose values can be calculated by a process of repeated substitution) coincides with the class of all functions that are effectively calculable—or computable. This claim is now known as Church's thesis—or as the Church-Turing thesis when stated in the form that any effectively calculable function can be calculated by a universal Turing machine, a type of abstract computer that Turing had introduced in the course of his proof.

In the summer of 1938 Turing returned from the United States to his fellowship at King's College. At the outbreak of hostilities with Germany in September 1939, he joined the wartime headquarters of the Government Code and Cypher School at Bletchley Park, Buckinghamshire. The British government had just been given the details of efforts

One of the Bombe machines designed by Alan Turing. The code-breaking capabilities of the Bombe machines were crucial to the efforts of Allied intelligence during the Second World War. SSPL/Getty Images

by the Poles, assisted by the French, to break the Enigma code, used by the German military for their radio communications. During 1939 and the spring of 1940, Turing and others designed a code-breaking machine known as the Bombe. Turing's ingenious Bombes kept the Allies supplied with intelligence for the remainder of the war. By early 1942 the Bletchley Park cryptanalysts were decoding about 39,000 intercepted messages each month, which rose subsequently to more than 84,000 per month. At the end of the war, Turing was made an officer of the Order of the British Empire for his code-breaking work.

Turing was a founding father of modern cognitive science and a leading early exponent of the hypothesis that the human brain is in large part a digital computing machine. He theorized that the cortex at birth is an "unorganised machine" that through "training" becomes organized "into a universal machine or something like it." A pioneer of artificial intelligence, Turing proposed (1950) what subsequently became known as the Turing test as a criterion for whether a machine thinks.

Ivan Matveyevich Vinogradov
(b. Sept. 2 [Sept. 14, New Style], 1891, Milolyub Russia—d. March 20, 1983, Moscow)

Ivan Vinogradov is known for his contributions to analytic number theory, especially his partial solution of the Goldbach conjecture (proposed in 1742), that every integer greater than two can be expressed as the sum of three prime numbers.

In 1914 Vinogradov graduated from the University of St. Petersburg (renamed the Leningrad State University in 1924 and the St. Petersburg State University in 1991). From 1918 to 1920 he taught at Perm State University—founded in 1916, originally as a branch of the University of St.

Petersburg—and was then appointed professor of mathematics at St. Petersburg. From 1925 he also served as head
of the department of number theory there. He became
director of the V.A. Steklov Institute of Mathematics,
Moscow, in 1932 and, in 1934, professor of mathematics
at Moscow State University. Because of his profound contributions to analytic number theory Vinogradov became
one of the leaders of Soviet mathematics, serving as a
member of the International Mathematical Association
when it met at Saint Andrews, Scotland, in 1958 and head-
ing the Soviet delegation to the International Congress of
Mathematicians (ICM)—the governing body that awards
the Fields medal—in Edinburgh that year. When the
Russian Academy of Sciences adopted a new constitution
in 1963, he was elected a member. In 1966, when the Soviet
Union hosted the ICM in Moscow, he was selected to give
one of the invited hour-long addresses.

Vinogradov's most famous result was his proof (1937;
"Some theorems concerning the theory of prime numbers") that every sufficiently large odd integer can be
expressed as the sum of three odd primes, which constituted a partial solution of Goldbach's conjecture. Among
his other published works are *The Method of Trigonometrical
Sums in the Theory of Numbers*, trans. and rev. by K. F. Roth
(1954; originally published in Russian, 1947), and *An
Introduction to the Theory of Numbers* (1955; reissued 1961;
trans. from Russian 6th ed., 1952). A collection of his work
in Russian is *Izbrannye trudy* (1952, reissued 1955).

JOHN VON NEUMANN
(b. Dec. 28, 1903, Budapest, Hung.—d. Feb. 8, 1957, Washington,
D.C., U.S.)

John von Neumann was a Hungarian-born American
mathematician. As an adult, he appended *von* to his

Mathematician John von Neumann (center) *chatted with graduate students during afternoon tea at Princeton University in 1947.* Alfred Eisenstaedt/ Time & Life Pictures/Getty Images

surname; the hereditary title had been granted his father in 1913. Von Neumann grew from child prodigy to one of the world's foremost mathematicians by his mid-twenties. Important work in set theory inaugurated a career that touched nearly every major branch of mathematics. Von Neumann's gift for applied mathematics took his work in directions that influenced quantum theory, automata theory, economics, and defense planning. Von Neumann pioneered game theory and, along with Alan Turing and Claude Shannon, was one of the conceptual inventors of the stored-program digital computer.

Von Neumann commenced his intellectual career at a time when the influence of David Hilbert and his program of establishing axiomatic foundations for mathematics was at a peak. A paper von Neumann wrote while still at the Lutheran Gymnasium ("The Introduction of Transfinite Ordinals," published 1923) supplied the now-conventional definition of an ordinal number as the set of all smaller ordinal numbers. This neatly avoids some of the complications raised by Georg Cantor's transfinite numbers. Von Neumann's "An Axiomatization of Set Theory" (1925) commanded the attention of Hilbert himself. From 1926 to 1927 von Neumann did postdoctoral work under Hilbert at the University of Göttingen. The goal of axiomatizing mathematics was defeated by Kurt Gödel's incompleteness theorems, a barrier that was understood immediately by Hilbert and von Neumann.

In 1933 von Neumann became one of the first professors at the Institute for Advanced Study (IAS), Princeton, N.J. The same year, Adolf Hitler came to power in Germany, and von Neumann relinquished his German academic posts. In late 1943 von Neumann began work on the Manhattan Project at the invitation of J. Robert Oppenheimer. Von Neumann was an expert in the nonlinear physics of hydrodynamics and shock waves, an expertise that he had already applied to chemical explosives in the British war effort. At Los Alamos, N.M., von Neumann worked on Seth Neddermeyer's implosion design for an atomic bomb. The Fat Man atomic bomb, dropped on the Japanese port of Nagasaki, used this design. Von Neumann participated in the selection of a Japanese target, arguing against bombing the Imperial Palace, Tokyo.

Overlapping with this work was von Neumann's magnum opus of applied math, *Theory of Games and Economic Behavior* (1944), cowritten with Princeton economist Oskar Morgenstern. The collaboration with Morgernstern burgeoned to 641 pages, the authors arguing for game theory as the "Newtonian science" underlying economic decisions.

In the postwar years, von Neumann spent increasing time as a consultant to government and industry. Starting

The design for the Fat Man atomic bomb, shown above, was developed with the help of John von Neumann during his time on the Manhattan Project. A bomb based on this design was dropped on Nagasaki, Japan, on Aug. 9, 1945, during the United States' attack against Japan in the Second World War. Hulton Archive/Getty Images

in 1944, he contributed important ideas to the U.S. Army's hard-wired ENIAC computer, designed by J. Presper Eckert, Jr., and John W. Mauchly. Most important, von Neumann modified the ENIAC to run as a stored-program machine. He then lobbied to build an improved computer at the Institute for Advanced Study. The IAS machine, which began operating in 1951, used binary arithmetic—the ENIAC had used decimal numbers—and shared the same memory for code and data, a design that greatly facilitated the "conditional loops" at the heart of all subsequent coding. Von Neumann's publications established the merit of a single-processor, stored-program computer—the widespread architecture now known as a von Neumann machine.

CHAPTER 3
NUMERICAL TERMS AND CONCEPTS

From the early days when humans developed basic number systems to the abstract number theories of the modern era, human understanding of what numbers can do has become ever more complex. Brief descriptions of some important numerical terms and concepts across the ages are included here.

ALGORITHM

An algorithm is a systematic procedure that produces—in a finite number of steps—the answer to a question or the solution of a problem. The name derives from the Latin translation, *Algoritmi de numero Indorum,* of the 9th-century Muslim mathematician Muḥammad ibn Mūsā al-Khwārizmī's arithmetic treatise "Al-Khwārizmī Concerning the Hindu Art of Reckoning."

For questions or problems with only a finite set of cases or values an algorithm always exists (at least in principle); it consists of a table of values of the answers. In general, it is not such a trivial procedure to answer questions or problems that have an infinite number of cases or values to consider, such as "Is the natural number (1, 2, 3, . . .) *a* prime?" or "What is the greatest common divisor of the natural numbers *a* and *b*?" The first of these questions belongs to a class called decidable; an algorithm that produces a yes or no answer is called a decision procedure. The second question belongs to a class called computable; an algorithm that leads to a specific number answer is called a computation procedure.

Algorithms exist for many such infinite classes of questions; Euclid's *Elements,* published about 300 BCE, contained one for finding the greatest common divisor of two natural numbers. Every elementary school student is drilled in long division, which is an algorithm for the question "Upon dividing a natural number a by another natural number b, what are the quotient and the remainder?" Use of this computational procedure leads to the answer to the decidable question "Does b divide a?" (the answer is yes if the remainder is zero). Repeated application of these algorithms eventually produces the answer to the decidable question "Is a prime?" (the answer is no if a is divisible by any smaller natural number besides 1).

Sometimes an algorithm cannot exist for solving an infinite class of problems, particularly when some further restriction is made upon the accepted method. For instance, two problems from Euclid's time requiring the use of only a compass and a straightedge (unmarked ruler)—trisecting an angle and constructing a square with an area equal to a given circle—were pursued for centuries before they were shown to be impossible. At the turn of the 20th century, the influential German mathematician David Hilbert proposed 23 problems for mathematicians to solve in the coming century. The second problem on his list asked for an investigation of the consistency of the axioms of arithmetic. Most mathematicians had little doubt of the eventual attainment of this goal until 1931, when the Austrian-born logician Kurt Gödel demonstrated the surprising result that there must exist arithmetic propositions (or questions) that cannot be proved or disproved. Essentially, any such proposition leads to a determination procedure that never ends (a condition known as the halting problem). In an unsuccessful effort to ascertain at least which propositions are unsolvable, the English mathematician and logician Alan Turing rigorously defined the loosely understood concept of an algorithm. Although Turing ended up proving that there must exist undecidable propositions, his description of the essential features of any general-purpose algorithm machine, or Turing machine, became the foundation of computer science. Today the issues of decidability and computability are central to the design of a computer program—a special type of algorithm.

ARITHMETIC FUNCTION

Any mathematical function defined for integers (. . ., -3, -2, -1, 0, 1, 2, 3, . . .) and dependent upon those properties of the integer itself as a number, in contrast to functions that are defined for other values (real numbers, complex numbers, or even other functions) and that involve various operations from algebra and calculus, is known as an arithmetic function. Examples of arithmetic functions include the following, which associate with each integer n: (1) the number of divisors of n; (2) the number of ways n can be represented as a sum or product of a specified number of integers; (3) the number of primes (integers not divisible by any number greater than one, except themselves) dividing n (including n itself). Arithmetic functions have applications in number theory, combinatorics, counting, probability theory, and analysis, in which they arise as the coefficients of power series.

ASSOCIATIVE LAWS

There are two associative laws relating to number operations of addition and multiplication—stated symbolically, they are $a + (b + c) = (a + b) + c$ and $a(bc) = (ab)c$; that is, the terms or factors may be associated in any way desired.

While associativity holds for ordinary arithmetic with real or imaginary numbers, there are certain applications—such as nonassociative algebras—in which it does not hold.

AXIOM OF CHOICE

The axiom of choice, sometimes called Zermelo's axiom of choice, is a statement in the language of set theory that makes it possible to form sets by choosing an element simultaneously from each member of an infinite collection of sets even when no algorithm exists for the selection. The axiom of choice has many mathematically equivalent formulations, some of which were not immediately realized to be equivalent. One version states that, given any collection of disjoint sets (sets having no common elements), there exists at least one set consisting of one element from each of the nonempty sets in the collection; collectively, these chosen elements make up the "choice set." Another common formulation is to say that for any set S there exists a function f (called a "choice function") such that, for any nonempty subset s of S, $f(s)$ is an element of s.

The axiom of choice was first formulated in 1904 by the German mathematician Ernst Zermelo in order to prove the "well-ordering theorem" (every set can be given an order relationship, such as less than, under which it is well ordered; i.e., every subset has a first element). Subsequently, it was shown that making any one of three assumptions—the axiom of choice, the well-ordering principle, or Zorn's lemma—enabled one to prove the other two; that is to say, all three are mathematically equivalent. The axiom of choice has the feature—not shared by other axioms of set theory—that it asserts the existence of a set without ever specifying its elements or any definite way to select them. In general, S could have many choice functions. The axiom of choice merely asserts that it has at least one, without saying how to construct it. This nonconstructive feature has led to some controversy regarding the acceptability of the axiom.

The axiom of choice is not needed for finite sets since the process of choosing elements must come to an end eventually. For infinite sets, however, it would take an infinite amount of time to choose elements one by one. Thus, infinite sets for which there does not exist some definite selection rule require the axiom of choice (or one of its equivalent formulations) in order to proceed with the choice set. The English mathematician-philosopher Bertrand Russell gave the following succinct example of this distinction: "To choose one sock from each of infinitely many pairs of socks requires the Axiom of Choice, but for shoes the Axiom is not needed." For example, one could simultaneously choose the left shoe from each member of the infinite set of shoes, but no rule exists to distinguish between the members of a pair of socks. Thus, without the axiom of choice, each sock would have to be chosen one by one—an eternal prospect.

Nonetheless, the axiom of choice does have some counterintuitive consequences. The best-known of these is the Banach-Tarski paradox. This shows that for a solid sphere there exists (in the sense that the axioms assert the existence of sets) a decomposition into a finite number of pieces that can be reassembled to produce a sphere with twice the radius of the original sphere. Of course, the pieces involved are nonmeasurable; that is, one cannot meaningfully assign volumes to them.

In 1939 the Austrian-born American logician Kurt Gödel proved that, if the other standard Zermelo-Fraenkel axioms (ZF) are consistent, then they do not disprove the axiom of choice. That is, the result of adding the axiom of choice to the other axioms (ZFC) remains consistent. Then in

1963 the American mathematician Paul Cohen completed the picture by showing, again under the assumption that ZF is consistent, that ZF does not yield a proof of the axiom of choice; that is, the axiom of choice is independent.

In general, the mathematical community accepts the axiom of choice because of its utility and its agreement with intuition regarding sets. On the other hand, lingering unease with certain consequences (such as well-ordering of the real numbers) has led to the convention of explicitly stating when the axiom of choice is utilized, a condition not imposed on the other axioms of set theory.

BINARY CODE

Binary code, which is used in digital computers, is based on a binary number system in which there are only two possible states, off and on, usually symbolized by 0 and 1. Whereas in a decimal system, which employs 10 digits, each digit position represents a power of 10 (100, 1,000, etc.), in a binary system each digit position represents a power of 2 (4, 8, 16, etc.). A binary code signal is a series of electrical pulses that represent numbers, characters, and operations to be performed. A device called a clock sends out regular pulses, and components such as transistors switch on (1) or off (0) to pass or block the pulses. In binary code, each decimal number (0–9) is represented by a set of four binary digits, or bits. The four fundamental arithmetic operations (addition, subtraction, multiplication, and division) can all be reduced to combinations of fundamental Boolean algebraic operations on binary numbers.

BINARY NUMBER SYSTEM

The binary number system is a positional numeral system employing 2 as the base and so requiring only two different symbols for its digits, 0 and 1, instead of the usual 10 different symbols needed in the decimal system. The importance of the binary system to information theory and computer technology derives mainly from the compact and reliable manner in which 0s and 1s can be represented in electromechanical devices with two states—such as "on-off," "open-closed," or "go–no go."

CANTOR'S THEOREM

Cantor's theorem states that the cardinality (numerical size) of a set is strictly less than the cardinality of its power set, or collection of subsets. In symbols, a finite set S with n elements contains 2^n subsets, so that the cardinality of the set S is n and its power set $P(S)$ is 2^n. While this is clear for finite sets, no one had seriously considered the case for infinite sets before the German mathematician Georg Cantor—who is universally recognized as the founder of modern set theory—began working in this area toward the end of the 19th century.

The 1891 proof of Cantor's theorem for infinite sets rested on a version of his so-called diagonalization argument, which he had earlier used to prove that the cardinality of the rational numbers is the same as the cardinality of the integers by putting them into a one-to-one correspondence. The notion that, in the case of infinite sets, the size of a set could be the same as one of its proper subsets was not too surprising, as before Cantor almost everyone assumed that there was only one size for infinity. However, Cantor's proof that some infinite sets are larger than others—for example, the real numbers are larger than the integers—was surprising, and it initially met with great resistance from some mathematicians, particularly the German Leopold Kronecker. Furthermore, Cantor's proof that the power set of any set, including any infinite set, is always larger than the original set led him to create an ever increasing hierarchy of cardinal numbers, $\aleph_0$, $\aleph_1$, $\aleph_2$. . ., known as transfinite numbers. Cantor proposed that there is no transfinite number between the first transfinite number $\aleph_0$, or the cardinality of the integers, and the continuum (*c*), or the cardinality of the real numbers; in other words, $c = \aleph_1$. This is now known as the continuum hypothesis, and it has been shown to be an undecidable proposition in standard set theory.

CHINESE REMAINDER THEOREM

The Chinese remainder theorem gives the conditions for multiple equations to have a simultaneous integer solution. The theorem has its origin in the work of the 3rd-century-CE Chinese mathematician Sun Zi, although the complete theorem was first given in 1247 by Qin Jiushao.

The Chinese remainder theorem addresses the following type of problem. One is asked to find a number that leaves a remainder of 0 when divided by 5, remainder 6 when divided by 7, and remainder 10 when divided by 12. The simplest solution is 370. Note that this solution is not unique, since any multiple of 5 × 7 × 12 (= 420) can be added to it and the result will still solve the problem.

The theorem can be expressed in modern general terms using congruence notation. Let $n_1, n_2, \ldots, n_k$ be integers that are greater than one and pairwise relatively prime (that is, the only common factor between any two of them is 1), and let $a_1, a_2, \ldots, a_k$ be any integers. Then there exists an integer solution *a* such that $a \equiv a_i \pmod{n_i}$ for each $i = 1, 2, \ldots, k$. Furthermore, for any other integer *b* that satisfies all the congruences, $b =^- a \pmod{N}$ where $N = n_1 n_2 \cdots n_k$. The theorem also gives a formula for finding a solution. Note that in the example above, 5, 7, and 12 ($n_1, n_2,$

and n_3 in congruence notation) are relatively prime. There is not necessarily any solution to such a system of equations when the moduli are not pairwise relatively prime.

CHURCH'S THESIS

Church's thesis (theorem), a principle formulated by the 20th-century American logician Alonzo Church, states that the recursive functions are the only functions that can be mechanically calculated. The theorem implies that the procedures of arithmetic cannot be used to decide the consistency of statements formulated in accordance with the laws of arithmetic.

COMMUTATIVE LAWS

There are two commutative laws relating to the number operations of addition and multiplication—stated symbolically, they are $a + b = b + a$ and $ab = ba$. From these laws it follows that any finite sum or product is unaltered by reordering its terms or factors. While commutativity holds for many systems, such as the real or complex numbers, there are other systems, such as the system of $n \times n$ matrices or the system of quaternions, in which commutativity of multiplication is invalid. Scalar multiplication of two vectors (to give the so-called dot product) is commutative (i.e., $a \cdot b = b \cdot a$), but vector multiplication (to give the cross product) is not (i.e., $a \times b = -b \times a$). The commutative law does not necessarily hold for multiplication of conditionally convergent series.

COMPLEX NUMBER

Complex numbers have the form $x + yi$, in which x and y are real numbers and i is the imaginary unit such that $i^2 = -1$.

CONTINUUM HYPOTHESIS

The continuum hypothesis states that the set of real numbers (the continuum) is in a sense as small as it can be. In 1873 the German mathematician Georg Cantor proved that the continuum is uncountable—that is, the real numbers are a larger infinity than the counting numbers—a key result in starting set theory as a mathematical subject. Furthermore, Cantor developed a way of classifying the size of infinite sets according to the number of its elements, or its cardinality. In these terms, the continuum hypothesis can be stated as follows: The cardinality of the continuum is the smallest uncountable cardinal number.

In Cantor's notation, the continuum hypothesis can be stated by the simple equation $2^{\aleph_0} = \aleph_1$, where $\aleph_0$ is the cardinal number of an infinite countable set (such as the set of natural numbers), and the cardinal numbers of larger "well-orderable sets" are $\aleph_1, \aleph_2, \ldots, \aleph_a, \ldots$, indexed by the ordinal numbers. The cardinality of the continuum can be shown to equal $2^{\aleph_0}$; thus, the continuum hypothesis rules out the existence of a set of size intermediate between the natural numbers and the continuum.

A stronger statement is the generalized continuum hypothesis (GCH): $2^{\aleph_a} = \aleph_{a+1}$ for each ordinal number a. The Polish mathematician Wacław Sierpiński proved that with GCH one can derive the axiom of choice.

As with the axiom of choice, the Austrian-born American mathematician Kurt Gödel proved in 1939 that, if the other standard Zermelo-Fraenkel axioms (ZF) are consistent, then they do not disprove the continuum hypothesis or even GCH. That is, the result of adding GCH to the other axioms remains consistent. Then in 1963 the American mathematician Paul Cohen completed the picture by showing, again under the assumption that

ZF is consistent, that ZF does not yield a proof of the continuum hypothesis.

Since ZF neither proves nor disproves the continuum hypothesis, there remains the question of whether to accept the continuum hypothesis based on an informal concept of what sets are. The general answer in the mathematical community has been negative: the continuum hypothesis is a limiting statement in a context where there is no known reason to impose a limit. In set theory, the power-set operation assigns to each set of cardinality $\aleph_a$ its set of all subsets, which has cardinality $2^{\aleph_a}$. There seems to be no reason to impose a limit on the variety of subsets that an infinite set might have.

DECIMAL NUMBER SYSTEM

The decimal number system—also called the Hindu-Arabic, or Arabic, number system—is a positional numeral system employing 10 as the base and requiring 10 different numerals, the digits 0, 1, 2, 3, 4, 5, 6, 7, 8, 9. It also requires a dot (decimal point) to represent decimal fractions. In this scheme, the numerals used in denoting a number take different place values depending upon position. In a base-10 system the number 543.21 represents the sum $(5 \times 10^2) + (4 \times 10^1) + (3 \times 10^0) + (2 \times 10^{-1}) + (1 \times 10^{-2})$.

This number system, with its associated arithmetic algorithms, has furnished the basis for the development of Western commerce and science since its introduction to the West in the 12th century CE.

DECISION PROBLEM

The decision problem, for a class of questions in mathematics and formal logic, involves finding, after choosing any question of the class, an algorithm or repetitive procedure that will yield a definite answer, "yes" or "no," to that question. The method consists of performing successively a finite number of steps determined by pre-assigned rules. In particular, the term is used for such procedures for finding whether—in a particular logistic system, logical calculus, or formal mathematical system— some given "well-formed formula" (generated in accordance with established formation rules) is or is not provable as a theorem of the system.

DEDEKIND CUT

In 1872 the German mathematician Richard Dedekind introduced a concept that combines an arithmetic formulation of the idea of continuity with a rigorous distinction between rational and irrational numbers. Dedekind reasoned that the real numbers form an ordered continuum, so that any two numbers x and y must satisfy one and only one of the conditions $x < y$, $x = y$, or $x > y$. He postulated a cut that separates the continuum into two subsets, say X and Y, such that if x is any member of X and y is any member of Y, then $x < y$. If the cut is made so that X has a largest rational member or Y a least member, then the cut corresponds to a rational number. If, however, the cut is made so that X has no largest rational member and Y no least rational member, then the cut corresponds to an irrational number.

For example, if X is the set of all real numbers x less than or equal to 22/7 and Y is the set of real numbers y greater than 22/7, then the largest member of X is the rational number 22/7. If, however, X is the set of all real numbers x such that x^2 is less than or equal to 2 and Y is the set of real numbers y such that y^2 is greater than 2, then X has no largest rational member and Y has no least rational member: the cut defines the irrational number $\sqrt{2}$.

DIOPHANTINE EQUATION

Diophantine equations involve only sums, products, and powers in which all the constants are integers and the only solutions of interest are integers. For example, $3x + 7y = 1$ or $x^2 - y^2 = z^3$, where x, y, and z are integers. Named in honour of the 3rd-century Greek mathematician Diophantus of Alexandria, these equations were first systematically solved by Hindu mathematicians beginning with aryabhata I (*c.* 476–550).

Diophantine equations fall into three classes: those with no solutions, those with only finitely many solutions, and those with infinitely many solutions. For example, the equation $6x - 9y = 29$ has no solutions, but the equation $6x - 9y = 30$, which upon division by 3 reduces to $2x - 3y = 10$, has infinitely many. For example, $x = 20$, $y = 10$ is a solution, and so is $x = 20 + 3t$, $y = 10 + 2t$ for every integer t, positive, negative, or zero. This is called a one-parameter family of solutions, with t being the arbitrary parameter.

Congruence methods provide a useful tool in determining the number of solutions to a Diophantine equation. Applied to the simplest Diophantine equation, $ax + by = c$, where a, b, and c are nonzero integers, these methods show that the equation has either no solutions or infinitely many, according to whether the greatest common divisor (GCD) of a and b divides c: if not, there are no solutions; if it does, there are infinitely many solutions, and they form a one-parameter family of solutions.

DIRICHLET'S THEOREM

Dirichlet's theorem states that there are infinitely many prime numbers contained in the collection of all numbers of the form $na + b$, in which the constants a and b are integers that have no common divisors except the number 1 (in which case the pair are known as being relatively prime) and the variable n is any natural number (1, 2, 3, . . .). For instance, because 3 and 4 are relatively prime, there must be infinitely many primes among numbers of the form $4n + 3$ (e.g., 7 when $n = 1$, 11 when $n = 2$, 19 when $n = 4$, and so forth). Conjectured by the late 18th–early 19th-century German mathematician Carl Friedrich Gauss, the statement was first proved in 1826 by the German mathematician Peter Gustav Lejeune Dirichlet.

DISTRIBUTIVE LAW

The distributive law relates the operations of multiplication and addition—stated symbolically, $a(b + c) = ab + ac$; that is, the monomial factor a is distributed, or separately applied, to each term of the binomial factor $b + c$, resulting in the product $ab + ac$. From this law it is easy to show that the result of first adding several numbers and then multiplying the sum by some number is the same as first multiplying each separately by the number and then adding the products.

EQUIVALENCE RELATION

The equivalence relation is a generalization of the idea of equality between elements of a set. All equivalence relations (e.g., that symbolized by the equals sign) obey three conditions: reflexivity (every element is in the relation to itself), symmetry (element A has the same relation to element B that B has to A), and transitivity. Congruence of triangles is an equivalence relation in geometry. Members of a set are said to be in the same equivalence class if they have an equivalence relation.

EUCLIDEAN ALGORITHM

The Euclidean algorithm is a procedure for finding the greatest common divisor (GCD) of two numbers. It was described by the Greek mathematician Euclid in his *Elements* (*c.* 300 BCE). The method is computationally efficient and, with minor modifications, is still used by computers.

The algorithm involves successively dividing and calculating remainders; it is best illustrated by example. For instance, to find the GCD of 56 and 12, first divide 56 by 12 and note that the quotient is 4 and the remainder is 8. This can be expressed as $56 = 4 \times 12 + 8$. Now take the divisor (12), divide it by the remainder (8), and write the result as

$12 = 1 \times 8 + 4$. Continuing in this manner, take the previous divisor (8), divide it by the previous remainder (4), and write the result as $8 = 2 \times 4 + 0$. Since the remainder is now 0, the process has finished and the last nonzero remainder, in this case 4, is the GCD.

The Euclidean algorithm is useful for reducing a common fraction to lowest terms. For example, the algorithm will show that

Greek mathematician Euclid, depicted here, was the most prominent mathematician of Greco-Roman antiquity. Best known for his treatise on geometry, the Elements, *he also wrote extensively on general mathematics.* Hulton Archive/Getty Images

the GCD of 765 and 714 is 51, and therefore 765/714 = 15/14. It also has a number of uses in more advanced mathematics. For example, it is the basic tool used to find integer solutions to linear equations $ax + by = c$, where a, b, and c are integers. The algorithm also provides, as the successive quotients obtained from the division process, the integers $a, b, \ldots, f$ needed for the expansion of a fraction p/q as a continued fraction:

$$a + 1/(b + 1/(c + 1/(d \ldots + 1/f)).$$

EUCLID'S TWIN PRIME CONJECTURE

Euclid's twin prime conjecture asserts that there are infinitely many twin primes, or pairs of primes that differ by 2. For example, 3 and 5, 5 and 7, 11 and 13, and 17 and 19 are twin primes. As numbers get larger, primes become less frequent and twin primes rarer still. Greek mathematician Euclid (flourished c. 300 BCE) gave the oldest known proof that there exist an infinite number of primes, and he conjectured that there are an infinite number of twin primes.

Very little progress was made on this conjecture until 1919, when Norwegian mathematician Viggo Brun showed that the sum of the reciprocals of the twin primes converges to a sum, now known as Brun's constant. (In contrast, the sum of the reciprocals of the primes diverges to infinity.) Brun's constant was calculated in 1976 as approximately 1.90216054 using the twin primes up to 100 billion. In 1994 American mathematician Thomas Nicely was using a personal computer equipped with the then new Pentium chip from the Intel Corporation when he discovered a flaw in the chip that was producing inconsistent results in his calculations of Brun's constant. Negative publicity from the mathematics community led Intel to offer free replacement chips that had been modified to correct the problem. In 2004 Nicely gave a value for Brun's constant of 1.902160582582 ± 0.000000001620 based on all twin primes less than 5×10^{15}.

The next big breakthrough occurred in 2003, when American mathematician Daniel Goldston and Turkish mathematician Cem Yildirim published a paper, "Small Gaps Between Primes," that established the existence of an infinite number of prime pairs within a small difference (16, with certain other assumptions). Although their proof was flawed, they corrected it with Hungarian mathematician János Pintz in 2005. Their introduction of new techniques may enable progress on the Riemann hypothesis, which is connected to the prime number theorem (a formula that gives an approximation of the number of primes less than any given value).

FACTOR

A factor is a number or algebraic expression that divides another number or expression evenly—i.e., with no remainder. For example, 3 and 6 are factors of 12 because $12 \div 3 = 4$ exactly and $12 \div 6 = 2$ exactly. The other factors of 12 are 1, 2, 4, and 12. A positive integer greater than 1, or an algebraic expression, that has only two factors (i.e., itself and 1) is termed prime; a positive integer or an algebraic expression that has more than two factors is termed composite. The prime factors of a number or an algebraic expression are those factors that are prime. By the fundamental theorem of arithmetic, except for the order in which the prime factors are written, every whole number larger than 1 can be uniquely expressed as the product of its prime factors; for example, 60 can be written as the product $2 \cdot 2 \cdot 3 \cdot 5$.

Methods for factoring large whole numbers are of great importance in public-key cryptography, and on such methods rests the security (or lack thereof) of data transmitted over the Internet. Factoring is also a particularly important step in the solution of many algebraic problems. For example, the polynomial equation $x^2 - x - 2 = 0$ can be factored as $(x - 2)(x + 1) = 0$. Since in an integral domain $a \cdot b = 0$ implies that either $a = 0$ or $b = 0$, the simpler equations $x - 2 = 0$ and $x + 1 = 0$ can be solved to yield the two solutions $x = 2$ and $x = -1$ of the original equation.

FACTORIAL

A factorial is the product of all positive integers less than or equal to a given positive integer and denoted by that integer and an exclamation point. Thus, factorial seven is written 7!, meaning $1 \times 2 \times 3 \times 4 \times 5 \times 6 \times 7$. Factorial zero is defined as equal to 1.

Factorials are commonly encountered in the evaluation of permutations and combinations and in the coefficients of terms of binomial expansions (see binomial theorem). Factorials have been generalized to include nonintegral values.

FERMAT PRIME

A Fermat prime is a number of the form $2^{2^n} + 1$, for some positive integer n. For example, $2^{2^3} + 1 = 2^8 + 1 = 257$ is a Fermat prime. On the basis of his knowledge that numbers of this form are prime for values of n from 1 through 4, the French mathematician Pierre de Fermat (1601–65) conjectured that all numbers of this form are prime. However, the Swiss mathematician Leonhard Euler

(1707–83) showed that Fermat's conjecture is false for $n = 5$: $2^{2^5} + 1 = 2^{32} + 1 = 4,294,967,297$, which is divisible by 641. In fact, it is known that numbers of this form are not prime for values of n from 5 through 30, placing doubt on the existence of any Fermat primes for values of $n > 4$.

FERMAT'S LAST THEOREM

Fermat's last theorem is the statement that there are no natural numbers (1, 2, 3, . . .) x, y, and z such that $xn + yn = zn$, in which n is a natural number greater than 2. For example, if $n = 3$, Fermat's theorem states that no natural numbers x, y, and z exist such that $x^3 + y^3 = z^3$ (i.e., the sum of two cubes is not a cube). In 1637 the French mathematician Pierre de Fermat wrote in his copy of the *Arithmetica* by Diophantus of Alexandria (*c.* 250 CE), "I have discovered a truly remarkable proof [of this theorem] but this margin is too small to contain it." For centuries mathematicians were baffled by this statement, for no one could prove or disprove Fermat's theorem. Proofs for many specific values of n were devised, however, and by 1993, with the help of computers, it was confirmed for all $n < 4,000,000$. Using sophisticated tools from algebraic geometry, the English mathematician Andrew Wiles, with help from his former student Richard Taylor, devised a proof of Fermat's last theorem that was published in 1995 in the journal *Annals of Mathematics*.

FERMAT'S LITTLE THEOREM

Fermat's little theorem, also known as Fermat's primality test, first given in 1640 by French mathematician Pierre de Fermat, states that for any prime number p and any integer a such that p does not divide a (the pair are relatively prime), p divides exactly into $ap - a$. Although a number n that does not divide exactly into $an - a$ for some a must be a composite number, the converse is not necessarily true. For example, let $a = 2$ and $n = 341$, then a and n are relatively prime and 341 divides exactly into $2^{341} - 2$. However, $341 = 11 \times 31$, so it is a composite number (a special type of composite number known as a pseudoprime). Thus, Fermat's theorem gives a test that is necessary but not sufficient for primality.

As with many of Fermat's theorems, no proof by him is known to exist. The first known published proof of this theorem was by Swiss mathematician Leonhard Euler in 1736, though a proof in an unpublished manuscript dating to about 1683 was given by German mathematician Gottfried Wilhelm Leibniz. A special case of Fermat's theorem, known as the Chinese hypothesis, may be some 2,000 years old. The Chinese hypothesis, which replaces a with 2, states that a number n is prime if and only if it divides exactly into $2n - 2$. As proved later in the West, the Chinese hypothesis is only half right.

FIBONACCI NUMBERS

Fibonacci numbers are the elements of the sequence of numbers 1, 1, 2, 3, 5, 8, 13, 21, . . ., each of which, after the second, is the sum of the two previous numbers. These numbers were first noted by the medieval Italian mathematician Leonardo Pisano ("Fibonacci") in his *Liber abaci* (1202; "Book of the Abacus"), which also popularized Hindu-Arabic numerals and the decimal number system in Europe.

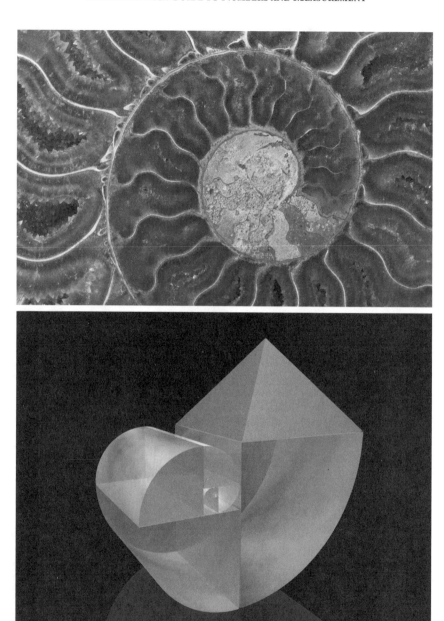

Top: *A naturally occurring Fibonacci sequence can be detected in this fossilized ammonite from the Jurassic period.* Shutterstock.com **Bottom:** *The golden ratio, a three-dimensional representation of which is shown above, is a significant irrational number. One reason for this is its occurrence in Fibonacci sequences in which two consecutive terms approach the value of the golden ratio (approximately 1.618) as the numbers increase.* Shutterstock.com

FRACTION

A fraction is a number expressed as a quotient, in which a numerator is divided by a denominator. In a simple fraction, both are integers. A complex fraction has a fraction in the numerator or denominator. In a proper fraction, the numerator is less than the denominator. If the numerator is greater, it is called an improper fraction and can also be written as a mixed number—a whole-number quotient with a proper-fraction remainder. Any fraction can be written in decimal form by carrying out the division of the numerator by the denominator. The result may end at some point, or one or more digits may repeat without end.

FUNDAMENTAL THEOREM OF ARITHMETIC

The fundamental theorem of arithmetic was proved by Carl Friedrich Gauss in 1801. It states that any integer greater than 1 can be expressed as the product of prime numbers in only one way.

GEOMETRIC SERIES

A geometric series is an infinite series of the form

$$a + ar + ar^2 + ar^3 + \cdots,$$

where r is known as the common ratio. A simple example is the geometric series for $a = 1$ and $r = 1/2$, or

$$1 + 1/2 + 1/4 + 1/8 + \cdots,$$

which converges to a sum of 2 (or 1 if the first term is excluded). The Achilles paradox is an example of the

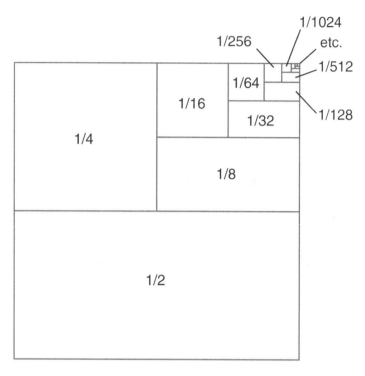

Clearly, the sum of the square's parts ($\frac{1}{2}$, $\frac{1}{4}$, $\frac{1}{8}$, etc.) is 1 (square). Thus, it can be seen that 1 is the limit of this series—that is, the value to which the partial sums converge. Encyclopædia Britannica, Inc.

difficulty that ancient Greek mathematicians had with the idea that an infinite series could produce a finite sum. The confusion around infinity did not abate until the 18th century, when mathematicians developed analysis and the concept of limits.

The sum of the first n terms of a geometric series is equal to $a(1 - rn)/(1 - r)$. If the absolute value of r is less than 1, the series converges to $a/(1 - r)$. For any other value of r, the series diverges.

GOLDBACH CONJECTURE

The Goldbach conjecture asserts, in modern terms, that every even counting number greater than 2 is equal to the sum of two prime numbers. The Russian mathematician Christian Goldbach first proposed this conjecture in a letter to the Swiss mathematician Leonhard Euler in 1742. More precisely, Goldbach claimed that "every number greater than 2 is an aggregate of three prime numbers." (In Goldbach's day, the convention was to consider 1 a prime number, so his statement is equivalent to the modern version in which the convention is to not include 1 among the prime numbers.)

Goldbach's conjecture was published in English mathematician Edward Waring's *Meditationes algebraicae* (1770), which also contained Waring's problem and what was later known as Vinogradov's theorem. The latter, which states that every sufficiently large odd integer can be expressed as the sum of three primes, was proved in 1937 by the Russian mathematician Ivan Matveyevich Vinogradov. Further progress on Goldbach's conjecture occurred in 1973, when the Chinese mathematician Chen Jing Run proved that every sufficiently large even number is the sum of a prime and a number with at most two prime factors.

HARMONIC SEQUENCE

A harmonic sequence is a sequence of numbers $a_1, a_2, a_3, \ldots$ such that their reciprocals $1/a_1, 1/a_2, 1/a_3, \ldots$ form an arithmetic sequence (numbers separated by a common difference). The best-known harmonic sequence, and the one typically meant when the harmonic sequence is mentioned, is $1, \frac{1}{2}, \frac{1}{3}, \frac{1}{4}, \ldots$, whose corresponding arithmetic sequence is simply the counting numbers 1, 2, 3, 4,. . ..

The study of harmonic sequences dates to at least the 6th century BCE, when the Greek philosopher and mathematician Pythagoras and his followers sought to explain through numbers the nature of the universe. One of the

An ancient Greek plays the kithara, a type of lyre. Harmonic sequences played a significant part in the way ancient Greeks played and understood their music. Hulton Archive/Getty Images

areas in which numbers were applied by the Pythagoreans was the study of music. In particular, Archytas of Tarentum, in the 4th century BCE, used the idea of regular numerical intervals to devise a theory of musical harmony (from the Greek *harmonia*, for agreement of sounds) and the enharmonic method of tuning musical instruments.

The sum of a sequence is known as a series, and the harmonic series is an example of an infinite series that does not converge to any limit. That is, the partial sums obtained by adding the successive terms grow without limit, or, put another way, the sum tends to infinity.

IMAGINARY NUMBER

An imaginary number is any product of the form ai, in which a is a real number and i is the imaginary unit defined as $\sqrt{-1}$.

INCOMPLETENESS THEOREMS

There are two incompleteness theorems, both of which were proved by the Austrian-born American logician Kurt Gödel. In 1931 Gödel published his first incompleteness theorem, "Über formal unentscheidbare Sätze der *Principia Mathematica* und verwandter Systeme" ("On Formally Undecidable Propositions of *Principia Mathematica* and Related Systems"), which stands as a major turning point of 20th-century logic. This theorem established that it is impossible to use the axiomatic method to construct a formal system for any branch of mathematics containing arithmetic that will entail all of its truths. In other words, no finite set of axioms can be devised that will produce all possible true mathematical statements, so no mechanical (or computer-like) approach will ever be able to exhaust the depths of mathematics. It is important to realize that if some particular statement is undecidable within a given formal system, it may be incorporated in another formal system as an axiom or be derived from the addition of other axioms. For example, German mathematician Georg Cantor's continuum hypothesis is undecidable in the standard axioms, or postulates, of set theory but could be added as an axiom.

The second incompleteness theorem follows as an immediate consequence, or corollary, from Gödel's paper.

Although it was not stated explicitly in the paper, Gödel was aware of it, and other mathematicians, such as the Hungarian-born American mathematician John von Neumann, realized immediately that it followed as a corollary. The second incompleteness theorem shows that a formal system containing arithmetic cannot prove its own consistency. In other words, there is no way to show that any useful formal system is free of false statements. The loss of certainty following the dissemination of Gödel's incompleteness theorems continues to have a profound effect on the philosophy of mathematics.

INEQUALITY

An inequality is a statement of an order relationship—greater than, greater than or equal to, less than, or less than or equal to—between two numbers or algebraic expressions. Inequalities can be posed either as questions, much like equations, and solved by similar techniques, or as statements of fact in the form of theorems. For example, the triangle inequality states that the sum of the lengths of any two sides of a triangle is greater than or equal to the length of the remaining side. Mathematical analysis relies on many such inequalities (e.g., the Cauchy-Schwarz inequality) in the proofs of its most important theorems.

INFINITE SERIES

An infinite series is the sum of infinitely many numbers related in a given way and listed in a given order. Infinite series are useful in mathematics and in such disciplines as physics, chemistry, biology, and engineering.

For an infinite series $a_1 + a_2 + a_3 + \cdots$, a quantity $sn = a_1 + a_2 + \cdots + an$, which involves adding only the first n

terms, is called a partial sum of the series. If *sn* approaches a fixed number S as n becomes larger and larger, the series is said to converge. In this case, S is called the sum of the series. An infinite series that does not converge is said to diverge. In the case of divergence, no value of a sum is assigned. For example, the nth partial sum of the infinite series $1 + 1 + 1 + \cdots$ is n. As more terms are added, the partial sum fails to approach any finite value (it grows without bound). Thus, the series diverges. An example of a convergent series is

$$1 + \frac{1}{2} + \frac{1}{4} + \cdots + \frac{1}{2^n} \quad .$$

As n becomes larger, the partial sum approaches 2, which is the sum of this infinite series. In fact, the series $1 + r + r^2 + r^3 + \cdots$ (in the example above r equals 1/2) converges to the sum $1/(1 - r)$ if $0 < r < 1$ and diverges if $r \geq 1$. This series is called the geometric series with ratio r and was one of the first infinite series to be studied. Its solution goes back to Zeno of Elea's paradox involving a race between Achilles and a tortoise.

Certain standard tests can be applied to determine the convergence or divergence of a given series, but such a determination is not always possible. In general, if the series $a_1 + a_2 + \cdots$ converges, then it must be true that *an* approaches 0 as n becomes larger. Furthermore, adding or deleting a finite number of terms from a series never affects whether or not the series converges. Furthermore, if all the terms in a series are positive, its partial sums will increase, either approaching a finite quantity (converging) or growing without bound (diverging). This observation leads to what is called the comparison test: if $0 \leq an \leq bn$ for all n and if $b_1 + b_2 + \cdots$ is a convergent infinite series, then $a_1 + a_2 + \cdots$ also converges. When the comparison test is applied to a geometric series, it is reformulated slightly and called the ratio test: if $an > 0$ and if $an_{+1}/an \leq r$ for some $r < 1$ for every n, then $a_1 + a_2 + \cdots$ converges. For example, the ratio test proves the convergence of the series

$$1 + \frac{1}{2} + \frac{1}{3 \cdot 2} + \frac{1}{4 \cdot 3 \cdot 2} + \cdots \quad .$$

Many mathematical problems that involve a complicated function can be solved directly and easily when the function can be expressed as an infinite series involving trigonometric functions (sine and cosine). The process of breaking up a rather arbitrary function into an infinite trigonometric series is called Fourier analysis or harmonic analysis and has numerous applications in the study of various wave phenomena.

INFINITY

Infinity is the concept of something that is unlimited, endless, without bound. The common symbol for infinity, ∞, was invented by the English mathematician John Wallis in 1657. Three main types of infinity may be distinguished: the mathematical, the physical, and the metaphysical. Mathematical infinities occur, for instance, as the number of points on a continuous line or as the size of the endless sequence of counting numbers: 1, 2, 3, ... Spatial and temporal concepts of infinity occur in physics when one asks if there are infinitely many stars or if the universe will last forever. In a metaphysical discussion of God or the Absolute, there are questions of whether an ultimate entity must be infinite and whether lesser things could be infinite as well.

INTEGER

The integers consist of zero and the whole-valued positive and negative numbers. The integers are generated from the set of counting numbers 1, 2, 3, . . . and the operation of subtraction. When a counting number is subtracted from itself, the result is zero. When a larger number is subtracted from a smaller number, the result is a negative whole number. In this way, every integer can be derived from the counting numbers, resulting in a set of numbers closed under the operation of subtraction (*see* group theory).

LAGRANGE'S FOUR-SQUARE THEOREM

Lagrange's four-square theorem states that every positive integer can be expressed as the sum of the squares of four integers. For example,

$$23 = 1^2 + 2^2 + 3^2 + 3^2.$$

The four-square theorem was first proposed by the Greek mathematician Diophantus of Alexandria in his treatise *Arithmetica* (3rd century CE). Credit for the first proof is given to the 17th-century French amateur mathematician Pierre de Fermat. (Although he did not publish this proof, his study of Diophantus led to Fermat's last

Joseph-Louis Lagrange, engraving by Robert Hart. Courtesy of the trustees of the British Museum; photograph, J.R. Freeman & Co. Ltd.

theorem.) The first published proof of the four-square theorem was in 1770 by the French mathematician Joseph-Louis Lagrange, for whom the theorem is now named.

The impetus for renewed interest in Diophantus and such problems in number theory was the Frenchman Claude-Gaspar Bachet de Méziriac, whose Latin translation *Diophanti* (1621) of *Arithmetica* brought the work to a wider audience. In addition to the proof of Diophantus's four-square theorem, study of the text led to a generalization of the theorem known as Waring's problem.

MERSENNE NUMBER

A Mersenne number is a number Mn of the form $2n - 1$, where n is a natural number. The numbers are named for the French theologian and mathematician Marin Mersenne, who asserted in the preface of *Cogitata Physica-Mathematica* (1644) that, for $n \leq 257$, Mn is a prime number only for 2, 3, 5, 7, 13, 17, 19, 31, 67, 127, and 257. His list, however, contained two numbers that produce composite numbers and omitted two numbers that produce primes. The corrected list is 2, 3, 5, 7, 13, 17, 19, 31, 61, 89, 107, and 127, which was not determined until 1947. This followed the work of numerous mathematicians through the centuries, starting with the Swiss mathematician Leonhard Euler, who first verified in 1750 that 31 produces a Mersenne prime.

It is now known that for M_n to be prime, n must be a prime (p), though not all M_p are prime. Every Mersenne prime is associated with an even perfect number—an even number that is equal to the sum of all its divisors (e.g., $6 = 1 + 2 + 3$)—given by $2^{n-1}(2^n - 1)$. (It is unknown if any odd perfect numbers exist.) For n prime, all known Mersenne numbers are squarefree, which means that they have no repeated divisors (e.g., $12 = 2 \times 2 \times 3$). It is not known if there are an infinite number of Mersenne primes, though they thin out so much that only 39 exist for values of *n* below 20,000,000, and only 7 more have been discovered for larger *n*.

The search for Mersenne primes is an active field in number theory and computer science. It is also one of the major applications for distributed computing, a process in which thousands of computers are linked through the Internet and cooperate in solving a problem. The Great Internet Mersenne Prime Search (GIMPS) in particular has enlisted more than 100,000 volunteers, who have downloaded special software to run on their personal computers. An added inducement for searching for large primes comes from the Electronic Frontier Foundation (EFF), which established prizes for the first verified prime with more than 1 million digits ($50,000; awarded in 2006), 10 million digits ($100,000; awarded in 2008), 100 million digits ($150,000), and 1 billion digits ($250,000). The largest known Mersenne prime, which won the prize for surpassing 10 million digits, is $2^{43,112,609} - 1$. As an interesting side note, Mersenne numbers consist of all 1s in base 2, or binary notation.

NUMBER

Numbers include any of the positive or negative integers, or any of the set of all real or complex numbers, the latter containing all numbers of the form $a + bi$, where a and b are real numbers and i denotes the square root of -1. (Numbers of the form bi are sometimes called pure imaginary numbers to distinguish them from "mixed" complex numbers.) The real numbers consist of rational and irrational numbers. Rational numbers, such as 12, $^{13}/_5$, or $-^4/_{11}$, are those numbers that can be expressed as integers or as the quotient of integers, whereas the irrational numbers, such as

$\sqrt{2}$, are those that cannot be so expressed. All rational numbers are also algebraic numbers—i.e., they can be expressed as the root of some polynomial equation with rational coefficients. Although some irrational numbers, such as $\sqrt{2}$, can be expressed as the solution of such a polynomial equation (in this case, $x^2 = 2$), many cannot. Those that cannot are called transcendental numbers. Among the transcendental numbers are e (the base of the natural logarithm), π, and certain combinations of these. The first number to be proved transcendental was e (by Charles Hermite in 1873), and π was shown to be transcendental in 1882 by Ferdinand von Lindemann.

Other classes of numbers include square numbers—i.e., those that are squares of integers; perfect numbers, those that are equal to the sum of their proper factors; random numbers, those that are representative of random selection procedures; and prime numbers, integers larger than 1 whose only positive divisors are themselves and 1.

PERFECT NUMBER

A perfect number is a positive integer that is equal to the sum of its proper divisors. The smallest perfect number is 6, which is the sum of 1, 2, and 3. Other perfect numbers are 28, 496, and 8,128. The discovery of such numbers is lost in prehistory. It is known, however, that the Pythagoreans (founded c. 525 BCE) studied perfect numbers for their "mystical" properties.

The mystical tradition was continued by the neo-Pythagorean philosopher Nicomachus of Gerasa (fl. c. 100 CE), who classified numbers as deficient, perfect, and superabundant according to whether the sum of their divisors was less than, equal to, or greater than the number, respectively. Nicomachus gave moral qualities to his definitions, and such ideas found credence among early

Christian theologians. Often the 28-day cycle of the Moon around the Earth was given as an example of a "Heavenly," hence perfect, event that naturally was a perfect number. The most famous example of such thinking is given by St. Augustine, who wrote in *The City of God* (413–426):

> *Six is a number perfect in itself, and not because God created all things in six days; rather, the converse is true. God created all things in six days because the number is perfect.*

The earliest extant mathematical result concerning perfect numbers occurs in Euclid's *Elements* (*c.* 300 BCE), where he proves the proposition:

> *If as many numbers as we please beginning from a unit [1] be set out continuously in double proportion, until the sum of all becomes a prime, and if the sum multiplied into the last make some number, the product will be perfect.*

Here "double proportion" means that each number is twice the preceding number, as in 1, 2, 4, 8, ... For example, 1 + 2 + 4 = 7 is prime; therefore, 7 × 4 = 28 ("the sum multiplied into the last") is a perfect number. Euclid's formula forces any perfect number obtained from it to be even, and in the 18th century the Swiss mathematician Leonhard Euler showed that any even perfect number must be obtainable from Euclid's formula. It is not known whether there are any odd perfect numbers.

PRIME

A prime is any positive integer greater than 1 that is divisible only by itself and 1; e.g., 2, 3, 5, 7, 11, 13, 17, 19, 23, ...

A key result of number theory, called the fundamental theorem of arithmetic, states that every positive integer greater than 1 can be expressed as the product of prime numbers in a unique fashion. Because of this, primes can be regarded as the multiplicative "building blocks" for the natural numbers (all whole numbers greater than zero; e.g., 1, 2, 3, . . .).

Primes have been recognized since antiquity, when they were studied by the Greek mathematicians Euclid (fl. c. 300 BCE) and Eratosthenes of Cyrene (c. 276–194 BCE), among others. In his *Elements*, Euclid gave the first known proof that there are infinitely many primes. Various formulas have been suggested for discovering primes, but all have been flawed. Two other famous results concerning the distribution of prime numbers merit special mention: the prime number theorem and the Riemann zeta function.

In the 20th century, with the help of computers, prime numbers with more than two million digits were discovered. Like efforts to generate ever more digits of π, such number theory research was thought to have no possible application—that is, until cryptographers discovered how large primes could be used to make nearly unbreakable codes.

PRIME NUMBER THEOREM

The prime number theorem gives an approximate value for the number of primes less than or equal to any given positive real number x. The usual notation for this number is $\pi(x)$, so that $\pi(2) = 1$, $\pi(3.5) = 2$, and $\pi(10) = 4$. The prime number theorem states that for large values of x, $\pi(x)$ is approximately equal to $x/\ln(x)$.

Ancient Greek mathematicians were the first to study the mathematical properties of prime numbers. (Earlier many people had studied such numbers for their supposed mystical or spiritual qualities.) While many people noticed that the primes seem to "thin out" as the numbers get larger, Euclid in his *Elements* (c. 300 BCE) may have been the first to prove that there is no largest prime; in other words, there are infinitely many primes. Over the ensuing centuries, mathematicians sought, and failed, to find some formula with which they could produce an unending sequence of primes. Failing in this quest for an explicit formula, others began to speculate about formulas that could describe the general distribution of primes. Thus, the prime number theorem first appeared in 1798 as a conjecture by the French mathematician Adrien-Marie Legendre. On the basis of his study of a table of primes up to 1,000,000, Legendre stated that if x is not greater than 1,000,000, then $x/(\ln(x) - 1.08366)$ is very close to $\pi(x)$. This result—indeed with any constant, not just 1.08366— is essentially equivalent to the prime number theorem, which states the result for constant 0. It is now known, however, that the constant that gives the best approximation to $\pi(x)$, for relatively small x, is 1.

The great German mathematician Carl Friedrich Gauss also conjectured an equivalent of the prime number theorem in his notebook, perhaps prior to 1800. However, the theorem was not proved until 1896, when the French mathematicians Jacques-Salomon Hadamard and Charles de la Valée Poussin independently showed that in the limit (as x increases to infinity) the ratio $x/\ln(x)$ equals $\pi(x)$.

Although the prime number theorem tells us that the difference between $\pi(x)$ and $x/\ln(x)$ becomes vanishingly small relative to the size of either of these numbers as x gets large, one can still ask for some estimate of that difference. The best estimate of this difference is conjectured to be given by $\sqrt{(x \ln(x))}$.

PSEUDOPRIME

A pseudoprime, also known as a Fermat pseudoprime, is a composite, or nonprime, number n such that it divides exactly into $a^n - a$ for some integer a. Thus, n is said to be a pseudoprime to the base a. In 1640 French mathematician Pierre de Fermat first asserted "Fermat's Little Theorem," also known as Fermat's primality test, which states that for any prime number p and any integer a such that p does not divide a (the pair are relatively prime), p divides exactly into $a^p - a$. Although a number n that does not divide exactly into $a^n - a$ for some a must be a composite number, the converse is not necessarily true. For example, let $a = 2$ and $n = 341$, then a and n are relatively prime and 341 divides exactly into $2^{341} - 2$. However, $341 = 11 \times 31$, so it is a composite number. (The smallest pseudoprime to base 2 is 341.) Thus, Fermat's primality test is a necessary but not sufficient test for primality. As with many of Fermat's theorems, no proof by him is known to exist. The first known proof of this theorem was published by Swiss mathematician Leonhard Euler in 1749.

There exist some numbers, such as 561 and 1,729, that are pseudoprime to any base. These are known as Carmichael numbers after their discovery in 1909 by American mathematician Robert D. Carmichael.

RATIONAL NUMBER

Rational numbers are numbers that can be represented as the quotient p/q of two integers such that $q \neq 0$. In addition to all the fractions, the set of rational numbers includes all the integers, each of which can be written as a quotient with the integer as the numerator and 1 as the denominator. In decimal form, rational numbers are either terminating or repeating decimals. For example, $1/7 = 0.\overline{142857}$, where the bar over 142857 indicates a pattern that repeats forever.

A real number that cannot be expressed as a quotient of two integers is known as an irrational number.

REAL NUMBER

Real numbers are quantities that can be expressed as an infinite decimal expansion. Real numbers are used in measurements of continuously varying quantities such as size and time, in contrast to the natural numbers 1, 2, 3, . . ., arising from counting. The word *real* distinguishes them from the complex numbers involving the symbol *i*, or $\sqrt{-1}$, used to simplify the mathematical interpretation of effects such as those occurring in electrical phenomena. The real numbers include the positive and negative integers and fractions (or rational numbers) and also the irrational numbers. The irrational numbers have decimal expansions that do not repeat themselves, in contrast to the rational numbers, the expansions of which always contain a digit or group of digits that repeats itself, as $1/6$ = 0.16666. . . or $2/7$ = 0.285714285714. . . . The decimal formed as 0.42442444244442 . . . has no regularly repeating group and is thus irrational.

The most familiar irrational numbers are algebraic numbers, which are the roots of algebraic equations with integer coefficients. For example, the solution to the equation $x^2 - 2 = 0$ is an algebraic irrational number, indicated by $\sqrt{2}$. Some numbers, such as π and e, are not the solutions of any such algebraic equation and are thus called transcendental irrational numbers. These numbers can often be represented as an infinite sum of fractions determined in some regular way, indeed the decimal expansion is one such sum.

The real numbers can be characterized by the important mathematical property of completeness, meaning that every nonempty set that has an upper bound has a smallest such bound, a property not possessed by the rational numbers. For example, the set of all rational numbers the squares of which are less than 2 has no smallest upper bound, because $\sqrt{2}$ is not a rational number. The irrational and rational numbers are both infinitely numerous, but the infinity of irrationals is "greater" than the infinity of rationals, in the sense that the rationals can be paired off with a subset of the irrationals, while the reverse pairing is not possible.

RIEMANN ZETA FUNCTION

The Riemann zeta function is useful for investigating properties of prime numbers. Written as $\zeta(x)$, it was originally defined as the infinite series

$$\zeta(x) = 1 + 2^{-x} + 3^{-x} + 4^{-x} + \cdots.$$

When $x = 1$, this series is called the harmonic series, which increases without bound—i.e., its sum is infinite. For values of x larger than 1, the series converges to a finite number as successive terms are added. If x is less than 1, the sum is again infinite. The zeta function was known to the Swiss mathematician Leonhard Euler in 1737, but it was first studied extensively by the German mathematician Bernhard Riemann.

In 1859 Riemann published a paper giving an explicit formula for the number of primes up to any preassigned limit—a decided improvement over the approximate value given by the prime number theorem. However, Riemann's formula depended on knowing the values at which a generalized version of the zeta function equals zero. (The Riemann zeta function is defined for all complex numbers—numbers of the form $x + iy$, where $i = \sqrt{-1}$—except for the line $x = 1$.) Riemann knew that the function equals zero for all negative even integers -2, -4, -6, . . . (so-called trivial zeros), and that it has an infinite number of zeros in the critical strip of complex numbers between the lines $x = 0$ and $x = 1$, and he also knew that all nontrivial zeros are symmetric with respect to the critical line $x = \frac{1}{2}$. Riemann conjectured that all of the nontrivial zeros are on the critical line, a conjecture that subsequently became known as the Riemann hypothesis.

In 1900 the German mathematician David Hilbert called the Riemann hypothesis one of the most important questions in all of mathematics, as indicated by its inclusion in his influential list of 23 unsolved problems with which he challenged 20th-century mathematicians. In 1915 the English mathematician Godfrey Hardy proved that an infinite number of zeros occur on the critical line, and by 1986 the first 1,500,000,001 nontrivial zeros were all shown to be on the critical line. Although the hypothesis may yet turn out to be false, investigations of this difficult problem have enriched the understanding of complex numbers.

ROOT

A root is a solution to an equation, usually expressed as a number or an algebraic formula.

In the 9th century, Arab writers usually called one of the equal factors of a number *jadhr* ("root"), and their medieval European translators used the Latin word *radix* (from which derives the adjective *radical*). If a is a positive real number and n a positive integer, there exists a unique positive real number x such that $x^n = a$. This number—the (principal) nth root of a—is written $\sqrt[n]{a}$ or $a^{1/n}$. The integer n is called the index of the root. For $n = 2$, the root is called the square root and is written a. The root $\sqrt[3]{a}$ is called the cube root of a. If a is negative and n is odd, the unique negative nth root of a is termed principal. For example, the principal cube root of -27 is -3.

If a whole number (positive integer) has a rational nth root—i.e., one that can be written as a common fraction—then this root must be an integer. Thus, 5 has no rational square root because 2^2 is less than 5 and 3^2 is greater than 5. Exactly n complex numbers satisfy the equation $x^n = 1$, and they are called the complex nth roots of unity. If a regular polygon of n sides is inscribed in a unit circle centred at the origin so that one vertex lies on the positive half of the x-axis, the radii to the vertices are the vectors representing the n complex nth roots of unity. If the root whose vector makes the smallest positive angle with the positive direction of the x-axis is denoted by the Greek letter omega, ω, then ω, ω^2, ω^3, . . ., $\omega_n = 1$ constitute all the nth roots of unity. For example, $\omega = -\frac{1}{2} + \frac{\sqrt{-3}}{2}$, $\omega^2 = -\frac{1}{2} - \frac{\sqrt{-3}}{2}$, and $\omega^3 = 1$ are all the cube roots of unity. Any root, symbolized by the Greek letter epsilon, ε, that has the property that ε, ε^2, . . ., $\varepsilon^n = 1$ give all the nth roots of unity is called primitive. Evidently the problem of finding the nth roots of unity is equivalent to the problem of inscribing a regular polygon of n sides in a circle. For every integer n, the nth roots of unity can be determined in terms of the rational numbers by means of rational operations and radicals; but they can be constructed by ruler and compasses (i.e., determined in terms of the ordinary operations of arithmetic and square roots) only if n is a product of distinct prime numbers of the form $2^b + 1$, or 2^k times such a product, or is of the form 2^k. If a is a complex number not 0, the equation $x^n = a$ has exactly n roots, and all the nth roots of a are the products of any one of these roots by the nth roots of unity.

The term *root* has been carried over from the equation $x^n = a$ to all polynomial equations. Thus, a solution of the equation $f(x) = a_0 x^n + a_1 x^{n-1} + . . . + a_{n-1} x + a_n = 0$, with $a_0 \neq 0$, is called a root of the equation. If the coefficients lie in the complex field, an equation of the nth degree has exactly n (not necessarily distinct) complex roots. If the coefficients are real and n is odd, there is a real root. But an equation does not always have a root in its coefficient field. Thus, $x^2 - 5 = 0$ has no rational root, although its coefficients (1 and –5) are rational numbers.

More generally, the term *root* may be applied to any number that satisfies any given equation, whether a polynomial equation or not. Thus π is a root of the equation $x \sin (x) = 0$.

RUSSELL'S PARADOX

Russell's paradox was devised by the English mathematician-philosopher Bertrand Russell to demonstrate a flaw in earlier efforts to axiomatize set theory.

Russell found the paradox in 1901 and communicated it in a letter to the German mathematician-logician Gottlob Frege in 1902. Russell's letter demonstrated an inconsistency in Frege's axiomatic system of set theory by deriving a paradox within it. (The German mathematician Ernst Zermelo had found the same paradox independently; since it could not be produced in his own axiomatic system of set theory, he did not publish the paradox.)

Frege had constructed a logical system employing an unrestricted comprehension principle. The comprehension principle is the statement that, given any condition expressible by a formula $\phi(x)$, it is possible to form the set of all sets x meeting that condition, denoted $\{x \mid \phi(x)\}$. For example, the set of all sets—the universal set—would be $\{x \mid x = x\}$.

It was noticed in the early days of set theory, however, that a completely unrestricted comprehension principle led to serious difficulties. In particular, Russell observed that it allowed the formation of $\{x \mid x \notin x\}$, the set of all non-self-membered sets, by taking $\phi(x)$ to be the formula $x \notin x$. Is this set—call it R—a member of itself? If it is a member of itself, then it must meet the condition of its

Bertrand Russell, shown above, left behind a multifaceted intellectual legacy. His accomplishments in the fields of logic and the philosophy of mathematics are matched by those he made as a social reformer and a champion of progressive thought. Baron/Hulton Archive/Getty Images

not being a member of itself. But if it is not a member of itself, then it precisely meets the condition of being a member of itself. This impossible situation is called Russell's paradox.

The significance of Russell's paradox is that it demonstrates in a simple and convincing way that one cannot both hold that there is meaningful totality of all sets and also allow an unfettered comprehension principle to construct sets that must then belong to that totality. (Russell spoke of this situation as a "vicious circle.")

Set theory avoids this paradox by imposing restrictions on the comprehension principle. The standard Zermelo-Fraenkel axiomatization (ZF) does not allow comprehension to form a set larger than previously constructed sets. (The role of constructing larger sets is given to the power-set operation.) This leads to a situation where there is no universal set—an acceptable set must not be as large as the universe of all sets.

A very different way of avoiding Russell's paradox was proposed in 1937 by the American logician Willard Van Orman Quine. In his paper "New Foundations for Mathematical Logic," the comprehension principle allows formation of $\{x \mid \phi(x)\}$ only for formulas $\phi(x)$ that can be written in a certain form that excludes the "vicious circle" leading to the paradox. In this approach, there is a universal set.

SET

Any collection of objects (elements), which may be mathematical (e.g., numbers, functions) or not, is known as a set. The intuitive idea of a set is probably even older than that of number. Members of a herd of animals, for example, could be matched with stones in a sack without members of either set actually being counted. The notion extends into the infinite. For example, the set of integers from 1 to 100 is finite, whereas the set of all integers is infinite. A set is commonly represented as a list of all its members enclosed in braces. A set with no members is called an empty, or null, set, and is denoted $\varnothing$. Because an infinite set cannot be listed, it is usually represented by a formula that generates its elements when applied to the elements of the set of counting numbers. Thus, $\{2x \mid x = 1,2,3,...\}$ represents the set of positive even numbers (the vertical bar means "such that").

SQUARE ROOT

A square root is a factor of a number that, when multiplied by itself, gives the original number. For example, both 3 and –3 are square roots of 9. As early as the 2nd millennium BCE, the Babylonians possessed effective methods for approximating square roots.

TRANSFINITE NUMBER

A transfinite number is the denotation of the size of an infinite collection of objects. Comparison of certain infinite collections suggests that they have different sizes even though they are all infinite. For example, the sets of integers, rational numbers, and real numbers are all infinite; but each is a subset of the next. Ordering the size of sets according to the subset relation results in too many classifications and gives no way of comparing the size of sets involving different elements. Sets of different elements can be compared by pairing them off and seeing which set has leftover elements. If the fractions are listed in a special way, they can be paired off with the integers with no numbers left over from either set. Any infinite set that can be thus paired off with the integers is called countably, or denumerably, infinite. It has been demonstrated that the real numbers cannot be paired off in this way; and so they are called uncountable or nondenumerable and are considered as larger sets. There are still larger sets, such as the set of all functions involving real numbers. The size of infinite sets is indicated by the cardinal numbers symbolized by the Hebrew letter aleph (alef>) with subscript. Aleph-null symbolizes the cardinality of any set that can be matched with the integers. The cardinality of the real numbers, or the continuum, is c. The continuum hypothesis asserts that c equals aleph-one, the next cardinal number; that is, no sets exist with cardinality between aleph-null and aleph-one. The set of all subsets of a given set has a larger cardinal number than the set itself, resulting in an infinite succession of cardinal numbers of increasing size.

TRANSITIVE LAW

The transitive law is the statement that if A bears some relation to B and B bears the same relation to C, then A

bears it to C. In arithmetic, the property of equality is transitive, for if $A = B$ and $B = C$, then $A = C$. Likewise is the property inequality if the two inequalities have the same sense: that is, if A is greater than B (i.e., $A > B$) and $B > C$, then $A > C$; and if A is less than B (i.e., $A < B$) and $B < C$, then $A < C$. An example of an intransitive relation is: if B is the daughter of A, and C is the daughter of B, then C is not the daughter of A; and of a nontransitive relation: if A loves B, and B loves C, then A *may* or *may not* love C.

TURING MACHINE

A Turing machine is a hypothetical computing device introduced in 1936 by the English mathematician and logician Alan M. Turing. Turing originally conceived the machine as a mathematical tool that could infallibly recognize undecidable propositions—i.e., those mathematical statements that, within a given formal axiom system, cannot be shown to be either true or false. (The mathematician Kurt Gödel had demonstrated that such undecidable propositions exist in any system powerful enough to contain arithmetic.) Turing instead proved that there can never exist any universal algorithmic method for determining whether a proposition is undecidable.

The Turing machine is not a machine in the ordinary sense but rather an idealized mathematical model that reduces the logical structure of any computing device to its essentials. As envisaged by Turing, the machine performs its functions in a sequence of discrete steps and assumes only one of a finite list of internal states at any given moment. The machine itself consists of an infinitely extensible tape, a tape head that is capable of performing various operations on the tape, and a modifiable control mechanism in the head that can store directions from a finite set of instructions. The tape is

Alan Turing, whose major achievements included developing the idea of the Turing machine and designing the code-breaking Bombe machine used during the Second World War. Life Magazine/ Time & Life Pictures/Getty Images

divided into squares, each of which is either blank or has printed on it one of a finite number of symbols. The tape head has the ability to move to, read, write, and erase any single square and can also change to another internal state at any moment. Any such act is determined by the internal state of the machine and the condition of the scanned square at a given moment. The output of the machine— i.e., the solution to a mathematical query—can be read from the system once the machine has stopped. (However, in the case of Gödel's undecidable propositions, the machine would never stop, and this became known as the "halting problem.")

By incorporating all the essential features of information processing, the Turing machine became the basis for all subsequent digital computers, which share the machine's basic scheme of an input/output device (tape and reader), memory (control mechanism's storage), and central processing unit (control mechanism).

VINOGRADOV'S THEOREM

Vinogradov's theorem states that all sufficiently large odd integers can be expressed as the sum of three prime numbers. As a corollary, all sufficiently large even integers can be expressed as the sum of three primes plus 3. The theorem was proved in 1937 by the Russian mathematician Ivan Matveyevich Vinogradov. The first statement of the theorem, however, dates to the publication of the English mathematician Edward Waring's *Meditationes Algebraicae* (1770; "Thoughts on Algebra"), which contained several other important ideas in number theory, including Waring's problem, Wilson's theorem, and the famous Goldbach conjecture.

WARING'S PROBLEM

Waring's problem is the conjecture that every positive integer is the sum of a fixed number $f(n)$ of nth powers that depends only on n. The conjecture was first published by the English mathematician Edward Waring in *Meditationes Algebraicae* (1770; "Thoughts on Algebra"), where he speculated that $f(2) = 4$, $f(3) = 9$, and $f(4) = 19$; that is, it takes no more than 4 squares, 9 cubes, or 19 fourth powers to express any integer.

Waring's conjecture built on the four-square theorem of the French mathematician Joseph-Louis Lagrange, who in 1770 proved that $f(2) \leq 4$. (The origin for the theorem, though, goes back to the 3rd century and the birth of number theory with Diophantus of Alexandria's publication of *Arithmetica*.) The general assertion concerning $f(n)$ was proved by the German mathematician David Hilbert in 1909. In 1912 the German mathematicians Arthur Wieferich and Aubrey Kempner proved that

$f(3) = 9$. In 1986 three mathematicians, Ramachandran Balasubramanian of India and Jean-Marc Deshouillers and François Dress of France, together showed that $f(4) = 19$. In 1964 the Chinese mathematician Chen Jingrun showed that $f(5) = 37$. A general formula for higher powers has been suggested but not proved true for all integers.

WILSON'S THEOREM

Wilson's theorem states that any prime p divides $(p - 1)! + 1$, where $n!$ is the factorial notation for $1 \times 2 \times 3 \times 4 \times \cdots \times n$. For example, 5 divides $(5 - 1)! + 1 = 4! + 1 = 25$. The conjecture was first published by the English mathematician Edward Waring in *Meditationes Algebraicae* (1770; "Thoughts on Algebra"), where he ascribed it to the English mathematician John Wilson.

The theorem was proved by the French mathematician Joseph-Louis Lagrange in 1771. The converse of the theorem is also true; that is, $(n - 1)! + 1$ is not divisible by a composite number n. In theory, these theorems provide a test for primes; in practice, the calculations are impractical for large numbers.

ZORN'S LEMMA

Zorn's lemma, also known as Kuratowski-Zorn lemma and originally called the maximum principle, is a statement in the language of set theory, equivalent to the axiom of choice, that is often used to prove the existence of a mathematical object when it cannot be explicitly produced.

In 1935 the German-born American mathematician Max Zorn proposed adding the maximum principle to the standard axioms of set theory. (Informally, a closed collection of sets contains a maximal member—a set that cannot be contained in any other set in the collection.) Although it is now known that Zorn was not the first to suggest the maximum principle (the Polish mathematician Kazimierz Kuratowski discovered it in 1922), he demonstrated how useful this particular formulation could be in applications, particularly in algebra and analysis. He also stated, but did not prove, that the maximum principle, the axiom of choice, and German mathematician Ernst Zermelo's well-ordering principle were equivalent; that is, accepting any one of them enables the other two to be proved.

A formal definition of Zorn's lemma requires some preliminary definitions. A collection C of sets is called a chain if, for each pair of members of C (C_i and C_j), one is a subset of the other ($C_i \subseteq C_j$). A collection S of sets is said to be "closed under unions of chains" if whenever a chain C is included in S (i.e., $C \subseteq S$), then its union belongs to S (i.e., $\cup\, C_k \in S$). A member of S is said to be maximal if it is not a subset of any other member of S. Zorn's lemma is the statement: Any collection of sets closed under unions of chains contains a maximal member.

As an example of an application of Zorn's lemma in algebra, consider the proof that any vector space V has a basis (a linearly independent subset that spans the vector space; informally, a subset of vectors that can be combined to obtain any other element in the space). Taking S to be the collection of all linearly independent sets of vectors in V, it can be shown that S is closed under unions of chains. Then by Zorn's lemma there exists a maximal linearly independent set of vectors, which by definition must be a basis for V. (It is known that, without the axiom of choice, it is possible for there to be a vector space without a basis.)

An informal argument for Zorn's lemma can be given as follows: Assume that S is closed under unions of chains. Then the empty set $\varnothing$, being the union of the empty chain, is in S. If it is not a maximal member, then some other member that includes it is chosen. This last step is then iterated for a very long time (i.e., transfinitely, by using ordinal numbers to index the stages in the construction). Whenever (at limit ordinal stages) a long chain of larger and larger sets has been formed, the union of that chain is taken and used to continue. Because S is a set (and not a proper class like the class of ordinal numbers), this construction ultimately must stop with a maximal member of S.

CHAPTER 4

MEASUREMENTS

Measurement is fundamental to the sciences; to engineering, construction, and other technical fields; and to almost all everyday activities. For that reason the elements, conditions, limitations, and theoretical foundations of measurement have been much studied.

Measurements may be made by unaided human senses, in which case they are often called estimates, or, more commonly, by the use of instruments, which may range in complexity from simple rules for measuring lengths to highly sophisticated systems designed to detect and measure quantities entirely beyond the capabilities of the senses, such as radio waves from a distant star or the magnetic moment of a subatomic particle.

Measurement begins with a definition of the quantity that is to be measured, and it always involves a comparison with some known quantity of the same kind. If the object or quantity to be measured is not accessible for direct comparison, it is converted or "transduced" into an analogous measurement signal. Since measurement always involves some interaction between the object and the observer or observing instrument, there is always an exchange of energy, which, although in everyday applications is negligible, can become considerable in some types of measurement and thereby limit accuracy.

MEASUREMENT SYSTEMS

Although the concept of weights and measures today includes such factors as temperature, luminosity, pressure, and electric current, it once consisted of only four basic measurements: mass (weight), distance or length, area, and volume (liquid or grain measure). The last three are, of course, closely related.

Basic to the whole idea of weights and measures are the concepts of uniformity, units, and standards. Uniformity, the essence of any system of weights and measures, requires accurate, reliable standards of mass and length and agreed-on units. A unit is the name of a quantity, such as kilogram or pound. A standard is the physical embodiment of a unit, such as the platinum-iridium cylinder kept by the International Bureau of Weights and Measures at Paris as the standard kilogram.

Two types of measurement systems are distinguished historically: an evolutionary system, such as the British Imperial, which grew more or less haphazardly out of custom, and a planned system, such as the International System of Units (French: Système Internationale d'Unités, or SI), in universal use by the world's scientific community and by most nations.

Early Units and Standards

Ancient Mediterranean Systems

Body measurements and common natural items probably provided the most convenient bases for early linear measurements; early weight units may have derived casually from the use of certain stones or containers or from determinations of what a person or animal could lift or haul.

The historical progression of units has followed a generally westward direction, the units of the ancient empires of the Middle East finding their way, mostly as a result of trade and conquest, to the Greek and then the Roman empires, thence to Gaul and Britain via Roman expansion.

The Egyptians

Although there is evidence that many early civilizations devised standards of measurement and some tools for measuring, the Egyptian cubit is generally recognized as having been the most ubiquitous standard of linear measurement in the ancient world. Developed about 3000 BCE, it was based on the length of the arm from the elbow to the extended fingertips and was standardized by a royal master cubit of black granite, against which all the cubit sticks or rules in use in Egypt were measured at regular intervals.

The royal cubit (524 mm, or 20.62 inches) was subdivided in an extraordinarily complicated way. The basic subunit was the digit, doubtlessly a finger's breadth, of which there were 28 in the royal cubit. Four digits equaled a palm, five a hand. Twelve digits, or three palms, equaled a small span. Fourteen digits, or one-half a cubit, equaled a large span. Sixteen digits, or four palms, made one *t'ser*. Twenty-four digits, or six palms, were a small cubit.

The digit was in turn subdivided. The 14th digit on a cubit stick was marked off into 16 equal parts. The next digit was divided into 15 parts, and so on, to the 28th digit, which was divided into 2 equal parts. Thus, measurement could be made to digit fractions with any denominator from 2 through 16. The smallest division, $^1/_{16}$ of a digit, was equal to $^1/_{448}$ part of a royal cubit.

The accuracy of the cubit stick is attested by the dimensions of the Great Pyramid of Giza; although thousands were employed in building it, its sides vary no more than 0.05 percent from the mean length of 230.364 metres (9,069.43 inches), which suggests the original dimensions were 440 by 440 royal cubits.

The Egyptians developed methods and instruments for measuring land at a very early date. The annual flood of the Nile River created a need for benchmarks and

The pyramids of Giza in Egypt, whose sizes attest to the accuracy of the cubit sticks used for measurement during their building. Shutterstock.com

surveying techniques so that property boundaries could be readily reestablished when the water receded.

The Egyptian weight system appears to have been founded on a unit called the *kite*, with a decimal ratio, 10 kites equaling 1 deben and 10 debens equaling 1 sep. Over the long duration of Egyptian history, the weight of the *kite* varied from period to period, ranging all the way from 4.5 to 29.9 grams (0.16 to 1.05 ounce). Approximately 3,500 different weights have been recovered from ancient Egypt, some in basic geometric shapes, others in human and animal forms.

Egyptian liquid measures, from large to small, were *ro, hin, hekat, khar,* and cubic cubit.

The Babylonians

Among the earliest of all known weights is the Babylonian mina, which in one surviving form weighed about 640 grams (about 23 ounces) and in another about 978 grams (about 34 ounces). Archaeologists have also found weights of 5 minas, in the shape of a duck, and a 30-mina weight in the form of a swan. The shekel, familiar from the Bible as a standard Hebrew coin and weight, was originally Babylonian. Most of the Babylonian weights and measures, carried in commerce throughout the Middle East, were gradually adopted by other countries. The basic Babylonian unit of length was the *kus* (about 530 mm, or 20.9 inches), also called the Babylonian cubit. The Babylonian *shusi*, defined as $^1/_{30}$ *kus*, was equal to 17.5 mm (0.69 inch). The Babylonian foot was $^2/_3$ *kus*.

The Babylonian liquid measure, *qa* (also spelled *ka*), was the volume of a cube of one handbreadth (about 99 to 102 millilitres, or about 6.04 to 6.23 cubic inches). The cube, however, had to contain a weight of one great mina of water. The *qa* was a subdivision of two other units; 300 *qa* equaled 60 *gin* or 1 *gur*. The *gur* represented a volume of almost 303 litres (80 U.S. gallons).

The Hittites, Assyrians, Phoenicians, and Hebrews derived their systems generally from the Babylonians and Egyptians. Hebrew standards were based on the relationship between the mina, the talent (the basic unit), and the shekel. The sacred mina was equal to 60 shekels, and the sacred talent to 3,000 shekels, or 50 sacred minas. The Talmudic mina equaled 25 shekels; the Talmudic talent equaled 1,500 shekels, or 60 Talmudic minas.

The volumes of the several Hebrew standards of liquid measure are not definitely known; the bat may have contained about 37 litres (nearly 10 U.S. gallons); if so, the *log* equaled slightly more than 0.5 litre (0.14 U.S. gallon), and the *hin* slightly more than 6 litres (1.6 U.S. gallons). The Hebrew system was notable for the close relationship between dry and liquid volumetric measures; the liquid *kor* was the same size as the dry *homer*, and the liquid bat corresponded to the dry *'efa*.

Greeks and Romans

In the 1st millennium BCE commercial domination of the Mediterranean passed into the hands of the Greeks and then the Romans. A basic Greek unit of length was the finger (19.3 mm, or 0.76 inch); 16 fingers equaled about 30 cm (about 1 foot), and 24 fingers equaled 1 Olympic cubit. The coincidence with the Egyptian 24 digits equaling 1 small cubit suggests what is altogether probable on the basis of the commercial history of the era, that the Greeks derived their measures partly from the Egyptians and partly from the Babylonians, probably via the Phoenicians who for a long time dominated vast expanses of the Mediterranean trade. The Greeks apparently used linear standards to establish their primary liquid measure, the *metrētēs*, equivalent to 39.4 litres (10.4 U.S. gallons). A basic Greek unit of weight was the talent (equal to 25.8 kg, or 56.9 pounds), obviously borrowed from Eastern neighbours.

Roman linear measures were based on the Roman standard foot (*pes*). This unit was divided into 16 digits or into 12 inches. In both cases its length was the same. Metrologists have come to differing conclusions concerning its exact length, but the currently accepted modern equivalents are 296 mm, or 11.65 inches. Expressed in terms of these equivalents, the digit (*digitus*), or $\frac{1}{16}$ foot, was 18.5 mm (0.73 inch); the inch (*uncia* or *pollicus*), or $\frac{1}{12}$ foot, was 24.67 mm (0.97 inch); and the palm (*palmus*), or $\frac{1}{4}$ foot, was 74 mm (2.91 inches).

Larger linear units were always expressed in feet. The cubit (*cubitum*) was $1\frac{1}{2}$ feet (444 mm, or 17.48 inches). Five Roman feet made the pace (*passus*), equivalent to 1.48 metres, or 4.86 feet.

The most frequently used itinerary measures were the furlong or stade (*stadium*), the mile (*mille passus*), and the league (*leuga*). The stade consisted of 625 feet (185 metres, or 606.9 feet), or 125 paces, and was equal to 1/8 mile. The mile was 5,000 feet (1,480 metres, or 4,856 feet), or 8 stades. The league had 7,500 feet (2,220 metres, or 7,283 feet), or 1,500 paces.

Prior to the 3rd century BCE the standard for all Roman weights was the *as*, or Old Etruscan or Oscan pound, of 4,210 grains (272.81 grams). It was divided into 12 ounces of 351 grains (22.73 grams) each. In 268 BCE a new standard was created when a silver *denarius* was struck to a weight of 70.5 grains (4.57 grams). Six of these *denarii*, or "pennyweights," were reckoned to the ounce (*uncia*) of 423 grains (27.41 grams), and 72 of them made the new pound (*libra*) of 12 ounces, or 5,076 grains (328.9 grams).

The principal Roman capacity measures were the *hemina, sextarius, modius*, and amphora for dry products and the *quartarus, sextarius, congius, urna*, and *amphora* for liquids. Since all of these were based on the *sextarius* and since no two extant *sextarii* are identical, a mean generally agreed upon today is 35.4 cubic inches, or nearly 1 pint (0.58 litre). The *hemina*, or half-*sextarius*, based on this mean was 17.7 cubic inches (0.29 litre). Sixteen of these *sextarii* made the *modius* of 566.4 cubic inches (9.28 litres), and 48 of them made the *amphora* of 1,699.2 cubic inches (27.84 litres).

In the liquid series, the *quartarus*, or one-fourth of a *sextarius* (35.4 cubic inches), was 8.85 cubic inches (0.145 litres). Six of these *sextarii* made the *congius* of 212.4 cubic inches (3.48 litres), 24 *sextarii* made the *urna* of 849.6 cubic inches (13.92 litres), and, as in dry products, 48 *sextarii* were equal to one *amphora*.

The Ancient Chinese System

Completely separated from the Mediterranean-European history of metrology is that of ancient China; yet the Chinese system exhibits all the principal characteristics of the Western. It employed parts of the body as a source of units — for example, the distance from the pulse to the base of the thumb. It was fundamentally chaotic in that there was no relationship between different types of units, such as those of length and those of volume. Finally, it was rich in variations. The *mou*, a unit of land measure, fluctuated from region to region from 0.08 to 0.13 hectare (0.2 to 0.3 acre). Variations were not limited to the geographic; a unit of length with the same name might be of one length for a carpenter, another for a mason, and still another for a tailor. This was a problem in Western weights and measures as well.

Shi Huang Di, who became the first emperor of China in 221 BCE, is celebrated for, among other things, his unification of the regulations fixing the basic units. The basic weight, the *shi*, or *dan*, was fixed at about 60 kg (132 pounds); the two basic measurements, the *zhi* and the *zhang*, were set at about 25 cm (9.8 inches) and 3 metres (9.8 feet), respectively. A noteworthy characteristic of the Chinese system, and one that represented a substantial advantage over the Mediterranean systems, was its predilection for a decimal notation, as demonstrated by foot rulers from the 6th century BCE. Measuring instruments, too, were of a high order.

A unique characteristic of the Chinese system was its inclusion of an acoustic dimension. A standard vessel used for measuring grain and wine was defined not only by the weight it could hold but by its pitch when struck; given a uniform shape and fixed weight, only a vessel of the proper volume would give the proper pitch. Thus the same word in old Chinese means "wine bowl," "grain measure," and "bell." Measures based on the length of a pitch pipe and its subdivision in terms of millet grains supplanted the old measurements based on the human body. The change brought a substantial increase in accuracy.

Medieval Systems

Medieval Europe inherited the Roman system, with its Greek, Babylonian, and Egyptian roots. It soon proliferated through daily use and language variations into a great number of national and regional variants, with elements borrowed from the Celtic, Anglo-Saxon, Germanic, Scandinavian, and Arabic influences and original contributions growing out of the needs of medieval life.

A determined effort by the Holy Roman emperor Charlemagne and many other medieval kings to impose uniformity at the beginning of the 9th century was in vain; differing usages hardened. The great trade fairs, such as those in Champagne during the 12th and 13th centuries, enforced rigid uniformity on merchants of all nationalities within the fairgrounds and had some effect on standardizing differences among regions, but the variations remained. A good example is the ell, the universal measure for wool cloth, the great trading staple of the Middle Ages. The ell of Champagne, 2 feet 6 inches, measured against an iron standard in the hands of the Keeper of the Fair, was accepted by Ypres and Ghent, both in modern Belgium; by Arras, in modern France; and by the other great cloth-manufacturing cities of northwestern Europe, even though their bolts varied in length. In several other parts of Europe, the ell itself varied, however. There were hundreds of thousands of such examples among measuring units throughout Europe.

The English and U.S. Customary Systems of Weights and Measures

The English System

Out of the welter of medieval weights and measures emerged several national systems, reformed and reorganized many times over the centuries; ultimately nearly all of these systems were replaced by the metric system. In Britain and in its American colonies, however, the altered medieval system survived.

BRITISH IMPERIAL AND U.S. CUSTOMARY SYSTEMS OF WEIGHTS AND MEASURES			
UNIT	ABBRE- VIATION OR SYMBOL	EQUIVALENTS IN OTHER UNITS OF SAME SYSTEM	METRIC EQUIVALENT
WEIGHT			
Avoirdupois[1]	avdp		
ton			
short ton		20 short hundredweight, or 2,000 pounds	0.907 metric ton
long ton		20 long hundredweight, or 2,240 pounds	1.016 metric tons
hundredweight	cwt		
short hundredweight		100 pounds, or 0.05 short ton	45.359 kilograms
long hundredweight		112 pounds, or 0.05 long ton	50.802 kilograms
pound	lb, lb avdp, or #	16 ounces, or 7,000 grains	0.454 kilogram
ounce	oz, or oz avdp	16 drams, 437.5 grains, or 0.0625 pound	28.350 grams
dram	dr, or dr avdp	27.344 grains, or 0.0625 ounce	1.772 grams
grain	gr	0.037 dram, or 0.002286 ounce	0.0648 gram
stone	st	0.14 short hundred-weight, or 14 pounds	6.35 kilograms

Unit	Abbre-viation or Symbol	Equivalents in Other Units of Same System	Metric Equivalent
Troy			
pound	lb t	12 ounces, 240 penny-weight, or 5,760 grains	0.373 kilogram
ounce	oz t	20 pennyweight, 480 grains, or 0.083 pound	31.103 grams
pennyweight	dwt, or pwt	24 grains, or 0.05 ounce	1.555 grams
grain	gr	0.042 pennyweight, or 0.002083 ounce	0.0648 gram
Apothecaries'			
pound	lb ap	12 ounces, or 5,760 grains	0.373 kilogram
ounce	oz ap	8 drams, 480 grains, or 0.083 pound	31.103 grams
dram	dr ap	3 scruples, or 60 grains	3.888 grams
scruple	s ap	20 grains, or 0.333 dram	1.296 grams
grain	gr	0.05 scruple, 0.002083 ounce, or 0.0166 dram	0.0648 gram
Capacity			
U.S. Liquid Measures			
gallon	gal	4 quarts	3.785 litres
quart	qt	2 pints	0.946 litre
pint	pt	4 gills	0.473 litre
gill	gi	4 fluid ounces	118.294 millilitres
fluid ounce	fl oz	8 fluid drams	29.573 millilitres
fluid dram	fl dr	60 minims	3.697 millilitres
minim	min	1/60 fluid dram	0.061610 millilitre

Unit	Abbre-viation or Symbol	Equivalents in Other Units of Same System	Metric Equivalent
U.S. Dry Measures			
bushel	bu	4 pecks	35.239 litres
peck	pk	8 quarts	8.810 litres
quart	qt	2 pints	1.101 litres
pint	pt	1/2 quart	0.551 litre
British Liquid and Dry Measure			
bushel	bu	4 pecks	0.036 cubic metre
peck	pk	2 gallons	0.0091 cubic metre
gallon	gal	4 quarts	4.546 litres
quart	qt	2 pints	1.136 litres
pint	pt	4 gills	568.26 cubic centimetres
gill	gi	5 fluid ounces	142.066 cubic centimetres
fluid ounce	fl oz	8 fluid drams	28.412 cubic centimetres
fluid dram	fl dr	60 minims	3.5516 cubic centimetres
minim	min	1/60 fluid dram	0.059194 cubic centimetre
Length			
nautical mile	nmi	6,076 feet, or 1.151 miles	1,852 metres
mile	mi	5,280 feet, 1,760 yards, or 320 rods	1.609 kilometres
furlong	fur	660 feet, 220 yards, or 1/8 mile	201 metres
rod	rd	5.50 yards, or 16.5 feet	5.029 metres

Unit	Abbreviation or Symbol	Equivalents in Other Units of Same System	Metric Equivalent
fathom	fth	6 feet, or 72 inches	1.829 metres
yard	yd	3 feet, or 36 inches	0.9144 metre
foot	ft, or '	12 inches, or 0.333 yard	30.48 centimetres
inch	in, or "	0.083 foot, or 0.028 yard	2.54 centimetres
AREA			
square mile	sq mi, or mi2	640 acres, or 102,400 square rods	2.590 square kilometres
acre		4,840 square yards, or 43,560 square feet	0.405 hectare, or 4,047 square metres
square rod	sq rd, or rd2	30.25 square yards, or 0.00625 acre	25.293 square metres
square yard	sq yd, or yd2	1,296 square inches, or 9 square feet	0.836 square metre
square foot	sq ft, or ft2	144 square inches, or 0.111 square yard	0.093 square metre
square inch	sq in, or in2	0.0069 square foot, or 0.00077 square yard	6.452 square centimetres
VOLUME			
cubic yard	cu yd, or yd3	27 cubic feet, or 46,656 cubic inches	0.765 cubic metre
cubic foot	cu ft, or ft3	1,728 cubic inches, or 0.0370 cubic yard	0.028 cubic metre
cubic inch	cu in, or in3	0.00058 cubic foot, or 0.000021 cubic yard	16.387 cubic centimetres
acre-foot	ac ft	43,560 cubic feet, or 1,613 cubic yards	1,233 cubic metres

UNIT	ABBRE-VIATION OR SYMBOL	EQUIVALENTS IN OTHER UNITS OF SAME SYSTEM	METRIC EQUIVALENT
board foot	bd ft	144 cubic inches, or 1/12 cubic foot	2.36 litres
cord	cd	128 cubic feet	3.62 cubic metres

1 The U.S. uses avoirdupois units as the common system of measuring weight.

By the time of the Magna Carta (1215), abuses of weights and measures were so common that a clause was inserted in the charter to correct those on grain and wine, demanding a common measure for both. A few years later a royal ordinance entitled "Assize of Weights and Measures" defined a broad list of units and standards so successfully that it remained in force for several centuries thereafter. A standard yard, "the Iron Yard of our Lord the King," was prescribed for the realm, divided into the traditional 3 feet, each of 12 inches, "neither more nor less." The perch (later the rod) was defined as 5.5 yards, or 16.5 feet. The inch was subdivided for instructional purposes into 3 barley corns.

The furlong (a "furrow long") was eventually standardized as 1/8 mile; the acre, from an Anglo-Saxon word, as an area 4 rods wide by 40 long. There were many other units standardized during this period.

The influence of the Champagne fairs may be seen in the separate English pounds for troy weight, perhaps from Troyes, one of the principal fair cities, and avoirdupois weight, the term used at the fairs for goods that had to be weighed—sugar, salt, alum, dyes, grain. The troy pound, for weighing gold and silver bullion, and the apothecaries' weight for drugs contained only 12 troy ounces.

A multiple of the English pound was the stone, which added a fresh element of confusion to the system by equaling neither 12 nor 16 but 14 pounds, among dozens of other pounds depending on the products involved. The sacks of raw wool, which were medieval England's principal export, weighed 26 stones, or 364 pounds; large standards, weighing 91 pounds, or one-fourth a sack, were employed in wool weighing. The sets of standards, which were sent out from London to the provincial towns, were usually of bronze or brass. Discrepancies crept into the system, and in 1496, following a Parliamentary inquiry, new standards were made and sent out, a procedure repeated in 1588, under Queen Elizabeth I. Reissues of standards were common throughout the Middle Ages and early modern period in all European countries.

No major revision occurred for nearly 200 years after Elizabeth's time, but several refinements and redefinitions were added. Edmund Gunter, a 17th-century mathematician, conceived the idea of taking the acre's breadth (4 perches, or 22 yards), calling it a chain, and dividing it into 100 links. In 1701 the corn bushel in dry measure was defined as "any round measure with a plain and even bottom, being 18.5 inches wide throughout and 8 inches deep." Similarly, in 1707 the wine gallon was defined as a round measure with an even bottom and containing 231 cubic inches; however, the ale gallon was retained at 282 cubic inches. There was also a corn gallon and an older, slightly smaller wine gallon. There were many other attempts made at standardization besides these, but it was not until the 19th century that a major overhaul occurred.

The Weights and Measures Act of 1824 sought to clear away some of the medieval tangle. A single gallon was decreed, defined as the volume occupied by

10 imperial pounds weight of distilled water weighed in air against brass weights with the water and the air at a temperature of 62 degrees of Fahrenheit's thermometer and with the barometer at 30 inches.

The same definition was reiterated in an Act of 1878, which redefined the yard:

the straight line or distance between the centres of two gold plugs or pins in the bronze bar . . . measured when the bar is at the temperature of sixty-two degrees of Fahrenheit's thermometer, and when it is supported by bronze rollers placed under it in such a manner as best to avoid flexure of the bar.

Other units were standardized during this era as well.

Finally, by an act of Parliament in 1963, all the English weights and measures were redefined in terms of the metric system, with a national changeover beginning two years later.

THE U.S. CUSTOMARY SYSTEM

In his first message to Congress in 1790, George Washington drew attention to the need for "uniformity in currency, weights and measures." Currency was settled in a decimal form, but the vast inertia of the English weights and measures system permeating industry and commerce and involving containers, measures, tools, and machines, as well as popular psychology, prevented the same approach from succeeding, though it was advocated by Thomas Jefferson. In these very years the metric system was coming into being in France, and in 1821 Secretary of State John Quincy Adams, in a famous report to Congress, called the metric system "worthy of acceptance . . . beyond a question." Yet Adams admitted the impossibility of winning acceptance for it in the United States, until a future time

when the example of its benefits, long and practically enjoyed, shall acquire that ascendancy over the opinions of other nations which gives motion to the springs and direction to the wheels of the power.

Instead of adopting metric units, the United States tried to bring its system into closer harmony with the English, from which various deviations had developed; for example, the United States still used "Queen Anne's gallon" of 231 cubic inches, which the British had discarded in 1824. Construction of standards was undertaken by the Office of Standard Weights and Measures, under the Treasury Department. The standard for the yard was one imported from London some years earlier, which guaranteed a close identity between the American and

A brass measure representing the size of half of the U.S. bushel. SSPL/ Getty Images

English yard; but Queen Anne's gallon was retained. The avoirdupois pound, at 7,000 grains, exactly corresponded with the British, as did the troy pound at 5,760 grains; however, the U.S. bushel, at 2,150.42 cubic inches, again deviated from the British. The U.S. bushel was derived from the "Winchester bushel," a surviving standard dating to the 15th century, which had been replaced in the British Act of 1824. It might be said that the U.S. gallon and bushel, smaller by about 17 percent and 3 percent, respectively, than the British, remain more truly medieval than their British counterparts.

At least the standards were fixed, however. From the mid-19th century, new states, as they were admitted to the union, were presented with sets of standards. Late in the century, pressure grew to enlarge the role of the Office of Standard Weights and Measures, which, by Act of Congress effective July 1, 1901, became the National Bureau of Standards (since 1988 the National Institute of Standards and Technology), part of the Commerce Department. Its functions, as defined by the Act of 1901, included, besides the construction of physical standards and cooperation in establishment of standard practices, such activities as developing methods for testing materials and structures; carrying out research in engineering, physical science, and mathematics; and compilation and publication of general scientific and technical data. One of the first acts of the bureau was to sponsor a national conference on weights and measures to coordinate standards among the states; one of the main functions of the annual conference became the updating of a model state law on weights and measures, which resulted in virtual uniformity in legislation.

Apart from this action, however, the U.S. government remained unique among major nations in refraining from exercising control at the national level. One noteworthy exception was the Metric Act of 1866, which permitted use of the metric system in the United States.

The Metric System of Measurement

The Development and Establishment of the Metric System

One of the most significant results of the French Revolution was the establishment of the metric system of weights and measures.

European scientists had for many years discussed the desirability of a new, rational, and uniform system to replace the national and regional variants that made scientific and commercial communication difficult. The first proposal closely to approximate what eventually became the metric system was made as early as 1670. Gabriel Mouton, the vicar of St. Paul's Church in Lyon, France, and a noted mathematician and astronomer, suggested a linear measure based on the arc of one minute of longitude, to be subdivided decimally. Mouton's proposal contained three of the major characteristics of the metric system: decimalization, rational prefixes, and the Earth's measurement as basis for a definition. Mouton's proposal was discussed, amended, criticized, and advocated for 120 years before the fall of the Bastille and the creation of the National Assembly made it a political possibility. In April of 1790 one of the foremost members of the assembly, Charles-Maurice de Talleyrand, introduced the subject and launched a debate that resulted in a directive to the French Academy of Sciences to prepare a report. After several months' study, the academy recommended that the length of the meridian passing through Paris be determined from the North Pole to the Equator, that 1/10,000,000 of this distance be termed the metre and form the basis of a new decimal linear system, and, further, that a new unit of weight should be derived from the weight of a cubic metre of water. A list of prefixes for decimal multiples and submultiples was proposed. The National Assembly endorsed the report and directed that the necessary meridional measurements be taken.

On June 19, 1791, a committee of 12 mathematicians, geodesists, and physicists met with King Louis XVI, who gave his formal approval. The next day, the king attempted to escape from France, was arrested, returned to Paris, and was imprisoned; a year later, from his cell, he issued the proclamation that directed several scientists including Jean Delambre and Pierre Mechain to perform the operations necessary to determine the length of the metre. The intervening time had been spent by the scientists and engineers in preliminary research; Delambre and Mechain now set to work to measure the distance on the meridian from Barcelona, Spain, to Dunkirk in northern France. The survey proved arduous; civil and foreign war so hampered the operation that it was not completed for six years. While Delambre and Mechain were struggling in the field, administrative details were being worked out in Paris. In 1793 a provisional metre was constructed from geodetic data already available. In 1795 the firm decision was taken to enact adoption of the metric system for France. The new law defined the length, mass, and capacity standards and listed the prefixes for multiples and submultiples. With the formal presentation to the assembly of the standard metre, as determined by Delambre and Mechain, the metric system became a fact in June 1799. The motto adopted for the new system was "For all people, for all time."

The standard metre was the Delambre-Mechain survey-derived "one ten-millionth part of a meridional quadrant of the earth." The gram, the basic unit of mass, was made equal to the mass of a cubic centimetre of pure water at the temperature of its maximum density (4 °C or 39.2 °F). A platinum cylinder known as the Kilogram of the Archives was declared the standard for 1,000 grams.

The litre was defined as the volume equivalent to the volume of a cube, each side of which had a length of 1 decimetre, or 10 centimetres.

The are was defined as the measure of area equal to a square 10 metres on a side. In practice the multiple hectare, 100 ares, became the principal unit of land measure.

The stere was defined as the unit of volume, equal to one cubic metre.

Names for multiples and submultiples of all units were made uniform, based on Greek and Latin prefixes.

The metric system's conquest of Europe was facilitated by the military successes of the French Revolution and Napoleon, but it required a long period of time to overcome the inertia of customary systems. Even in France Napoleon found it expedient to issue a decree permitting use of the old medieval system. Nonetheless, in the competition between the two systems existing side by side, the advantages of metrics proved decisive; in 1840 it was established as the legal monopoly in France, and from that point forward its progress throughout the world has been steady, though it is worth observing that in many cases the metric system was adopted during the course of a political upheaval, just as in its original French beginning. Notable examples are Latin America, the Soviet Union, and China. In Japan the adoption of the metric system came about following the peaceful but far-reaching political changes associated with the Meiji Restoration of 1868.

In Britain, the Commonwealth nations, and the United States, the progress of the metric system has been discernible. The United States became a signatory to the Metric Convention of 1875 and received copies of the International

Prototype Metre and the International Prototype Kilogram in 1890. Three years later the Office of Weights and Measures announced that the prototype metre and kilogram would be regarded as fundamental standards from which the customary units, the yard and the pound, would be derived.

Throughout the 20th century, use of the metric system in various segments of commerce and industry increased spontaneously in Britain and the United States; it became almost universally employed in the scientific and medical professions. The automobile, electronics, chemical, and electric power industries have all adopted metrics at least in part, as have such fields as optometry and photography. Legislative proposals to adopt metrics generally have been made in the U.S. Congress and British Parliament. In 1968 the former passed legislation calling for a program of investigation, research, and survey to determine the impact on the United States of increasing worldwide use of the metric system. The program concluded with a report to Congress in July 1971 that stated:

> On the basis of evidence marshalled in the U.S. metric study, this report (D.V. Simone, "Metric America, A Decision whose Time has Come," National Bureau of Standards Special Publication 345) recommends that the United States change to the International Metric System.

Parliament went further and established a long-range program of changeover.

The International System of Units

Just as the original conception of the metric system had grown out of the problems scientists encountered in dealing with the medieval system, so a new system grew out of the problems a vastly enlarged scientific community faced in the proliferation of subsystems improvised to serve particular disciplines. At the same time, it had long been known that the original 18th-century standards were not accurate to the degree demanded by 20th-century scientific operations; new definitions were required. After lengthy discussion the 11th General Conference on Weights and Measures (11th CGPM), meeting in Paris in October 1960, formulated a new International System of Units (abbreviated SI). The SI was amended by subsequent convocations of the CGPM. The following base units have been adopted and defined:

Length: Metre

Since 1983 the metre has been defined as the distance traveled by light in a vacuum in 1/299,792,458 second.

Mass: Kilogram

The standard for the unit of mass, the kilogram, is a cylinder of platinum-iridium alloy kept by the International Bureau of Weights and Measures, located in Sèvres, near Paris. A duplicate in the custody of the National Institute

The metric system is used extensively throughout the world, as evidenced by the customers above who wait to buy rice by the kilogram in the Philippines. Romeo Gacad/AFP/Getty Images

of Standards and Technology serves as the mass standard for the United States. (This is the only base unit still defined by an artifact.)

Time: Second

The second is defined as the duration of 9,192,631,770 cycles of the radiation associated with a specified transition, or change in energy level, of the cesium-133 atom.

Electric Current: Ampere

The ampere is defined as the magnitude of the current that, when flowing through each of two long parallel wires separated by one metre in free space, results in a force between the two wires (due to their magnetic fields) of 2 ×

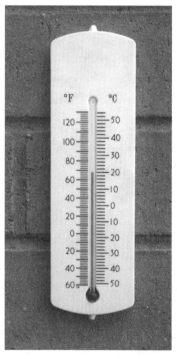

A thermometer showing temperature readings on both the Fahrenheit and Celsius scales. Shutterstock.com

10^{-7} newton (the newton is a unit of force equal to about 0.2 pound) for each metre of length.

Thermodynamic Temperature: Kelvin

The thermodynamic, or Kelvin, scale of temperature used in SI has its origin or zero point at absolute zero and has a fixed point at the triple point of water (the temperature and pressure at which ice, liquid water, and water vapour are in equilibrium), defined as 273.16 kelvins. The Celsius temperature scale is derived from the Kelvin scale. The triple point is defined as 0.01 degree on the Celsius scale, which is approximately 32.02 degrees on the Fahrenheit temperature scale.

Amount of Substance: Mole

The mole is defined as the amount of substance containing the same number of chemical units (atoms, molecules, ions, electrons, or other specified entities or groups of entities) as exactly 12 grams of carbon-12.

Light (Luminous) Intensity: Candela

The candela is defined as the luminous intensity in a given direction of a source that emits monochromatic radiation at a frequency of 540×10^{12} hertz and that has a radiant intensity in the same direction of $1/683$ watt per steradian (unit solid angle).

MEASUREMENT INSTRUMENTS AND SYSTEMS

In general, measuring systems comprise a number of functional elements. One element is required to discriminate the object and sense its dimensions or frequency. This information is then transmitted throughout the system by physical signals. If the object is itself active, such as water flow, it may power the signal; if passive, it must trigger the signal by interaction either with an energetic probe, such as a light source or X-ray tube, or with a carrier signal. Eventually the physical signal is compared with a reference signal of known quantity that has been subdivided or multiplied to suit the range of measurement required. The reference signal is derived from objects of known quantity by a process called calibration. The comparison may be an analog process in which signals in a continuous dimension are brought to equality. An alternative comparison process is quantization by counting, i.e., dividing the signal into parts of equal and known size and adding up the number of parts.

Other functions of measurement systems facilitate the basic process described above. Amplification ensures that the physical signal is strong enough to complete the measurement. In order to reduce degradation of the measurement as it progresses through the system, the signal may be converted to coded or digital form. Magnification, enlarging the measurement signal without increasing its power, is often necessary to match the output of one element of the system with the input of another, such as matching the size of the readout meter with the discerning power of the human eye.

One important type of measurement is the analysis of resonance, or the frequency of variation within a physical system. This is determined by harmonic analysis, commonly exhibited in the sorting of signals by a radio receiver. Computation is another important measurement process, in which measurement signals are manipulated mathematically, typically by some form of analog or digital computer. Computers may also provide a control function in monitoring system performance.

Measuring systems may also include devices for transmitting signals over great distances. All measuring systems, even highly automated ones, include some method of displaying the signal to an observer. Visual display systems may comprise a calibrated chart and a pointer, an integrated display on a cathode-ray tube, or a digital readout. Measurement systems often include elements for recording. A common type utilizes a writing stylus that records measurements on a moving chart. Electrical recorders may include feedback reading devices for greater accuracy.

The actual performance of measuring instruments is affected by numerous external and internal factors. Among external factors are noise and interference, both of which tend to mask or distort the measurement signal. Internal factors include linearity, resolution, precision, and accuracy, all of which are characteristic of a given instrument or system, and dynamic response, drift, and hysteresis, which are effects produced in the process of measurement itself. The general question of error in measurement raises the topic of measurement theory.

MEASUREMENT THEORY

Measurement theory is the study of how numbers are assigned to objects and phenomena, and its concerns include the kinds of things that can be measured, how different measures relate to each other, and the problem of error in the measurement process. Any general theory of measurement must come to grips with three basic problems: error; representation, which is the justification of number assignment; and uniqueness, which is the degree to which the kind of representation chosen approaches being the only one possible for the object or phenomenon in question.

Various systems of axioms, or basic rules and assumptions, have been formulated as a basis for measurement theory. Some of the most important types of axioms include axioms of order, axioms of extension, axioms of difference, axioms of conjointness, and axioms of geometry. Axioms of order ensure that the order imposed on objects by the assignment of numbers is the same order attained in actual observation or measurement. Axioms of extension deal with the representation of such attributes as time duration, length, and mass, which can be combined, or concatenated, for multiple objects exhibiting the attribute in question. Axioms of difference govern the measuring of intervals. Axioms of conjointness postulate that attributes that cannot be measured empirically (for example, loudness, intelligence, or hunger) can be measured by observing the way their component dimensions change in relation to each other. Axioms of geometry govern the representation of dimensionally complex attributes by pairs of numbers, triples of numbers, or even *n*-tuples of numbers.

The problem of error is one of the central concerns of measurement theory. At one time it was believed that errors of measurement could eventually be eliminated through the refinement of scientific principles and equipment. This belief is no longer held by most scientists, and almost all physical measurements reported today are accompanied by some indication of the limitation of accuracy or the probable degree of error. Among the various types of error that must be taken into account are errors of observation (which include instrumental errors, personal errors, systematic errors, and random errors), errors of sampling, and direct and indirect errors (in which one erroneous measurement is used in computing other measurements).

Measurement theory dates back to the 4th century BCE, when a theory of magnitudes developed by the Greek mathematicians Eudoxus of Cnidus and Thaeatetus was included in Euclid's Elements. The first systematic work on observational error was produced by the English mathematician Thomas Simpson in 1757, but the fundamental work on error theory was done by two 18th-century French astronomers, Joseph-Louis Lagrange and Pierre-Simon Laplace. The first attempt to incorporate measurement theory into the social sciences also occurred in the 18th century, when Jeremy Bentham, a British utilitarian moralist, attempted to create a theory for the measurement of value. Modern axiomatic theories of measurement derive from the work of two German scientists, Hermann von Helmholtz and Otto Hölder, and contemporary work on the application of measurement theory to psychology and economics derives in large part from the work of Oskar Morgenstern and John von Neumann.

Since most social theories are speculative in nature, attempts to establish standard measuring sequences or techniques for them have met with limited success. Some of the problems involved in social measurement include the lack of universally accepted theoretical frameworks and thus of quantifiable measures, sampling errors, problems associated with the intrusion of the measurer on the object being measured, and the subjective nature of the information received from human subjects. Economics is probably the social science that has had the most success in adopting measurement theories, primarily because many economic variables (like price and quantity) can be measured easily and objectively. Demography has successfully employed measurement techniques as well, particularly in the area of mortality tables.

CHAPTER 5
MEASUREMENT
PIONEERS

They ranged in profession from civil engineers to astronomers to mechanical instrument makers, but they shared a common passion: creating standards that allowed others to set objective measurements. The following brief biographies highlight the work of a few of these influential measurement pioneers.

NORMAN ROBERT CAMPBELL
(b. March 7, 1880, London, Eng.—d. May 18, 1949, Nottingham)

Norman Campbell is best known for his contributions to the theory and practice of physical measurements.

Campbell was a research assistant at the Cavendish Laboratory at Cambridge, where he worked under the great experimental physicist Sir J. J. Thomson and contributed to the study of spontaneous ionization in gases and radioactivity. In 1910 Campbell joined Sir William Bragg's research group at the University of Leeds, where he studied X-ray ionization on an honorary basis until a formal position was created for him in 1912. During this period at Leeds, Campbell met and married Edith Utley Sowerbutts, who taught science at the Leeds Girls' High School. In 1914 Campbell joined the electrotechnics and photometry department of the British National Physical Laboratory, where he worked under physicist Clifford Patterson on military research. Following the end of World War I, Campbell was recruited by Patterson to form part of the research staff for what later became the General Electric Company Research Laboratory, where he spent the rest of his career.

Before joining Patterson in 1919, however, the Campbells adopted two babies, a boy and a girl, and withdrew for nine months to adjust to family life. During this self-imposed retreat, Campbell wrote *Physics: The Elements* (1920; republished posthumously in 1957 in an expanded edition as *Foundations of Science: The Philosophy of Theory and Experiment*), which is still influential for its consideration of philosophical issues related to physical measurements and epistemology.

During World War II, Campbell's son was killed in action in 1941 by a torpedo in the Mediterranean, which led the grieving couple to retire and move to Dorset. In 1944 the Campbell's home was destroyed by a stray German bomb, which left Norman virtually unharmed but severely injured Edith. Following her death in 1948, he moved in with his daughter and her children.

Campbell's major works include *Modern Electrical Theory* (1907), which rejected the existence of the so-called ether and foreshadowed certain ideas of relativity; *The Principles of Electricity* (1912); *What Is Science?* (1921); and *An Account of the Principles of Measurement and Calculation* (1928).

ANDERS CELSIUS

(b. Nov. 27, 1701, Uppsala, Sweden—d. April 25, 1744, Uppsala)

Anders Celsius was an astronomer and inventor of the Celsius temperature scale (often called the centigrade scale).

Celsius was professor of astronomy at Uppsala University from 1730 to 1744, and in 1740 he built the Uppsala Observatory. In 1733 Celsius published a collection of 316 observations of the aurora borealis, or northern lights, made by himself and others from 1716 to 1732. He advocated the measurement of an arc of a meridian in Lapland and in 1736 took part in an expedition organized for that

Anders Celsius, for whom the Celsius tempera-ture scale is named. Frederic Lewis/Hulton Archive/Getty Images

purpose, which ver-ified Isaac Newton's theory that the Earth is somewhat flattened at the poles. In 1742 he described his ther-mometer in a paper read before the Swedish Academy of Sciences. His other works include *Dissertatio de Nova Methodo Distantiam Solis a Terra Deter-minandi* (1730; "A Dissertation on a New Method of Determining the Distance of the Sun from the Earth") and *De Observationibus pro Figura Telluris Determinanda in Gallia Habitis, Disquisitio* (1738; "Disquisition on Obser-vations Made in France for Determining the Shape of the Earth").

GIOVANNI GIORGI

(b. Nov. 27, 1871, Lucca, Italy—d. Aug. 19, 1950, Castiglioncello)

Giovanni Giorgi proposed a widely used system for the definition of electrical, magnetic, and mechanical units of measurement.

Giorgi studied civil engineering at the Institute of Technology in Rome and from 1906 to 1923 directed the Technology Office of Rome. He taught (1913–39) at the University of Rome and also held appointments at the universities of Cagliari and Palermo and at the Royal Institute for Higher Mathematics. He is best known for developing the Giorgi International System of Measurement (also known as the MKSA system) in 1901. This system proposed as units of scientific measurement the metre, kilogram, second, and joule and was endorsed in 1960 by the General Conference of Weights and Measures (with the ampere instead of the joule as the unit of energy).

Giorgi also contributed to the development of hydroelectric installations, electric distribution networks, and urban trolley systems.

EDMUND GUNTER

(b. 1581, Hertfordshire, Eng.—d. Dec. 10, 1626, London)

Edmund Gunter invented many useful measuring devices, including a forerunner of the slide rule.

Gunter was professor of astronomy at Gresham College, London, from 1619 until his death. Descriptions of some of his inventions were given in his treatises on the sector, cross-staff, bow, quadrant, and other instruments. In *Canon Triangulorum, or Table of Artificial Sines and Tangents* (1620), the first published table of common logarithms of the sine and tangent functions, he introduced the terms cosine and cotangent. He also suggested to his friend Henry Briggs, the inventor of common logarithms, the use of the arithmetical complement.

Gunter's practical inventions included Gunter's chain. Commonly used for surveying, it was 22 yards (20.1 metres) long and was divided into 100 links. Gunter's quadrant was used to find the hour of the day, the sun's azimuth, and the altitude of an object in degrees. Gunter's scale, or Gunter's line, generally called the gunter by seamen, was a large plane scale with logarithmic divisions plotted on it.

Edmund Gunter's quadrant, used to calculate the time of day. SSPL/Getty Images

With the aid of a pair of compasses, it was used to multiply and divide. Gunter's scale was an important step in the development of the slide rule.

JOSEPH-LOUIS LAGRANGE

(b. Jan. 25, 1736, Turin, Sardinia-Piedmont [Italy]—d. April 10, 1813, Paris, France)

Joseph-Louis Lagrange made great contributions to number theory and to analytic and celestial mechanics. His most important book, *Mécanique analytique* (1788; "Analytic Mechanics"), was the basis for all later work in this field.

The French Revolution, which began in 1789, pressed Lagrange into work on the committee to reform the metric system. When the École Centrale des Travaux Publics (later renamed the École Polytechnique) was opened in 1794, he became, with Gaspard Monge, its leading professor of mathematics.

Napoleon honoured the aging mathematician, making him a senator and a count of the empire, but he remained the quiet, unobtrusive academician, a venerable figure wrapped in his thoughts.

PIERRE-SIMON LAPLACE

(b. March 23, 1749, Beaumount-en-Auge, Normandy, France—d. March 5, 1827, Paris)

Pierre-Simon Laplace is best known for his investigations into the stability of the solar system.

Laplace successfully accounted for all the observed deviations of the planets from their theoretical orbits by applying Sir Isaac Newton's theory of gravitation to the solar system, and he developed a conceptual view of evolutionary change in the structure of the solar system. He also demonstrated the usefulness of probability for interpreting scientific data.

Probably because he did not hold strong political views and was not a member of the aristocracy, he escaped imprisonment and execution during the French Revolution. Laplace was president of the Board of Longitude, aided in the organization of the metric system, helped found the scientific Society of Arcueil, and was created a marquis. He served for six weeks as minister of the interior under Napoleon, who famously reminisced that Laplace "carried the spirit of the infinitesimal into administration."

PIERRE MECHAIN

(b. Aug. 16, 1744, Laon, France—d. Sept. 20, 1804, Castellón de la Plana, Spain)

Pierre Mechain, with Jean Delambre, measured the meridian arc from Dunkirk, France, to Barcelona, Spain. The measurement was made between 1792 and 1798 to establish a basis for the unit of length in the metric system called for by the French national legislature. Mechain also discovered 11 comets and calculated the orbits of these and other known comets.

Born the son of a master ceiling plasterer, Mechain early in life showed mathematical prowess and worked as a hydrographer for the Naval Map Archives at Versailles during the 1770s. He turned to astronomy, and in 1782 his work with comets won him admission to the Académie Royale des Sciences. In addition, Mechain discovered numerous nebulae that were later incorporated by Charles Messier into his famous catalog of clusters and nebulae.

JESSE RAMSDEN

(b. Oct. 6, 1735, Halifax, Yorkshire, Eng.—d. Nov. 5, 1800, Brighton, Sussex)

Jesse Ramsden was a pioneer in the design of precision tools.

Ramsden was apprenticed as a boy to a cloth worker, but in 1758 he apprenticed himself to a mathematical instrument maker. He went into business for himself in London in 1762. He designed dividing engines of great accuracy for both circles and straight lines and produced highly accurate sextants, theodolites, and vertical circles for astronomical observatories. He also built barometers, manometers, assay balances, and other instruments. He was elected to the Royal Society in 1786 and awarded the Copley Medal in 1795.

CHAPTER 6
MEASUREMENT TERMS AND CONCEPTS

There are many reasons why it is important to measure everything from liquids to light to land. Accurate measurements can help to make trades fair, help scientists quantify their work, and ensure that recipes can come out correctly. Brief descriptions of some important or historical measurement terms and concepts are included here.

ACRE

The acre is a unit of land measurement in the British Imperial and U.S. Customary systems, equal to 43,560 square feet, or 160 square rods. One acre is equivalent to 0.4047 hectares (4,047 square metres). Derived from Middle English *aker* (from Old English *aecer*) and akin to Latin *ager* ("field"), the acre had one origin in the typical area that could be plowed in one day with a yoke of oxen pulling a wooden plow. The Anglo-Saxon acre was defined as a strip of land 1 × $^1/_{10}$ furlong, or 40 × 4 rods (660 × 66 feet). One acre gradually came to denote a piece of land of any shape measuring the present 4,840 square yards. Larger and smaller variant acres, ranging from 0.19 to 0.911 hectares, were once employed throughout the British Isles.

AMPHORA

The amphora is an ancient Roman unit of capacity for grain and liquid products equal to 48 *sextarii* and equivalent to about 27.84 litres (7.36 U.S. gallons). The term *amphora* was borrowed from the Greeks, who used it to

A Roman amphora. An amphora was both a type of vessel and a measurement. Vincenzo Pinto/ AFP/Getty Images

designate a measure équal to about 34 litres (9 U.S. gallons).

ANGSTROM (Å)

The angstrom, a unit of length used chiefly in measuring wavelengths of light, is equal to 10^{-10} metre, or 0.1 nanometer. It is named for the 19th-century Swedish physicist Anders Jonas Ångström. The angstrom and multiples of it, the micron (10^4 Å) and the millimicron (10 Å), are also used to measure such quantities as molecular diameters and the thickness of films on liquids.

APOTHECARIES' WEIGHT

Apothecaries' weight is a traditional system of weight in the British Isles used for the measuring and dispensing of pharmaceutical items and based on the grain, scruple (20 grains), dram (3 scruples), ounce (8 drams), and pound (12 ounces). The apothecaries' grain is equal to the troy and avoirdupois grains and represents $1/5,760$ part of the troy and apothecaries' pound and $1/7,000$ part of the avoirdupois pound. One apothecaries' pound equals approximately 0.82 avoirdupois pound, 373.24 grams, and 0.37 kilogram.

Apothecaries' weight was used officially in both the United States and Great Britain until 1858. In that year,

Old pharmaceutical canisters. Shutterstock.com

under the authority of the Medical Act, Great Britain adopted the avoirdupois system for dispensing medicines. Apothecaries' weight is still common in the United States. In recent years, however, the metric system has gradually replaced it for dispensing medicines.

ARE

The are is a basic unit of area in the metric system, equal to 100 square metres and the equivalent of 0.0247 acre. Its multiple, the hectare (equal to 100 ares), is the principal unit of land measurement for most of the world.

AVOIRDUPOIS WEIGHT

Avoirdupois weight is a traditional system of weight in the British Imperial System and the U.S. Customary System of weights and measures. The name derives ultimately from French *avoir de pois* ("goods of weight" or "property").

The avoirdupois pound contains 7,000 grains, or 256 drams of 27.344 grains each, or 16 ounces of 437 ½ grains each. It is used for all products not subject to apothecaries' weight (for pharmaceutical items) or troy weight (for precious metals). It is equal to about 1.22 apothecaries' or troy pounds. Since 1959 the avoirdupois pound has been officially defined in most English-speaking countries as 0.45359237 kg.

BARREL

The barrel is a unit of both liquid and dry measure in the British Imperial and U.S. Customary systems, ranging from 31.5 to 42 gallons for liquids and fixed at 7,056 cubic inches (105 dry quarts, or 115.63 litres) for most fruits, vegetables, and other dry commodities. The cranberry barrel, however, measures 5,826 cubic inches. In liquid measure, the wine barrel of 126 quarts (31.5 gallons, or 119.24 litres) and the ale and beer barrel of 144 quarts (36 gallons, or 136.27 litres) probably were defined by the traditional size of the actual wooden barrels used in these trades. In the United States a 40-gallon barrel for proof spirits has been legally recognized, and federal taxes on fermented liquors are calculated on a barrel of 31 gallons. A petroleum barrel of 42 gallons may have become standard in the American Southwest because casks of this capacity were readily available. Dry-weight barrels include the barrel of 200 pounds for fish, beef, and pork and that of 376 pounds for cement, among others.

BAT

The bat (baht or bath), also called an ephah, is an ancient Hebrew unit of liquid and dry capacity. Estimated at 37 litres (about 6.5 gallons) and approximately equivalent to the Greek *metre-te-s*, the bat contained 10 *omers*, 1 *omer* being the quantity (based on tradition) of manna allotted to each Israelite for every day of the 40-year sojourn in the desert recorded in the Bible.

BRITISH IMPERIAL SYSTEM

The British Imperial System is a traditional system of weights and measures used officially in Great Britain from 1824 until the adoption of the metric system beginning in 1965. The U.S. Customary System of weights and measures is derived from it. British Imperial units are now legally defined in metric terms.

The British Imperial System evolved from the thousands of Roman, Celtic, Anglo-Saxon, and customary local units employed in the Middle Ages. Traditional names such as pound, foot, and gallon were widely used, but the values so designated varied with time, place, trade, product specifications, and dozens of other requirements. Early royal standards established to enforce uniformity took the name Winchester, after the ancient capital of Britain, where the 10th-century Saxon king Edgar the Peaceable kept a royal bushel measure and quite possibly others. Fourteenth-century statutes recorded a yard (perhaps based originally on a rod or stick) of 3 feet, each foot containing 12 inches, each inch equaling the length of three barleycorns (employed merely as a learning device since the actual standard was the space between two marks on a yard bar). Units of capacity and weight were also specified. In the late 15th century, King Henry VII reaffirmed the customary Winchester standards for capacity and length and distributed royal standards (physical embodiments of the approved units) throughout the realm. This process was repeated about a century later in the reign of Queen Elizabeth I. In the 16th century the rod (5.5 yards, or 16.5 feet) was defined (once again as a learning device and not as a standard) as the length of the left feet of 16 men lined up heel to toe as they emerged from church. By the 17th century usage and statute had established the acre, rod, and furlong at their present values (4,840 square yards, 16.5 feet, and 660 feet, respectively), together with other historic units. The several trade pounds in common use were reduced to just two: the troy pound, primarily for precious metals, and the pound avoirdupois, for other goods sold by weight.

The Weights and Measures Act of 1824 and the Act of 1878 established the British Imperial System on the basis of precise definitions of selected existing units. The 1824 act sanctioned a single imperial gallon to replace the wine, ale, and corn (wheat) gallons then in general use. The new gallon was defined as equal in volume to 10 pounds avoirdupois of distilled water weighed at 62 °F with the barometer at 30 inches, or 277.274 cubic inches (later corrected to 277.421 cubic inches). The two new basic standard units were the imperial standard yard and the troy pound, which was later restricted to weighing drugs, precious metals, and jewels. A 1963 act abolished such archaic measures as the rod and chaldron (a measure of coal equal to 36 bushels) and redefined the standard yard and pound as 0.9144 metres and 0.45359237 kg respectively. The gallon now equals the space occupied by 10 pounds of distilled water of density 0.998859 gram per millilitre weighed in air of density 0.001217 gram per millilitre against weights of density 8.136 grams per millilitre.

While the British were reforming their weights and measures in the 19th century, the Americans were just adopting units based on those discarded by the act of 1824. The standard U.S. gallon is based on the Queen Anne wine gallon of 231 cubic inches and is about 17 percent smaller than the British imperial gallon. The U.S. bushel of 2,150.42

cubic inches, derived from the Winchester bushel abandoned in Britain, is approximately 3 percent smaller than the British imperial bushel. In the British system, units of dry and liquid capacity are the same, while in the United States they differ; the liquid and dry pint in Britain both equal 0.568 cubic decimetre, while the U.S. liquid pint is 0.473 cubic decimetre, and the U.S. dry pint is 0.551 cubic decimetre. British and American units of linear measure and weight are essentially the same. Notable exceptions are the British stone of 14 pounds, which is not used in the United States, and a divergence in definition of the hundredweight (100 pounds in the United States, 112 in Britain) that yields two different tons, the short U.S. ton of 2,000 pounds and the long British ton of 2,240 pounds. In 1959 major English-speaking nations adopted common metric definitions of the inch (2.54 cm), the yard (0.9144 metres), and the pound (0.4536 kg).

BUSHEL

The bushel is a unit of capacity in the British Imperial and the U.S. Customary systems of measurement. In the British system the units of liquid and dry capacity are the same, and since 1824 a bushel has been defined as 8 imperial gallons, or 2,219.36 cubic inches (36,375.31 cubic cm). In the United States the bushel is used only for dry measure. The U.S. level bushel (or struck bushel) is equal to 2,150.42 cubic inches (35,245.38 cubic cm) and is considered the equivalent of the Winchester bushel, a measure used in England from the 15th century until 1824. A U.S. level bushel is made up of 4 pecks, or 32 dry quarts. Two bushels make up a unit called a strike. In 1912 the U.S. Court of Customs defined a "heaped bushel" for measuring quantities of apples as 2,747.715 cubic inches (45,035.04 cubic cm). In the British Isles various cubic capacities and

Bushels of apples. Shutterstock.com

weights for the bushel have existed since the 13th century depending on the product to be sold or transported. It derived ultimately from the Old French *boissel*, from *boisse*, a measure of grain.

CENTIMETRE (CM)

The centimetre is a unit of length equal to 0.01 metre in the metric system and the equivalent of 0.3937 inch.

CORD

The cord is a unit of volume for measuring stacked firewood. A cord is generally equivalent to a stack $4 \times 4 \times 8$ feet (128 cubic feet), and its principal subdivision is the cord foot, which measures $4 \times 4 \times 1$ feet. A standard cord consists of sticks or pieces 4 feet long stacked in a 4×8-foot rick. A short cord is a 4×8-foot rick of pieces shorter than 4 feet, and a long cord is a similar rick of pieces longer than 4 feet. A face cord is a 4×8-foot stack of pieces 1 foot long. The cord was originally devised in order to measure firewood and was so named because a line, string, or cord was used to tie the wood into a bundle.

The useful amount of wood a cord actually contains varies greatly, depending upon such factors as the type of wood, the size and straightness of the pieces, and the amount of bark present. A tree with a usable height of 40 feet and a circumference of 6.25 feet will contain about one cord of wood.

CUBIT

The cubit is a unit of linear measure used by many ancient and medieval peoples. It may have originated in Egypt about 3000 BCE; it thereafter became ubiquitous in the ancient world. The cubit, generally taken as equal to 18 inches (457 mm), was based on the length of the arm from the elbow to the tip of the middle finger and was considered the equivalent of 6 palms or 2 spans. In some ancient cultures it was as long as 21 inches (531 mm).

CUP

The cup is a unit of volume in the British Imperial and U.S. Customary systems of measurement. The U.S. liquid cup is equal to 14 $7/16$ cubic inches, or 236.59 cubic cm; the more rarely used U.S. dry cup is equal to 1.164 liquid cups. In Great Britain a single cup is used for both types of measurement, equal to 1.201 U.S. liquid cups (284.14 cubic cm). In either system a cup contains two gills, and two cups are contained in a pint.

DRAM

The dram is a unit of weight in the apothecaries' and avoirdupois systems. An apothecaries' dram contains 3 scruples

(3.888 grams) of 20 grains each and is equal to one-eighth apothecaries' ounce of 480 grains. The avoirdupois dram contains 27.344 grains (1.772 grams) and is equal to one-sixteenth avoirdupois ounce of 437 $^1/_2$ grains. The term also refers to the fluid dram, a measure of capacity equal to 1/8 fluid ounce.

In England *dram* came to mean a small draught of cordial or alcohol; hence the term *dram-house* for the taverns where one could purchase a dram. *Dram* is ultimately derived from the Greek drachma, designating an ancient coin and weight that probably originated as the amount one could hold in one's hands. The use of the dram as a measuring unit has largely been superseded by metric measures.

FATHOM

The fathom is an old English measure of length, now standardized at 6 feet (1.83 metre), which has long been used as a nautical unit of depth. The longest of many units derived from an anatomical measurement, the fathom originated as the distance from the middle fingertip of one hand to the middle fingertip of the other hand of a large man holding his arms fully extended. The name comes from the Old English *faedm* or *faethm*, meaning outstretched arms.

FINGER

The finger is an ancient and medieval measure of $^1/_8$ yard, or 4 $^1/_2$ inches (11.4 cm), used primarily to measure lengths of cloth. The finger derives ultimately from the *digitus*, the smallest of the basic Roman linear measures. From the *digitus* came the English nail, which equaled $^3/_4$ inch, or $^1/_{16}$ foot. The nail also came to mean the 16th part of a yard—2 $^1/_4$ inches—as well as the 16th part of other measures. The one-nail length was also defined as the half finger, the length from the tip of the middle finger to the centre of the second joint from the tip. Thus, the finger became double the nail, or the length of the whole finger, tip to knuckle.

Leonardo da Vinci employed a "finger" measurement, but his was actually a finger's breadth (0.75 inch). Four of da Vinci's finger units equaled a palm, and six palms equaled a cubit.

FOOT

The foot (plural: feet) includes any of numerous ancient, medieval, and modern linear measures (commonly 25 to 34 cm) based on the length of the human foot and used exclusively in English-speaking countries, where it generally consists of 12 inches or 1/3 yard. In most countries and in all scientific applications, the foot, with its multiples and subdivisions, has been superseded by the metre, the basic linear unit in the metric system. In the United States the definition of the foot as exactly 30.48 cm took effect in 1959.

FURLONG

The furlong is an old English unit of length, based on the length of an average plowed furrow (hence "furrow-long," or furlong) in the English open- or common-field system. Each furrow ran the length of a 40 × 4-rod acre, or 660 modern feet. The standardization of such linear units as the yard, foot, and inch—begun by government enactment sometime between 1266 and 1303—recognized the traditional sizes of rods, furlongs, and acres as fixed and therefore simply redefined them in terms of the newly standardized units. Thus, the furlong, often measured as 625 northern

(German) feet, became 660 standard English feet, and the mile, always 8 furlongs, became 5,280 feet. Today, the furlong is used almost exclusively in horse racing.

GAL

The gal is a unit of acceleration, named in honour of the Italian physicist and astronomer Galileo Galilei (1564–1642) and used especially in measurements of gravity. One gal equals a change in rate of motion of one centimetre (0.3937 inch) per second per second.

GILL

The gill, also spelled jill, is a unit of volume in the British Imperial and U.S. Customary systems. It is used almost exclusively for the measurement of liquids. Although its capacity has varied with time and location, in the United States it is defined as half a cup, or four U.S. fluid ounces, which equals 7.219 cubic inches, or 118.29 cubic cm; in Great Britain the gill is 5 British fluid ounces, which equals 8.669 cubic inches, 1/4 pint, or 142.07 cubic cm.

The gill was introduced in the 14th century to measure individual servings of whiskey or wine. The term *jill* appears in the nursery rhyme "Jack and Jill." Soon after ascending to the throne of England in 1625, King Charles I scaled down the jack or jackpot (sometimes known as a double jigger) in order to collect higher sales taxes. The jill, by definition twice the size of the jack, was automatically reduced also and "came tumbling after."

GRAIN

The grain is a unit of weight equal to 0.065 gram, or $1/7,000$ pound avoirdupois. One of the earliest units of common measure and the smallest, it is a uniform unit in the avoirdupois, apothecaries', and troy systems. The ancient grain, varying from one culture to the next, was defined as the weight of a designated number of dry wheat (or other edible grain) kernels taken from the middle of the ear. It was also used as the original basis for the medieval English inch, which was defined for instructional purposes as the length of 3 medium-sized barleycorns placed end to end (about 2.54 cm). The Sumerian shekel equaled the weight of 180 wheat grains; the British silver penny sterling was set at the weight of 32 wheat grains. The metric grain of 50 mg is used to weigh precious stones.

GRAM (GM OR G)

The gram is a unit of mass or weight that is used especially in the centimetre-gram-second system of measurement. One gram is equal to 0.001 kg. The gram is very nearly equal (it was originally intended to be equal) to the mass of one cubic centimetre of pure water at 4 °C (39.2 °F), the temperature at which water reaches its maximum density under normal terrestrial pressures. The gram of force is equal to the weight of a gram of mass under standard gravity. For greater precision, the mass may be weighed at a point at which the acceleration due to gravity is 980.655 cm/sec^2.

GUNTER'S CHAIN

Gunter's chain, also called a surveyor's chain, is a measuring device and arbitrary measurement unit still widely used for surveying in English-speaking countries. Invented by the English mathematician Edmund Gunter in the early 17th century, Gunter's chain is exactly 22 yards (about 20 m) long and divided into 100 links. In the device, each link is a solid bar. Measurement of the public land systems of the United States and Canada is based on Gunter's chain. An area of 10 square chains is equal to one acre.

HAND

The hand is an ancient unit of length, now standardized at 4 inches (10.16 cm) and used today primarily for measuring the height of horses from the ground to the withers (top of the shoulders). The unit was originally defined as the breadth of the palm including the thumb. A statute of King Henry VIII of England established the hand at 4 inches. Units of various lengths were used by the ancient Egyptians, Hebrews, Greeks, Romans, and others.

HECTARE

The hectare is a unit of area in the metric system equal to 100 ares, or 10,000 square metres, and the equivalent of 2.471 acres in the British Imperial System and the United States Customary measure. The term is derived from the Latin *area* and from *hect*, an irregular contraction of the Greek word for hundred. Although the are is the primary metric unit of land measurement, in practice the hectare is more commonly used. The hectare is, by subsequent definition, equal to a *djerib* in Turkey, a *jerib* in Iran, a *gong qing* in mainland China, a *manzana* in Argentina, and a *bunder* in The Netherlands.

INCH

The inch is a unit of British Imperial and U.S. Customary measure equal to $^1/_{36}$ of a yard. The unit derives from the Old English *ince*, or *ynce*, which in turn came from the Latin unit *uncia*, which was "one-twelfth" of a Roman foot, or *pes*. (The Latin word *uncia* was the source of the name of another English unit, the ounce.) The old English *ynce* was defined by King David I of Scotland about 1150 as the breadth of a man's thumb at the base of the nail. To help maintain consistency of the unit, the measure was usually achieved by adding the thumb breadth of three men—one small, one medium, and

David I, King of Scotland. Hulton Archive/Getty Images

one large—and then dividing the figure by three. During the reign of King Edward II, in the early 14th century, the inch was defined as "three grains of barley, dry and round, placed end to end lengthwise." At various times the inch has also been defined as the combined lengths of 12 poppyseeds. Since 1959 the inch has been defined officially as 2.54 cm.

INTERNATIONAL BUREAU OF WEIGHTS AND MEASURES

The International Bureau of Weights and Measures (French: *Bureau International des Poids et Mesures*, or BIPM) is an international organization founded to bring about the unification of measurement systems, to establish and preserve fundamental international standards and prototypes, to verify national standards, and to determine fundamental physical constants. The bureau was established by a convention signed in Paris on May 20, 1875, effective January 1876. In 1921 a modified convention was signed.

The convention provides for a General Conference that meets every four years to consider required improvements or modifications in standards. An International Committee of Weights and Measures, composed of 18 scientists elected by the conference, meets annually to monitor worldwide uniformity in units of measure. The bureau headquarters at Sèvres, France, serves as a depository for the primary international standards and as a laboratory for certification and comparison of national standard copies.

INTERNATIONAL SYSTEM OF UNITS

The International System of Units (French: Système Internationale d'Unités, or SI) is an international decimal system of weights and measures derived from and extending the metric system of units. Adopted by the 11th General Conference on Weights and Measures in 1960, it is abbreviated SI in all languages.

Rapid advances in science and technology in the 19th and 20th centuries fostered the development of several overlapping systems of units of measurements as scientists improvised to meet the practical needs of their disciplines. The early international system devised to rectify this situation was called the metre-kilogram-second (MKS) system. The General Conference on Weights and Measures added three new units (among others) in 1948: a unit of force (the newton), defined as that force which gives to a mass of one kilogram an acceleration of one metre per second per second; a unit of energy (the joule), defined as the work done when the point of application of a newton is displaced one metre in the direction of the force; and a unit of power (the watt), which is the power that in one second gives rise to energy of one joule. All three units are named for eminent scientists.

The 1960 International System builds on the MKS system. Its seven basic units, from which other units are derived, are currently defined as follows: for length, the metre, defined as the distance traveled by light in a vacuum in $^1/_{299,792,458}$ second; for mass, the kilogram, which equals 1,000 grams as defined by the international prototype kilogram of platinum-iridium in the keeping of the International Bureau of Weights and Measures in Sèvres, France; for time, the second, the duration of 9,192,631,770 periods of radiation associated with a specified transition of the cesium-133 atom; for electric current, the ampere, which is the current that, if maintained in two wires placed one metre apart in a vacuum, would produce a force of 2×10^{-7} newton per metre of length; for luminous intensity, the candela, defined as the intensity in a given direction of a source emitting radiation of frequency 540×10^{12} hertz and that has a radiant intensity in that direction of $^7/_{16}$ watt per steradian; for amount of substance, the mole, defined as containing as many elementary entities of a substance as there are atoms in 0.012 kg of carbon-12; and for thermo-dynamic temperature, the kelvin.

INTERNATIONAL UNIT (IU)

The international unit, as used in pharmacology, is a quantity of a substance, such as a vitamin, hormone, or toxin, that produces a specified effect when tested according to an internationally accepted biological procedure. For certain substances, the IU has been identified with a weight of a particular purified form of the material; for example, one gram of vitamin A acetate contains 2.904×10^6 IU.

KILOMETRE (KM)

The kilometre is a unit of length equal to 1,000 metres and the equivalent of 0.6214 mile.

Four speedometers (top left, top right, bottom left, bottom centre), *showing various readings of velocity in miles per hour and kilometres per hour.* Shutterstock.com

KNOT

The knot is a measure of speed at sea, equal to one nautical mile per hour (approximately 1.15 statute miles per hour). Thus, a ship moving at 20 knots is traveling as fast as a land vehicle at about 23 mph (37 km/hr). The term *knot* derives from its former use as a length measure on ships' log lines, which were used to measure the speed of a ship through the water. Such a line was marked off at intervals by knots tied in the rope. Each interval, or knot, was about 47 feet (14.3 metres) long. When the log was tossed overboard, it remained more or less stationary while its attached log line trailed out from the vessel as the latter moved forward. After 28 seconds had elapsed, the number of knots that had passed overboard was counted. The number of knots that ran out in 28 seconds was roughly the speed of the ship in nautical miles per hour.

LEAGUE

A league is any of several European units of measurement ranging from 2.4 to 4.6 statute miles (3.9 to 7.4 km). In English-speaking countries the land league is generally accepted as 3 statute miles (4.83 km), although varying lengths from 7,500 feet to 15,000 feet (2.29 to 4.57 km) were sometimes employed. An ancient unit derived from the Gauls and introduced into England by the Normans, the league was estimated by the Romans to be equal to 1,500 paces — a pace, or *passus*, in Roman measure being nearly 5 feet (1.5 metres).

Land leagues of about 2.63 miles (4.23 km) were used by the Spanish in early surveys of parts of the American Southwest. At one time the term was also used as a unit of area measurement. Old California surveys show square leagues equal to 4,439 acres (1,796 hectares). In the late 18th century the league also came to refer to the distance a cannon shot could be fired at menacing ships offshore. This resulted in the 3-mile offshore territorial limit.

LIBRA

The libra was the basic Roman unit of weight; after 268 BCE it was about 5,076 English grains or equal to 0.722

pounds avoirdupois (0.329 kg). This pound was brought to Britain and other provinces where it became the standard for weighing gold and silver and for use in all commercial transactions. The abbreviation *lb* for pound is derived from libra. One-twelfth of the libra, the Roman uncia, is the ancestor of the English ounce.

The libra is one of the nonmetric units of weight still used in Spain, Portugal, and several Spanish-speaking countries of the Americas. Most of the New World libras weigh about the same as the U.S. avoirdupois pound.

LITRE (L)

The litre is a unit of volume in the metric system, equal to one cubic decimetre (0.001 cubic metre). From 1901 to 1964 the litre was defined as the volume of 1 kilogram of pure water at 4 °C (39.2 °F) and standard atmospheric pressure; in 1964 the original, present value was reinstated. One litre is equivalent to approximately 1.0567 U.S. quart.

Bottles of milk around the world, such as this bottle from the Netherlands, are often sold in units of litres. Patrik Stollarz/Getty Images

LOG

The log, also called a maritime log, is an instrument for measuring the speed of a ship through water. The first practical log, developed about 1600, consisted of a pie-shaped log chip with a lead weight on its curved edge that caused it to float upright and resist towing. When the log was tossed overboard, it remained more or less stationary while an attached line (marked off with equally spaced knots) was let out behind the vessel for a measured interval of time (measured with a sandglass). The line and log were then hauled aboard and the speed of the ship determined by dividing the length of the line by the time interval.

In the 19th century the log chip was replaced by a towed rotor or propeller connected by a line to automatic speed- and distance-measuring equipment. Two logs in use today are the pitometre log and the electronic log. The pitometre uses a pitot tube projecting through the bottom of the ship. The tube has one forward facing and two side facing orifices. When the ship is moving, pressure in the forward-facing tube exceeds the pressure in the side tubes; this differential is transmitted to equipment that translates it into a speed measurement. In the electronic log, which also protrudes through the bottom of the ship, a water-driven rotor turns a small electric generator, the current from which is proportional to the speed of the ship. This current is similarly used to produce a speed measurement.

METRE

The metre is the fundamental unit of length in the metric system and in the International System of Units (SI). It is equal to approximately 39.37 inches in the British Imperial and U.S. Customary systems. The metre was historically defined by the French Academy of Sciences in 1791 as $^1/_{10,000,000}$ of the quadrant of the Earth's circumference running from the North Pole through Paris to the equator. The International Bureau of Weights and Measures in 1889 established the international prototype metre as the distance between two lines on a standard bar of 90 percent platinum and 10 percent iridium. By 1960 advances in the techniques of measuring light waves had made it possible to establish an accurate and easily reproducible standard independent of any physical artifact. In 1960 the metre was thus defined in the SI system as equal to 1,650,763.73 wavelengths of the orange-red line in the spectrum of the krypton-86 atom in a vacuum.

By the 1980s, advances in laser measurement techniques had yielded values for the speed of light in a vacuum of an unprecedented accuracy, and it was decided in 1983 by the General Conference on Weights and Measures that the accepted value for this constant would be exactly 299,792,458 metres per second. The metre is now thus defined as the distance traveled by light in a vacuum in $^1/_{299,792,458}$ of a second.

METRĒTĒS

Metrētēs was the primary liquid measure of the ancient Greeks, equivalent to 39.4 litres, or about 9 gallons. In the Greek system, of which the smallest capacity unit was the *kotyle* (16.5 cubic inches; 0.475 pint; 270 cubic cm), the *metrētēs* equaled 144 *kotyle*, or 12 *khous*, or 2 *xestes*. Reconstructed earthenware cylinders excavated in the Acropolis in Athens furnish the oldest known evidence of the Greek system of liquid measurement.

METRIC SYSTEM

The metric system is an international decimal system of weights and measures, based on the metre for length and the kilogram for mass, that was adopted in France in 1795 and is now used officially in almost all countries.

The French Revolution of 1789 provided an opportunity to pursue the frequently discussed idea of replacing the confusing welter of thousands of traditional units of measure with a rational system based on multiples of 10. In 1791 the French National Assembly directed the French Academy of Sciences to address the chaotic state of French weights and measures. It was decided that the new system would be based on a natural physical unit to ensure immutability. The academy settled on the length of $^{1}/_{10,000,000}$ of a quadrant of a great circle of the Earth, measured around the poles of the meridian passing through Paris. An arduous six-year survey led by such luminaries as Jean Delambre, Jacques-Dominique Cassini, Pierre Mechain, Adrien-Marie Legendre, and others to determine the arc of the meridian from Barcelona, Spain, to Dunkirk, France, eventually yielded a value of 39.37008 inches for the new unit to be called the metre, from Greek *metron*, meaning "measure."

By 1795 all metric units were derived from the metre, including the gram for weight (one cubic centimetre of water at its maximum density) and the litre for capacity ($^{1}/_{1,000}$ of a cubic metre). Greek prefixes were established for multiples of 10, *myria* (10,000), *kilo* (1,000), *hecto* (100), and *deca* (10), while Latin prefixes were selected for the submultiples, *milli* (0.001), *centi* (0.01), and *deci* (0.1). Thus, a kilogram equals 1,000 grams, a millimetre $^{1}/_{1,000}$ of a metre. In 1799 the Metre and Kilogram of the Archives, platinum embodiments of the new units, were declared the legal standards for all measurements in France, and the motto of the metric system expressed the hope that the new units would be "for all people, for all time." Not until 1875 did an international conference meet in Paris to establish an International Bureau of Weights and Measures. The Treaty of the Metre signed there provided for a permanent laboratory in Sèvres, near Paris, where international standards are kept, national standard copies inspected, and metrological research conducted. The General Conference of Weights and Measures, with diplomatic representatives of some 40 countries, meets every six years to consider reform. The conference selects 18 scientists who form the International Committee of Weights and Measures that governs the bureau.

For a time, the international prototype metre and kilogram were based, for convenience, on the archive standards rather than directly on actual measurement of the Earth. Definition by natural constants was readopted in 1960, when the metre was redefined as 1,650,763.73 wavelengths of the orange-red line in the krypton-86 spectrum, and again in 1983, when it was redefined as the distance traveled by light in a vacuum in $1/299,792,458$ second. The kilogram is still defined as the mass of the international prototype at Sèvres.

In the 20th century the metric system generated derived systems needed in science and technology to express physical properties more complicated than simple length, weight, and volume. The centimetre-gram-second (CGS) and the metre-kilogram-second (MKS) systems were the chief systems so used until the establishment of the International System of Units.

MICROMETRE

The micrometre, also called a micron, is a metric unit of measure for length equal to 0.001 mm, or about 0.000039 inch. Its symbol is μm. The micrometre is commonly employed to measure the thickness or diameter of microscopic objects, such as microorganisms and colloidal particles. Minute distances, as, for example, the wavelengths of infrared radiation, are also given in micrometres.

MILE

The mile includes any of various units of distance, such as the statute mile of 5,280 feet (1.609 km). It originated from the Roman *mille passus*, or "thousand paces," which measured 5,000 Roman feet.

About the year 1500 the "old London" mile was defined as eight furlongs. At that time the furlong, measured by a larger northern (German) foot, was 625 feet, and thus the mile equaled 5,000 feet. During the reign of Queen Elizabeth I, the mile gained an additional 280 feet—to 5,280—under a statute of 1593 that confirmed the use of a shorter foot that made the length of the furlong 660 feet.

Elsewhere in the British Isles, longer miles were used, including the Irish mile of 6,720 feet (2.048 km) and the Scottish mile of 5,952 English feet (1.814 km).

A nautical mile was originally defined as the length on the Earth's surface of one minute ($1/60$ of a degree) of arc along a meridian (north-south line of longitude). Because of a slight flattening of the Earth in polar latitudes, however, the measurement of a nautical mile increases slightly toward the poles. For many years the British nautical mile, or admiralty mile, was set at 6,080 feet (1.85318 km), while the U.S. nautical mile was set at 6,080.20 feet (1.85324 km). In 1929 the nautical mile was redefined as exactly 1.852 km (about 6,076.11549 feet or 1.1508 statute miles) at an international conference held in Monaco, although the United States did not change over to the new international nautical mile until 1954. The measure remains in universal use in both marine and air transportation. The knot is one nautical mile per hour.

MILLIMETRE (MM)

The millimetre is a unit of length equal to 0.001 metre in the metric system and the equivalent of 0.03937 inch.

MINA

The mina is the earliest of all known units of weight, created by the Babylonians and used by the Hittites, Phoenicians, Assyrians, Egyptians, Hebrews, and Greeks. Its weight and relationship to its major subdivisions varied at different times and places in the ancient world. In one surviving form, from the Babylonian period, the mina weighs about 640 grams, while in another it weighs 978 grams.

The mina, or minah, was a basic standard of weight among the ancient Hebrews. In the sacred system of weights, the sacred mina was equal to 60 shekels, and 50 sacred minas equaled one sacred talent. In the Talmudist system, one Talmudist mina equaled 25 shekels, and 60 Talmudist minas equaled one Talmudist talent. The Hebrew sacred mina has been estimated at 499 grams. The Greek, or Attic, mina, equal to 100 drachmas, has been estimated at 431 grams.

MOU

The *mou* is a Chinese unit of land measurement that varies with location but is commonly 806.65 square yards (0.165 acre, or 666.5 square metres). Based on the *chi*, a unit of length after 1860 measuring 14.1 inches, the *mou* has been defined by customs treaty as 920.417 square yards. In ancient China, where units of measure displayed great regional and functional variety, the *mou* ranged from $^1/_{30}$ to $^1/_8$ hectare (333.333 to 1,250 square metres).

OUNCE

The ounce is a unit of weight in the avoirdupois system, equal to $^1/_{16}$ pound (437 $^1/_2$ grains), and in the troy and apothecaries' systems, equal to 480 grains, or $^1/_{12}$ pound. The avoirdupois ounce is equal to 28.35 grams and the troy and apothecaries' ounce to 31.103 grams. As a unit of volume, the fluid ounce is equal to $^1/_{16}$ of a pint, or 29.57 millilitres, in the U.S. Customary System and to $^1/_{20}$ of a pint, or 28.41 millilitres, in the British Imperial System. As a unit of weight, the ounce derives from the Roman *uncia* (meaning "twelfth part"), which was $^1/_{12}$ of a Roman foot or ounce. The standard or physical embodiment of the Roman foot, a copper bar, constituted the Roman pound standard and was divided along its length into 12 equal parts, called *unciae*. Thus, *uncia* designated both a unit of weight and one of length and is the source of the modern terms "inch" and "ounce."

PECK

The peck is a unit of capacity in the U.S. Customary and the British Imperial Systems of measurement. In the United States the peck is used only for dry measure and is equal to 8 dry quarts, or 537.6 cubic inches (8.810 litres). In Great Britain the peck may be used for either liquid or dry measure and is equal to 8 imperial quarts (2 imperial gallons), or 1/4 imperial bushel, or 554.84 cubic inches (9.092 litres). The peck has been in use since the early 14th century, when it was introduced as a measure for flour. The term referred to varying quantities, however, until the modern units were defined in the 19th century.

PINT

The pint is a unit of capacity in the British Imperial and U.S. Customary systems of measurement. In the British system the units for dry measure and liquid measure are identical; the single British pint is equal to 34.68 cubic inches (568.26 cubic cm) or one-eighth gallon. In the United States the unit for dry measure is slightly different from that for liquid measure; a U.S. dry pint is 33.6 cubic inches (550.6 cubic cm), while a U.S. liquid pint is 28.9 cubic inches (473.2 cubic cm). In each system, two cups make a pint, and two pints equal a quart.

A U.S. liquid pint holds 1.042 pounds of water at room temperature, a fact that gave rise to the saying "a pint's a pound the world around." The pint has been a common unit of measure in Great Britain since the 14th century. The actual volume of the pint, however, has varied considerably over the years; in the medieval and early modern British Isles it varied from 0.446 to 1.887 litres.

POUND

The pound is a unit of avoirdupois weight, equal to 16 ounces, 7,000 grains, or 0.4536 kg, and of troy and apothecaries' weight, equal to 12 ounces, 5,760 grains, or 0.37 kg. The Roman ancestor of the modern pound, the libra, is the source of the abbreviation *lb*. In medieval England several derivations of the libra vied for general acceptance. Among the earliest of these, the Tower pound, so called because its standard was kept in the Royal Mint in the Tower of London, was applied to precious metals and drugs and contained 5,400 grains, or 0.350 kg, while the mercantile pound contained 6,750 grains, or 0.437 kg. The troy pound, believed to have originated in Troyes, France, superseded the lighter Tower pound in 1527 as the gold and silver standard. Increased trade with France led also to the adoption of the 16-ounce avoirdupois pound in the 16th century to replace the mercantile pound.

The British monetary pound is historically linked with the minting of

Scales in supermarkets frequently give weight measurements in terms of pounds and ounces.
© www.istockphoto.com/Michael Krinke

silver coins (sterlings) from the Tower pound. Large payments were reckoned in "pounds of sterlings," later shortened to "pounds sterling."

QA

The *qa*, also spelled *qû* or *ka*, was an ancient Babylonian liquid measure equal to the volume of a cube whose dimensions are each one handbreadth (3.9 to 4 inches, or 9.9 to 10.2 cm) in length. The cube held one great mina (about 2 pounds, or 1 kg) of water by weight. Five *qa* made up a *šiqlu*, 100 *qa* equaled an *imēru* (donkey load), and 300 *qa* equaled a *gur*. The gur was the equivalent of about 80 U.S. gallons (302 litres).

QUART

The quart is a unit of capacity in the British Imperial and U.S. Customary systems of measurement. For both liquid and dry measure, the British system uses 1 standard quart, which is equal to 2 imperial pints, or 1/4 imperial gallon (69.36 cubic inches, or 1,136.52 cubic cm). The U.S. system has two units called a quart, one for liquid measure and a slightly larger unit for dry measure. The U.S. liquid quart is equal to 2 liquid pints, or 1/4 U.S. gallon (57.75 cubic inches, or 946.35 cubic cm); and the dry quart is equal to 2 dry pints, or $^1/_{32}$ bushel (67.2 cubic inches, or 1,101.22 cubic cm).

The quart was originally a medieval English unit for dry and liquid measures that varied between 0.95 and 1.16 litres, relatively close to its modern equivalents. In Geoffrey Chaucer's *Miller's Tale* (about 1370), it was used as a measure for ale.

ROD

The rod is an old English measure of distance equal to 16.5 feet (5.029 metres), with variations from 9 to 28 feet (2.743 to 8.534 metres) also being used. It was also called a perch or pole. The word *rod* derives from Old English *rodd* and is akin to Old Norse *rudda* ("club"). Etymologically *rod* is also akin to the Dutch *rood*, which referred to a land area of 40 square rods, equal to 1/4 acre, or 10,890 square feet (1,012 square metres). It also denoted just 1 square rod, or 272.25 square feet (25.29 square metres). The rood also was a British linear unit, containing 660 feet (201.2 metres).

SCRUPLE

The scruple is a unit of weight in the apothecaries' system, equal to 20 grains, or 1/3 dram, and equivalent to 1.296

grams. It was sometimes mistakenly assigned to the avoirdupois system. In ancient times, when coinage weights customarily furnished the lower subdivisions of weight systems, the scruple (from Latin *scrupulus*, "small stone" or "pebble") was a unit of Roman commercial weight as well as a unit of coinage weight. One drachma, the basic Greek silver unit, consisted of three scruples.

SHI

The *shi*, also called a *dan*, was the basic unit of weight in ancient China. The *shi* was created by Shi Huang Di, who became the first emperor of China in 221 BCE and who is celebrated for his unification of regulations fixing the basic units. He fixed the *shi* at about 60 kg (132 pounds). The modern *shi* is equivalent to 71.68 kg (157.89 pounds).

STERADIAN

The steradian is a unit of solid-angle measure in the International System of Units (SI), defined as the solid angle of a sphere subtended by a portion of the surface whose area is equal to the square of the sphere's radius. Since the complete surface area of a sphere is 4π times the square of its radius, the total solid angle around a point is equal to 4π steradians. Derived from the Greek word for "solid" and the English word *radian*, a steradian is, in effect, a solid radian; the radian is an SI unit of plane-angle measurement defined as the angle of a circle subtended by an arc equal in length to the circle's radius.

STERE

The stere is a metric unit of volume equal to 1 cubic metre, or 1,000 litres. The stere (from Greek *stereos*, "solid") was originally defined by law and used in France in 1793, primarily as a measure for firewood. It is thus the metric counterpart of the cord, one standard cord (128 cubic feet of stacked wood) being equal to 3.625 steres. A stere is made up of 10 decisteres, and 100 steres make up a hectostere. Very large volumes may be expressed in kilosteres, equal to 1,000 steres.

STONE

The stone is a British unit of weight for dry products generally equivalent to 14 pounds avoirdupois (6.35 kg), though it varied from 4 to 32 pounds (1.814 to 14.515 kg) for various items over time. Originally any good-sized rock chosen as a local standard, the stone came to be widely used as a unit of weight in trade, its value fluctuating with the commodity and region. In the 14th century England's exportation of raw wool to Florence necessitated a fixed standard. In 1389 a royal statute fixed the stone of wool at 14 pounds and the sack of wool at 26 stones. Trade stones of variant weights persist, such as the glass stone of 5 pounds. The stone is still commonly used in Britain to designate the weights of people and large animals.

TALENT

The talent was a unit of weight used by many ancient civilizations, such as the Hebrews, Egyptians, Greeks, and Romans. The weight of a talent and its relationship to its major subdivision, the mina, varied considerably over time and location in the ancient world. The most common ratio of the talent to the mina was probably 1:60.

The Hebrew talent, or *kikka-r*, probably of Babylonian origin, was the basic unit of weight among the ancient

Hebrews. In the sacred system of weights, the Talmudic talent was equal to 60 Talmudic minas.

The talent was also an important unit of weight among the Greeks, who undoubtedly borrowed it from eastern neighbours. The Attic talent, which equaled 60 Attic minas, is estimated to have weighed about 56.9 pounds (25.8 kg). It was certainly smaller than the Hebrew talent.

TON

The ton is a unit of weight in the avoirdupois system equal to 2,000 pounds (907.18 kg) in the United States (the short ton) and 2,240 pounds (1,016.05 kg) in Britain (the long ton). The metric ton used in most other countries is 1,000 kg, equivalent to 2,204.6 pounds avoirdupois. The term derives from *tun*, denoting a large barrel used in the wine trade and named from the French *tonnerre*, or "thunder," in turn named for the rumbling it produced when rolled. Ton came to mean any large weight, until it was standardized at 20 hundredweight although the total weight could be 2,000, 2,160, 2,240, or 2,400 pounds (from 907.18 to 1,088.62 kg) depending on whether the corresponding hundredweight contained 100, 108, 112, or 120 pounds.

Ton, as a unit of volume, may also refer to the cargo capacity of ships or to the freight itself. The register ton is defined as 100 cubic feet, the freight or measurement ton as 40 cubic feet; an older measure of a ship's displacement was based on the volume of a long ton of seawater, or 35 cubic feet. Variant tons of capacity have existed for specific commodities, such as the English water ton, used to measure petroleum products and equal to 224 British Imperial System gallons; the timber ton of 40 cubic feet; and the wheat ton of 20 U.S. bushels.

TROY WEIGHT

Troy weight is a traditional system of weight in the British Isles based on the grain, pennyweight (24 grains), ounce (20 pennyweights), and pound (12 ounces). The troy grain, pennyweight, and ounce have been used since the Middle Ages to weigh gold, silver, and other precious metals and stones. The name supposedly derives from the city of Troyes in France, site of one of the major medieval fairs. The troy pound was adopted by the U.S. Mint for the regulation of coinage in 1828.

The troy pound is equal to the apothecaries' pound and to approximately 0.82 avoirdupois pound and 0.373 kilogram.

ZHANG

The *zhang* was an old Chinese measure of length equal to 10 *chi*, or 3.58 metres (11 feet 9 inches). The value was agreed upon by China in treaties (1842–44 and 1858–60) with England and France. It was thereafter used by Chinese maritime customs as the standard value for assessing all tariff duties. The length of one *chi* varied throughout China from 27.9 to 40 cm (11 to 15.8 inches). The so-called treaty *chi* was defined for customs purposes as 35.8 cm (14.1 inches).

Glossary

arithmetic Branch of mathematics that studies numbers and the relationships between numbers. It generally refers to basic operations and computation, such as addition, subtraction, multiplication, and division.

associative law Property of addition and multiplication stating that for any numbers, for example a, b, and c, any grouping of those numbers will produce the same result when they are added or multiplied. This can be illustrated by the following: $(a + b) + c = a + (b + c)$ or $(ab)c = a(bc)$.

base A number greater than 1 in terms of which further unit groupings can be made.

binary system A numeric system with a base of 2, whose only digits are 0 and 1.

cardinality Numeration of elements in a given set.

ciphered numeral system Numeral system in which the multiples of a base, b, in addition to b and the number 1, are designated by special and unrelated names.

commutative law Property of addition and multiplication stating that any numbers, for example a, b, and c, can be added or multiplied in any order. This can be illustrated by the following: $a + b + c = b + c + a$ or $abc = bca$.

cuneiform numeral Babylonian representation of a number formed by impressing a wedge shape in clay.

decimal number system Also called the Hindu-Arabic or Arabic system. A type of positional numeral system with 10 as a base and with digits 0, 1, 2, 3, 4, 5, 6, 7, 8, and 9. A decimal point (dot) is used to signify an alternate expression of fractions.

distributive law Property of arithmetic stating that multiplying the sum of two or more numbers, for example, *b* and *c*, by a factor, *a*, is equivalent to multiplying each number by that factor and then adding the sums. This can be illustrated by the following: $a(b + c) = ab + ac$.

divisor An integer (factor) that divides another evenly.

exponent An expression of the product of $a \times a \times a...$, wherein *a* represents any number (the base) and any number *n* is signified as a superscript of the base, such that *an* is equivalent to *a* multiplied by itself *n* times.

factor A number that divides another number without leaving a remainder.

fundamental theorem of arithmetic Theorem that states that any integer larger than 1 can be uniquely represented as a product of prime numbers.

integer Any positive or negative whole number or zero.

irrational number A number that cannot be expressed as a ratio of two nonzero integers. Decimals with no repeating pattern of digits that continue infinitely are expressions of irrational numbers.

logarithm The exponent (*x*) that a base (*b*) must have in order to produce a given number (*y*). If $b^x = y$, then *x* is the logarithm of *y* to base *b*, or alternately, $\log b\, (y) = x$.

measurement theory The study of number assignment to objects and the determination of what can be measured, the relationships between measurements, and error in measurement processes.

multiplicative grouping system Numeral system in which certain levels of numbers are designated by special characters or symbols. For example, if 10 is represented by *X* and 100 is represented by *C*, but the digits between 1 and 9 are represented normally, the number 752 would be 7*C*5*X*2.

natural number A positive integer. Zero may also be included in the set of natural numbers if the set includes all non-negative numbers.

positional numeral system A number system in which all digits less than a given base, b, receive unique names, with larger numbers expressed as sequences of these digits.

prime number An integer greater than 1 that can only be divided by itself and the number 1.

prime number theorem Formula that approximates the number of prime numbers below a given positive real number (x). If the number of primes below x is designated as $p(x)$, then it can be approximated by the formula $x/\ln(x)$.

rational number The quotient of any two nonzero integers, including integers themselves. Decimals that terminate or repeat infinitely are also rational numbers.

set A grouping of a finite or infinite number of elements, which may or may not be mathematical, that is treated as a single unit.

set theory Branch of mathematics that deals with the properties of sets

transfinite number Measure of the size of infinite sets.

BIBLIOGRAPHY

NUMERALS AND NUMERAL SYSTEMS

An accessible history of ancient and non-Western number systems is David Eugene Smith, *History of Mathematics*, 2 vol. (1923–25, reissued 1968). Graham Flegg (ed.), *Numbers Through the Ages* (1989), explores the history of counting systems, including basic techniques of calculation. Karl Menninger, *Number Words and Number Symbols: A Cultural History of Numbers* (1969, reissued 1992; trans. from German 2nd ed., 1957–58), is considered a classic on the origins of numbers. Georges Ifrah, *The Universal History of Numbers: From Prehistory to the Invention of the Computer* (1998, reissued 2000; originally published in French, 1981), is encyclopaedic in its scope.

ARITHMETIC

Constance Reid, *From Zero to Infinity: What Makes Numbers Interesting*, 4th ed. (1992), is an introduction to elementary number theory accessible to nonmathematicians. Other introductory works include Robert L. Hershey, *How to Think with Numbers* (1982), an analysis of consumer applications of arithmetic; Peter Hilton and Jean Pedersen, and Gary L. Musser, William F. Burger, and Blake E. Peterson, *Mathematics for Elementary Teachers: A Contemporary Approach*, 5th updated ed. (2001), are written from the point of view of education.

Frank J. Swetz, *Capitalism and Arithmetic: The New Math of the 15th Century* (1987), translates the *Treviso Arithmetic* (or *Arte dell'abbaco*) of 1478, an early work

274

demonstrating methods and applications of arithmetic, and analyzes its content and impact. J.L. Berggren, *Episodes in the Mathematics of Medieval Islam* (1986), chronicles the history of Islamic mathematics.

SET THEORY

I. Grattan-Guinness, *The Search for Mathematical Roots, 1870–1940* (2000), is the most complete mathematical account of the development of set theory and includes an extensive bibliography. José Ferreirós, *Labyrinth of Thought: A History of Set Theory and Its Role in Modern Mathematics* (1999), focuses on the motivation and institutions behind the research programs in set theory between 1850 and 1940. Jean van Heijenoort (ed.), *From Frege to Gödel: A Source Book in Mathematical Logic, 1879–1931* (1967, reissued 2002), has 36 of the most important papers in mathematical logic and set theory.

Standard introductions for advanced undergraduate or beginning graduate-level students are Herbert B. Enderton, *Elements of Set Theory* (1977); and Keith J. Devlin, *The Joy of Sets: Fundamentals of Contemporary Set Theory*, 2nd rev. ed. (1993; originally published as *Fundamentals of Contemporary Set Theory*, 1979). Robert L. Vaught, *Set Theory: An Introduction*, 2nd ed. (1995, reissued 2001), is an undergraduate textbook that includes answers to exercises, increasing its usefulness for self-study. Paul R. Halmos, *Naive Set Theory* (1960, reissued 1998), is a concise overview of basic set theory ideas for nonspecialist mathematics students.

NUMBER THEORY

Øystein Ore, *Number Theory and Its History* (1948; reprinted with supplement, 1988), is a popular introduction to this fascinating subject and a timeless classic. More demanding mathematically is a book by a major figure in 20th-century mathematics, André Weil, *Number Theory: An Approach through History from Hammurapi to Legendre* (1984), which gives special attention to the work of Fermat and Euler. A dated but immense treatise is Leonard Eugene Dickson, *History of the Theory of Numbers*, 3 vol. (1919–23, reprinted 1999), which, though lacking material on 20th-century mathematics, provides a minutely detailed account of the development of number theory to that point. Morris Kline, *Mathematical Thought from Ancient to Modern Times* (1972, reissued in 3 vol., 1990), is an encyclopaedic survey of the history of mathematics—including many sections on the history of number theory.

Recreational aspects of number theory are presented in Albert H. Beiler, *Recreations in the Theory of Numbers: The Queen of Mathematics Entertains*, 2nd ed. (1966), and John H. Conway and Richard K. Guy, *The Book of Numbers* (1996, reprinted with corrections, 1998). Simon Singh, *Fermat's Enigma: The Epic Quest to Solve the World's Greatest Mathematical Problem* (1997), presents the historical development of modern number theory through the story of the solution of Fermat's last theorem.

MEASUREMENT SYSTEM

The understanding and development of systems of physical measurements, from early elementary to sophisticated modern ones, are discussed in A.E. Berriman, *Historical Metrology: A New Analysis of the Yardsticks of the Universe* (1984); O.A.W. Dilke, *Mathematics and Measurement* (1987); Witold Kula, *Measures and Men* (1986; originally published in Polish, 1970); and Ronald E. Zupko, *British Weights and Measures: A History from Antiquity to the Seventeenth Century* (1977), and *Revolution in Measurement: Western European Weights and Measures Since the Age of Science* (1990).

Advance toward modern systems of measurement is traced in Arthur E. Kennelly, *Vestiges of Pre-Metric Weights and Measures Persisting in Metric-System Europe, 1926–1927* (1928); *Landmarks in Metrology—1983* (1983).

INDEX

set, description of, 193
sets, operations on, 73–74
set theory, 71–72, 81, 89, 125, 127, 156, 160
  axiomatic set theory, 80, 94, 96, 124, 191
  axiom of restriction, 89, 91
  axiom schema of replacement, 87
  axiom schema of separation, 83, 84, 86
  Cantorian set theory, 75–80, 81
  limitations of, 92–94
  naive set theory, 72–73, 80, 84
  principle of abstraction in, 76–77
  relations in, 74–75
  Zermelo-Fraenkel set theory, 81
Set Theory and the Continuum Hypothesis (Cohen), 128
Shannon, Claude, 147
shi (measurement), 267
Shi Huang Di, 208, 267
Shnirelman, Lev Genrikhovich, 119
Shushu jiuzhang (Qin), 110
Sierpiński, Wacław, 159
Simpson, Thomas, 228
Simson, Robert, 108
Skolem, Thoralf Albert, 81, 82, 86
Sowerbutts, Edith Utley, 230, 231
square root, description of, 193
St. Augustine, 183
Steinitz, Ernst, 47
steradian (measurement), 237
stere (measurement), 267–268

stone (measurement), 268
subtraction, 40
Sun Zi (Sun Tzu), 50, 60, 157
symbols, number
  history of, 21–22

T

talent (measurement), 268–269
Talleyrand, Charles-Maurice de, 219
tally system, 21
Taylor, Richard, 69
Thabit ibn Qurrah, 61
Theory of Games and Economic Behavior (von Neumann and Morgenstern), 148
Thomson, J. J., 230
ton (measurement), 269
Torricelli, Evangelista, 121
transfinite numbers, 125, 127, 147, 194
transitive law, 194–195
trigonometry, 55
troy weight, 270
Turing, Alan Mathison, 142–144, 147, 152, 195
Turing machine, 143, 195–196
Turing test, 144

V

Vallée-Poussin, Charles Jean de la, 68, 185
Varahamihira, 97
Vienna Circle, 136, 137–138
vigesimal system, 23
Vinogradov, Ivan Matveyevich, 119, 144–145, 173, 197
Vinogradov's theorem, 197